ALASKAN SLED DOG TALES

TRUE STORIES OF THE STEADFAST COMPANIONS OF THE NORTH COUNTRY

1925 New York Times headlines the Serum Run to Nome.

~ Helen Hegener ~

NORTHERN LIGHT MEDIA

ALASKAN SLED DOG TALES
TRUE STORIES OF THE
STEADFAST COMPANIONS
OF THE NORTH COUNTRY

by Helen Hegener

© 2016 by Helen Hegener, Northern Light Media. All rights reserved. This book may not be reproduced in whole or in part without written permission from the author and publisher.

The author very gratefully acknowledges multiple sources for the history and photographs in this book, including but not limited to the Alaska State Library, the University of Alaska Fairbanks, Alaska's Digital Archives, the Library of Congress, and the National Archives. Addresses and websites in the appendix.

First printing May 14, 2016 by Northern Light Media.
Printed in the United States of America.

ISBN-10 0692668470
ISBN-13 978-0692668474

Northern Light Media
Post Office Box 870515
Wasilla, Alaska 99687

http://northernlightmedia.wordpress.com
email: northernlightmedia@gmail.com

Alaskan Sled Dog Tales

For Michael and Collin, and in memory of Snoopy.

*But you can't tell me God would have Heaven
So a man couldn't mix with his friends;
That we're doomed to meet disappointment
When we come to the place the trail ends.
That would be a low-grade sort of Heaven
And I'd never regret a damned sin
If I mush up to the gate, white and pearly,
And they don't let my malamutes in.*
*~ Old Yukon: Tails, Trails and Trials
by James Wickersham (1938)*

Alaskan Sled Dog Tales

TABLE OF CONTENTS

6............**Maps of Alaska**
12..........**Author's Preface** ~ *Why I Wrote this Book*
18..........**Introduction**
22..........**Writing Alaska's History** ~ Sled Dogs Did Heavy Lifting
26..........**Riding the Arctic Circuit** ~ Judge James Wickersham
38..........**The 1925 Serum Run to Nome** ~ with Leonhard Seppala
46..........**From Nome to Washington, D.C.** ~ Story of Eli A. Smith
54..........**Colonel Goodwin** ~ The 1908 Iditarod Trail
58..........**An Alaskan "Mush" to Presbytery** ~ by Rev. S. Hall Young
76..........**Mary Joyce** ~ Mushing from Juneau to Fairbanks
80..........**Mush, You Malamutes!** ~ Father Bernard R. Hubbard
86..........**An Ode to Mushing** ~ by Rev. S. Hall Young
88..........**Olympic Sled Dogs** ~ Seppala and St. Godard Competed
94..........**Dog Team Doctor** ~ Dr. Joseph Romig
96..........**All Alaska Sweepstakes** ~ From Nome to Candle
106........**Dog Team Delivery** ~ Sled Dog Mail Teams
114........**Sled Dog News** ~ Reporting History
118........**The Huskies and the Reindeer** ~ S. Jackson vs. H. Stuck
128........**Sled Dog Magazine Covers** ~ Dashing Through the Snow
134........**Racing Down to Golovin** ~ Seppala's Epic Serum Run

Alaskan Sled Dog Tales

140........**Split-the-Wind** ~ "....the greatest musher...."
146........**Alaska Nellie's Adventures** ~ Rescue in Hell's Acres
158........**Seppala's Dogs** ~ Togo, Fritz and Balto
164........**Jujiro Wada** ~ Legendary Alaskan Trailblazer
178........**Gold on the Iditarod Trail** ~ "3,400 ounces of gold"
184........**Slim Williams** ~ Alaska Highway Trailblazer
190........**John "Iron Man" Johnson** ~ 1910 Sweepstakes Champion
196........**Baldy of Nome** ~ Scotty Allan's Legendary Lead Dog
202........**King of the Arctic Trail** ~ Allan Alexander "Scotty" Allan
210........**A Dog-Puncher on the Yukon** ~ Arthur Treadwell Walden
218........**Ten Thousand Miles with a Dog Sled** ~ Hudson Stuck
226........**Military Sled Dogs** ~ They Received the Croix de Guerre
238........**Ernest de Koven Leffingwell** ~ Mapping Arctic Coastline
244........**Caribou Bill** ~ World Tour with a Dog Team
250........**The Cheechakos** ~ Alaska's First Motion Picture
258........**Margaret Murie** ~ Over the Valdez-Fairbanks Trail
264........**Dog Team Postcards** ~ Sled Dogs in the Mail
274........**Ed Biederman** ~ Delivering the Mail on the Yukon
278........**Esther Birdsall Darling** ~ Alaskan Author
282........**The Great Dog Races of Nome** ~ Esther Birdsall Darling

Alaskan Sled Dog Tales

MAPS OF ALASKA

~

From a 1920 Alaska Road Commission Map

On the following pages, close-ups of the map below show dashed lines indicating the trails most frequently traveled by dog teams. Many of these trails later became roads, and many of the names are original roadhouse locations.

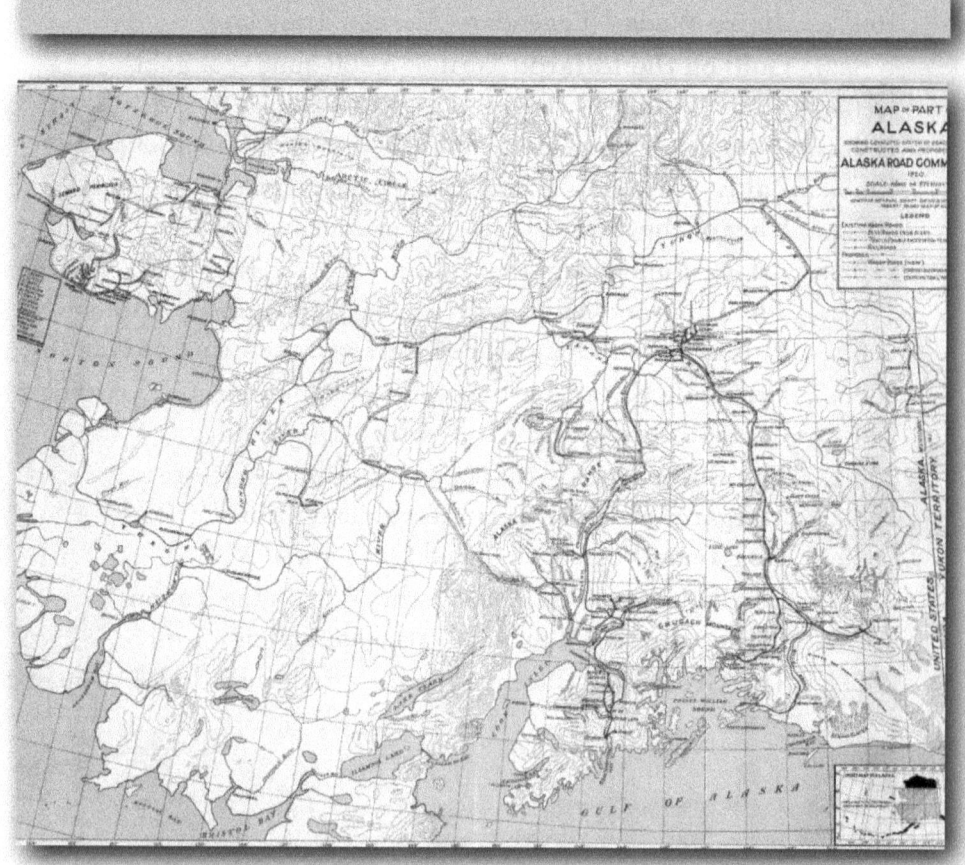

Online at: http://vilda.alaska.edu/cdm/singleitem/collection/cdmg11/id/13475/rec/4

Alaskan Sled Dog Tales

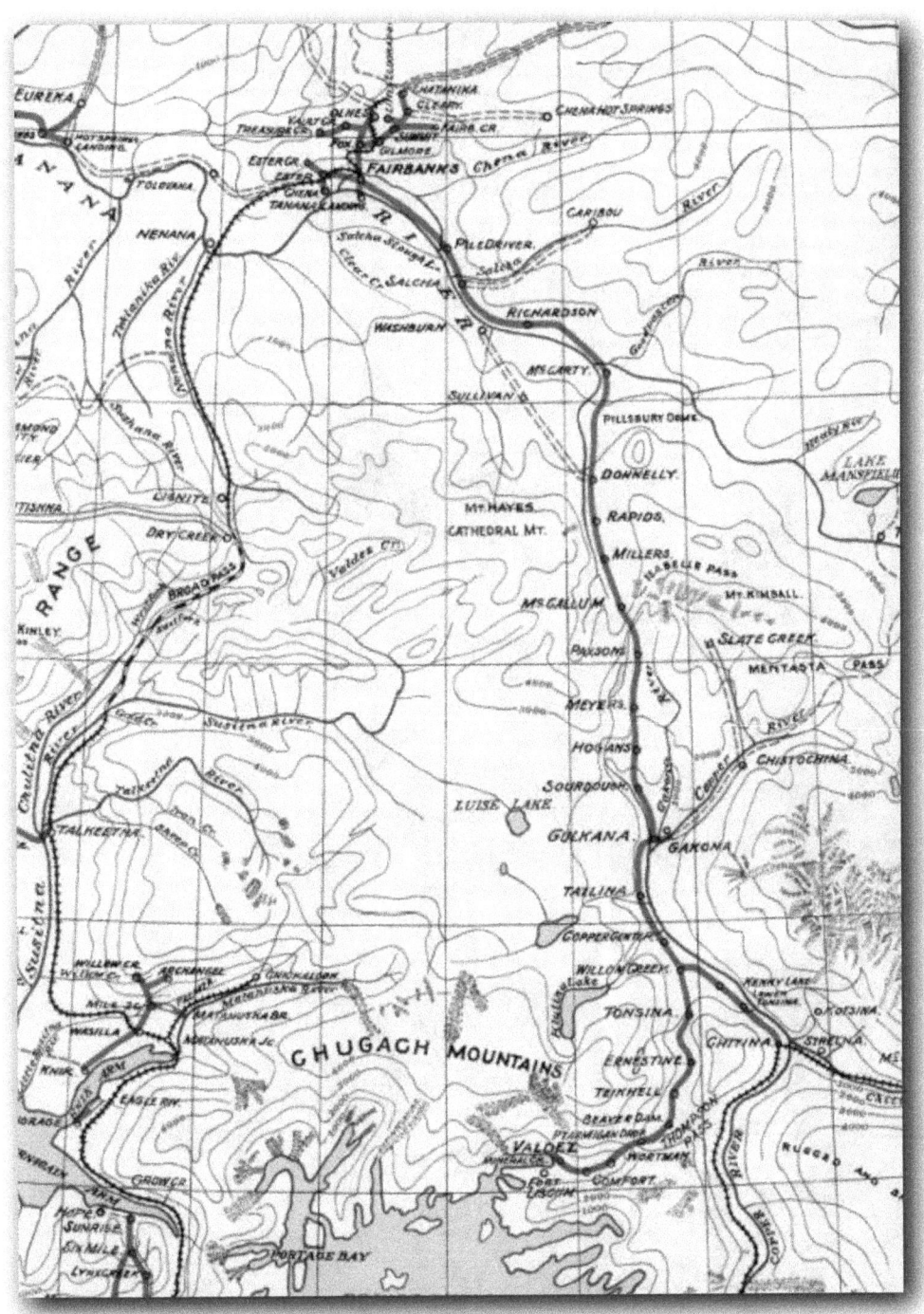

Alaskan Sled Dog Tales

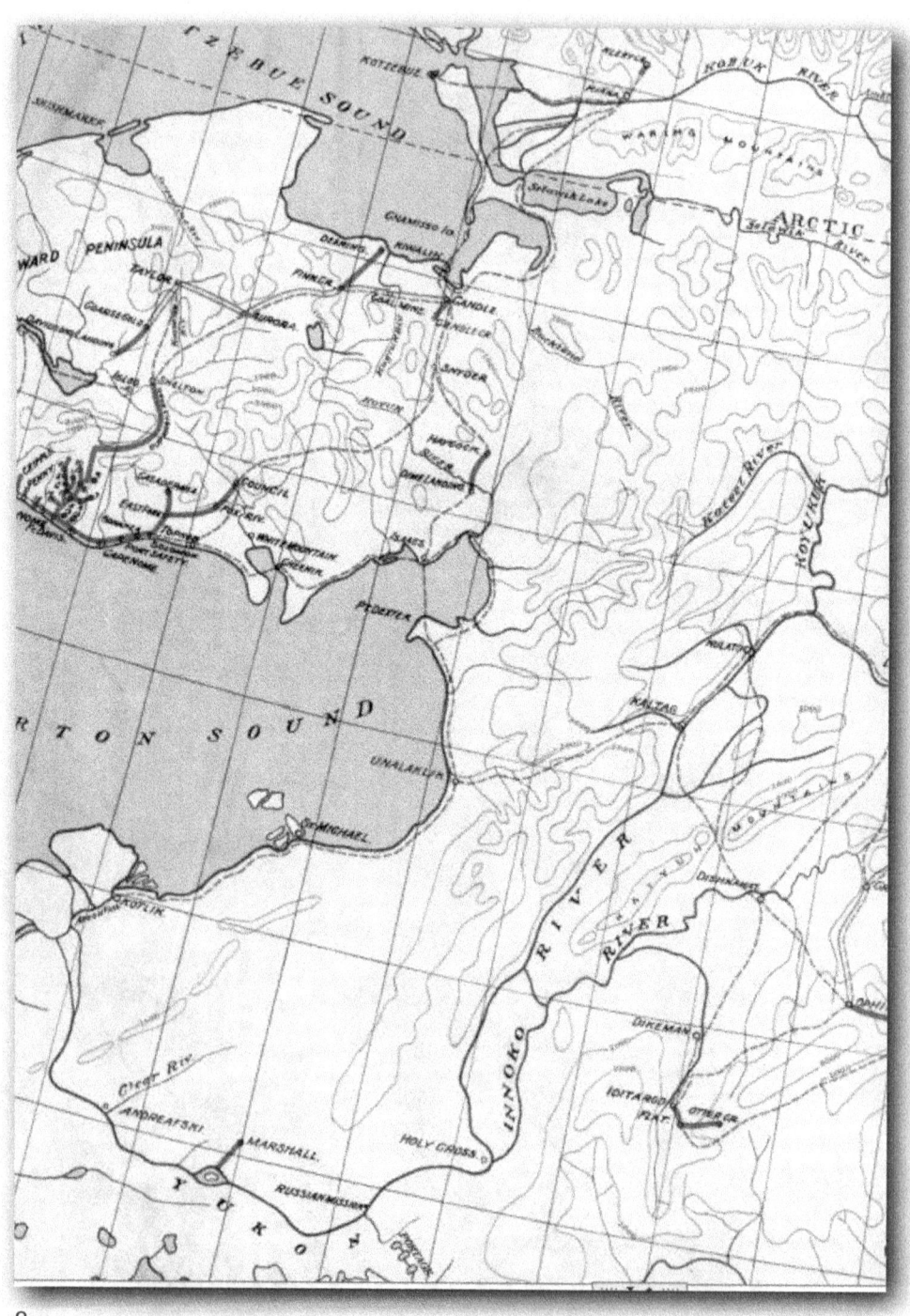

Alaskan Sled Dog Tales

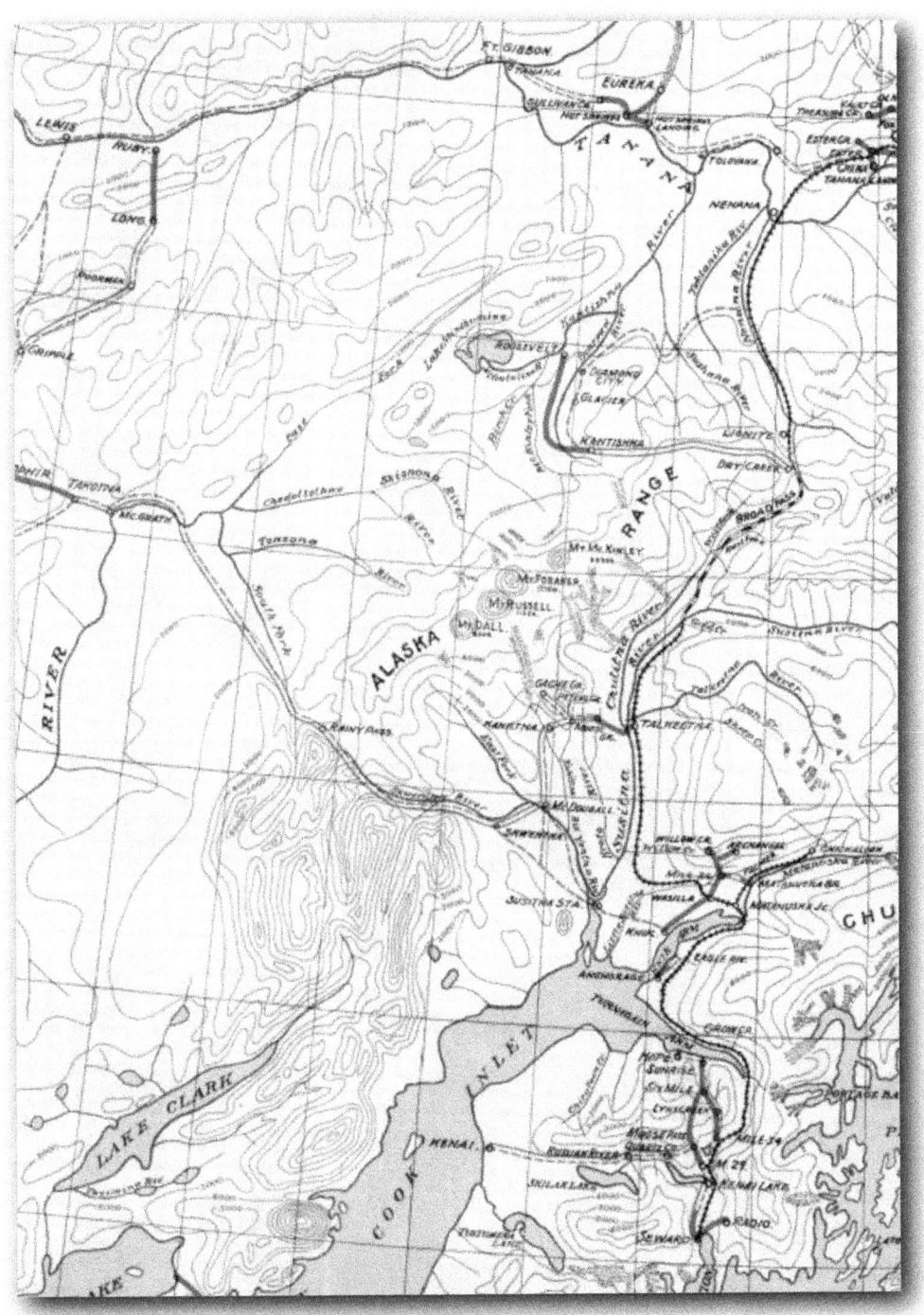

Alaskan Sled Dog Tales

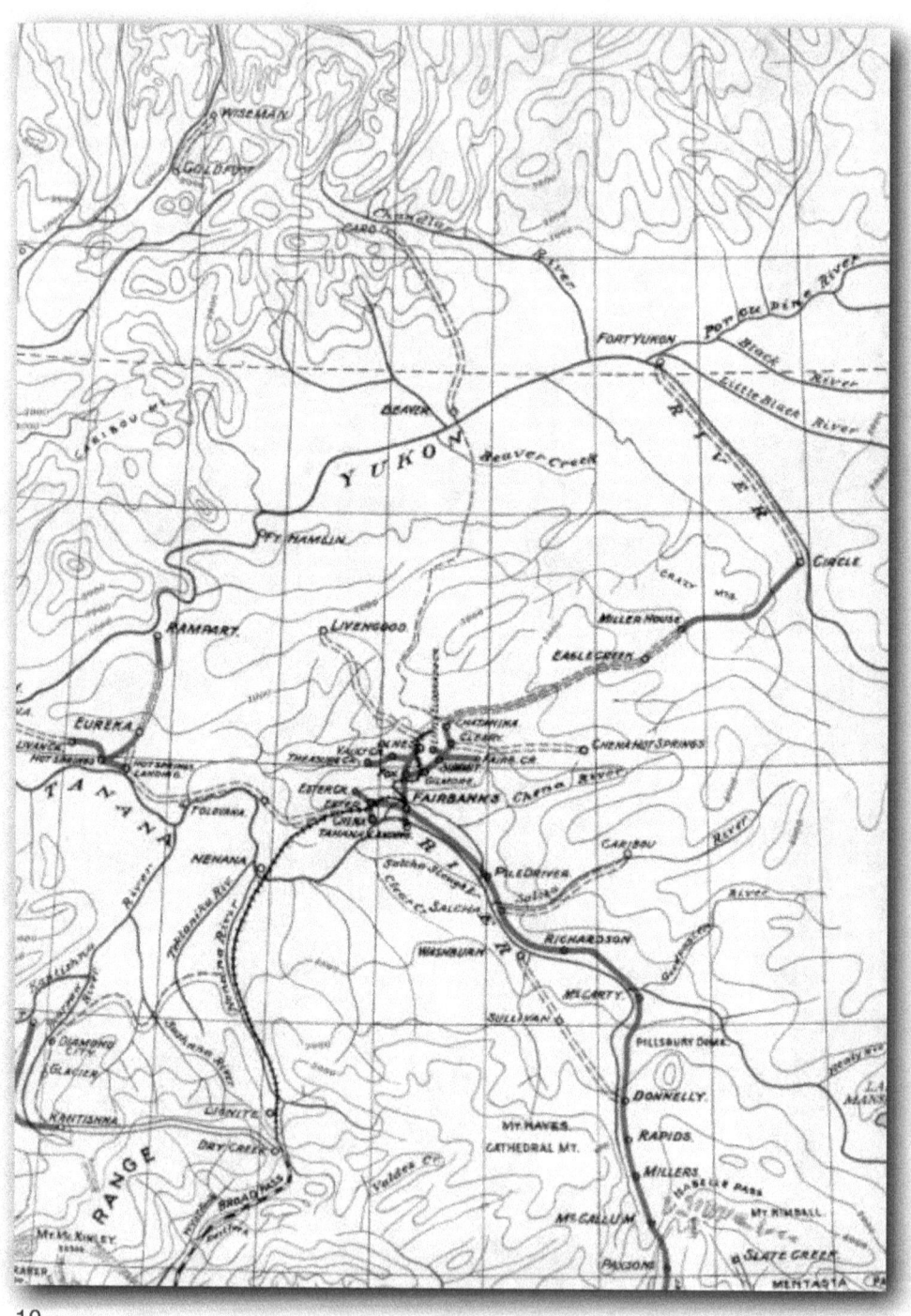

Alaskan Sled Dog Tales

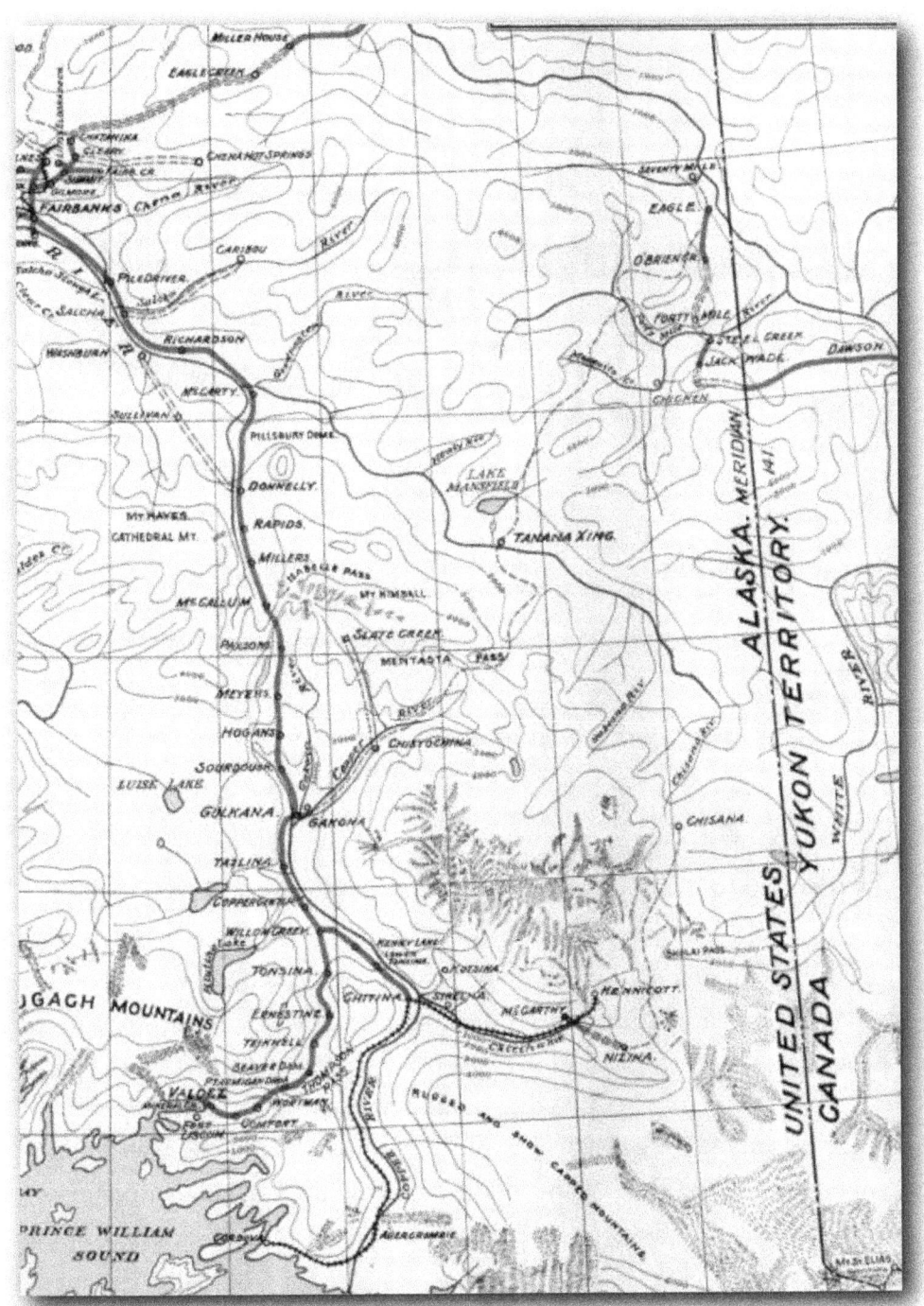

Benjamin S. Downing departing Dawson City on the Yukon River with the U.S. mail, 1900. Between 1897 and his death in 1906, Downing carried mail and passengers along what some called "the world's loneliest mail route." [Alaska State Library]

AUTHOR'S PREFACE, OR WHY I WROTE THIS BOOK

My fascination with sled dogs and mushing started when I was a teenager, just barely turned 15. I had come to Alaska with my parents in the late summer of 1965, and one of the first dogs I met was a huge wolfish-looking gray husky who roamed the campground at Eagle River, where we stayed for a few weeks until our military housing was ready to move into. I called him Wolfie, and he became my trusted companion on many long explorations up and down the banks of the glacier-fed Eagle

Alaskan Sled Dog Tales

River, 13 miles north of Anchorage. Around the same time we left the campground and moved to nearby Fort Richardson, the big dog was taken in by close friends of my parents, and their extended card games with my parents left plenty of time for Wolfie and I to go exploring together. I had a favorite place to sit above Eagle River, on a hill high above the river with a grand view of the surrounding landscape, and the big gray husky would lay there beside me gazing out across the river to the mountains beyond. Watching him, I could easily imagine he was thinking of the travels of his ancestors across that land, both his wolfish forebears and the closer relatives who pulled freighters, miners, and the U.S. mail over frozen trails.

That winter we all became fans of the exciting sprint races run by legends such as George Attla, Doc Lombard, and Emmitt Peters, the "Yukon Fox." That Christmas my parents gave me a tricolor malemute mix puppy, who joined the big gray and I on our adventures, and those two dogs left an indelible mark on my heart, forever securing a love for the beautiful and gentle Alaskan husky.

By 1972 I was married and living in a log cabin my husband and I had built near Wasilla, and of course we had a small dog team which we used for hauling water and firewood. A local musher named Joe Redington started talking about a sled dog race from Anchorage to Nome, 1,000 miles across a then little-known route called the Iditarod Trail. Close friends were helping Joe with the planning and logistics, and they got my husband and I involved with the effort as well.

I had a friend who worked for what was at that time the largest newspaper in Alaska, the *Anchorage Daily Times*, and I brought him out to meet Joe Redington and listen to his dreams of a new kind of race. My husband got interested in joining the adventure with our small team and some additional dogs which were offered, but his father passed away suddenly that winter and life took us in quite a different direction. It

Alaskan Sled Dog Tales

would be more than thirty-five years before sled dogs became an important part of my life again.

In 2007 I was co-owner of a small production company which filmed and interviewed Lance Mackey, son of the 1978 Iditarod champion Dick Mackey and, already a three-time Yukon Quest champion, on his way to winning a record-breaking four consecutive Iditarod championships. I wrote the script and then edited the film and audio recordings into a 45-minute documentary DVD we titled *Appetite and Attitude,* so named because those were two primary qualities Lance looked for in his dogs. When the production company partnership dissolved I kept the company, Northern Light Media, and turned the focus toward my first love, publishing books on Alaska's history.

The next several years brought endless hours of research, writing, and the publication of several books relating to the history of sled dogs and the great long distance races such as the All Alaska Sweepstakes, the Yukon Quest, and the Iditarod Trail Sled Dog Race. The research was fortified with hands-on experience as I became a volunteer for popular mid-distance races such as the Northern Lights 300 and the Copper Basin 300, and the 1,000-mile Yukon Quest. I also became a columnist for *Alaska Dispatch* and a frequent contributor to publications such as *Mushing, Last Frontier,* and *Alaska* magazines, traveling to the races I was writing about.

In the course of my travels, research, and a growing fascination for the history of mushing, I developed an extensive collection of old books, articles, newspaper clippings, postcards, and memorabilia relating to the history of sled dogs in Alaska. There have been many wonderful books published about this subject, most notably Lorna Coppinger's *The World of Sled Dogs* and Elsie Noble Caldwell's *Alaska Trail Dogs,* but I wanted to share a different perspective, to bring a new approach, and *Along Alaskan Trails* was my first book which focused on the histories of the mushers and their trail dogs.

Alaskan Sled Dog Tales

My first effort shared stories of mushers such as Jujiro Wada, the Japanese long distance musher whose exploits included helping to found the city of Fairbanks and becoming a key player in the opening of the Iditarod Trail from Seward to Nome. Other chapters told of Slim Williams, who mushed his team from Glennallen to Washington, D.C. in 1933 to help promote the idea of building a highway to Alaska; and Mary Joyce, who drove her team of huskies through the trackless wilderness from Juneau to Fairbanks; Hudson Stuck, the Episcopal Archdeacon who wrote *Ten Thousand Miles with a Dog Team*; Scotty Allan, champion of the All Alaska Sweepstakes; and Leonhard Seppala, hero of the 1925 Serum Run to Nome. Their stories have all been included in this new book, along with the compelling true stories of many other mushers and memorable dogs such as Togo, Baldy, Wolf and Kolyma.

Early Alaskan postcard of a dog team in Keystone Canyon, near Valdez.

Alaskan Sled Dog Tales

Dog stories have always been a popular staple of literature, witness the multiple reprinting of classics such as *Lassie Come Home*, *Old Yeller*, *Beautiful Joe*, and *Big Red*. And then there are the North's own classics, among them *Baldy of Nome*, *White Fang*, and *The Call of the Wild*. But the dog stories in these pages are all true, at least as true as the vagaries of time allow. But we know these dogs actually walked the Great Land, steadfast companions of the men they traveled with, and the history of Alaska would be quite different without the countless teams of stalwart sled dogs who, in exchange for food and a minimum of care, provided a reliable way to cross the frozen tundra, rugged mountains, and endless lakes and rivers of the Great Land.

A colorful reminder of the past, sled dogs played an important role in the early transportation networks of the territory of Alaska. When the intrepid Arctic explorers traveled across the unknown lands of the north the dog teams were their mode of transport. When the miners crossed the high mountain ranges in search of the next El Dorado the dog teams carried their freight and supplies and even the prospectors themselves. When the U.S. mail needed to go through in winter it was the hardy dog teams which carried it to far-flung corners of Alaska.

Alaskan sled dogs are still running the trails hauling freight and supplies and excited tourists, and entertaining thousands of fans across the world as they race in the increasingly popular sprint, mid- and long-distance races every winter and into the long spring days.

This book is my tribute to them all.

Helen Hegener, Meadow Lakes, Alaska ~ May, 2016

Alaskan Sled Dog Tales

Cover art for a 1936 issue of The Saturday Evening Post

"*They were new dogs, utterly transformed by the harness. All passiveness and unconcern had dropped from them. They were alert and active, anxious that the work should go well, and fiercely irritable with whatever, by delay or confusion, retarded that work. The toil of the traces seemed the supreme expression of their being, and all that they lived for and the only thing in which they took delight.*"

~From *The Call of the Wild,* by Jack London

Alaskan Sled Dog Tales

"Baldy of Nome," Scotty Allan's famous leader, winner of $25,000 in Sweepstakes prizes.

INTRODUCTION

The history of Alaska would be very different without the criss-crossing trails of thousands of sled dog teams. Man's dependence on these canine workhorses of the north can be seen in photo after photo: A dog team carrying passengers on the Richardson Trail, a dog team hauling freight across the Iditarod Trail, two dog teams loaded with the U.S. Mail and bound for Anchorage from Seward, a dog team on patrol from Fort Gibbon near Tanana, a dog team making its way along the frozen Yukon River to the next missionary stopover...

Sifting through hundreds of photos of Alaskan dog teams makes clear their important role in the history of this land. Before cars, trucks, ships, trains and airplanes, there were sled dogs. In every part of this great land, from the misty fjords of southeastern Alaska to the farthest northern tip of the continent, sled dogs were the most dependable - and often the only - form of transportation.

Alaskan Sled Dog Tales

In a slim collection of stories titled *Alaska Trail Dogs* (1945, Richard R. Smith), author Elsie Noble Caldwell cites a number which may or may not be accurate: "More than thirty-five thousand dogs have played a part in the development of Alaskan resources..."

Whatever their numbers, the importance of sled dogs in the history of the north is undisputed, and the stories in this book illustrate the many ways in which the dog team made travel and moving loads over otherwise impassable trails possible.

In *The Cruelest Miles* (2003, W.W. Norton & Co.) Gay and Laney Salisbury wrote: "On the Alaskan trail, sled dogs became partners in a game of survival. Drivers depended on their dogs so that they could make a living as freighters, mailmen, and trappers, and relied on the animals' skill and intelligence to get them safely across the rough, dangerous terrain."

Typical Alaskan sled dogs were not always the photogenic lot depicted in movies or on posters of Sgt. Preston of the Mounties with his faithful sidekick Yukon King. They were more often odd-sized, dock-tailed, and funny-colored, for as the Salisburys noted, "The demand for sled dogs was so high, particularly during the northern gold rushes, that the supply of dogs ran out and a black market for dogs sprang up in the states. Any dog that looked as if it could pull a sled or carry a saddlebag--whether or not it was suited to withstand the cold--was kidnapped and sold in the north."

In his book, *Ten Thousand Miles with a Dog Sled* (1914, Charles Scribner's), gold-rush era missionary and Episcopal Archdeacon Hudson Stuck, who summited Mt. McKinley in 1913 with the aid of dog teams, wrote that the original Native sled dogs had been extensively mated with setters, pointers, hounds, mastiffs, Saint Bernards and Newfoundlands, creating "a general admixture of breeds, so that the work dogs of Alaska are a heterogeneous lot..."

Alaskan Sled Dog Tales

Despite their often questionable backgrounds, most sled dogs share a love of being on the trail and going someplace new with their teammates and their driver, a term which originated with drivers of oxen and horses, but by which mushers have always been known in Alaska. Sled dogs were, and still are, working animals, but according to their nature and in keeping with their role as Man's Best Friend, sled dogs were often much more than just beasts of burden. When Scotty Allen was elected to the Alaska Legislature and moved to the capitol city of Juneau, his faithful lead dog Baldy, who had once saved his life, went along. And when Scotty Allan retired to California, once again Baldy accompanied his master along strange and unknown trails. Leonhard Seppala was rarely without the faithful Togo, until he retired his peerless leader to a life of comfort with his friend Elizabeth Ricker.

In an often unforgiving land of intrepid men and heroic dogs it was not uncommon to find a trail-wise husky at the heels of almost any miner, trapper, logger, hunter, surveyor, explorer, or any other reason a man found to be in the wilds of Alaska. Many men's lives depended on the speed and intelligence of these dogs, and many courageous men cried when they lost one of their faithful team members. From the wise leaders who could find a trail buried in a blizzard, to the strong wheel dogs who could shift an entire sled out of danger in an instant, each dog in every team was an important part of the writing of Alaska's history.

Today's sled dog races are a continuing testament to the courage and stamina of these incredibly tough animals, showcasing their continuing endurance and exhibiting their sheer joyous love of running. The sled dogs running today's races are very often the direct descendants of canine royalty, strong brave dogs who worked side-by-side with the men who built Alaska. Stalwart companions of the north country. A few of their stories are in this book. ~•~

Alaskan Sled Dog Tales

A dog team travels through a canyon on the Dyea Trail, 1899.

Alaskan Sled Dog Tales

"Dogs being the only means of transport during those long winter months when the going is toughest, I guess it's natural that men in the Arctic are overly partial to their huskies and malamutes. I figure I've mushed more than twenty thousand miles of snowy trail, and I'm convinced there's nothing to compare with careering along behind a dog team—sled creaking and crunching over the drifts, snow flying up from padded feet, every ear alert and every tail curled proudly over a sleek, rippling back."

~Grant Pearson, My Life of High Adventure (Prentice-Hall, 1962)

"1905, photo taken at Ponto's Road House 20 miles from Valdez. This malamute dog team held the speed record between Valdez and Fairbanks - over 400 miles in a little over 4 days."
Photograph by Ocha Potter [UAF-2003-163-6m, Ocha Potter Papers]

Alaskan Sled Dog Tales

WRITING ALASKA'S HISTORY
Dog Teams Did the Heavy Lifting

"Well, all I know about dogs is not much, but when I was up in Alaska . . . their whole existence tangles around dogs . . . the backbone of the arctic is a dog's backbone." ~American humorist Will Rogers, in the final column he wrote, August, 1935. It was recovered from the plane crash near Barrow which killed Rogers and his friend and pilot, noted aviator Wiley Post.

Imagine for a moment that you're traveling through the snowy landscape of the Alaskan wilderness one hundred years ago, as a passenger snuggled into frost-rimmed furs piled onto a long freight sled being hauled by a team of hardy sled dogs. Behind you, a slim weather-beaten man urges the dogs on with a ceaseless patter and an occasional swear word uttered as levelly as the faint praise he gives them for keeping their traces taut and maintaining a steady gait.

The dogs' feet hitting the trail produces a soft murmuring noise which you've grown accustomed to hearing as the miles go by, and as the driver continues his non-stop encouragement you gaze upward at snowy peaks which disappear into the clouds. You fondly remember the tasty thick soup and warm bread proffered at the last roadhouse, and hope there will be a similar serving at the establishment ahead. At the very least you hope there will be a warm fire and a mug of hot tea or coffee.

Alaskan Sled Dog Tales

Winter travel by dog team was the norm in Alaska for many years, and a sturdy, well-conditioned team was a prized possession for anyone who made their living hauling freight, mail, passengers or supplies over the long cold trails. The dogs might be of uncertain origin, but then, more often than not, so were the drivers. Many had come north with the gold rushes, either as hopeful prospectors or hoping to earn better than usual wages working for those who were doing the mining. Between 1890 and 1900 the population of the territory of Alaska nearly doubled, and everyone was searching for a means to make a living. A team of dogs, needing only food and care in exchange for an honest day's hard work, seemed like a good investment to many.

In Alaska, around the turn of the century, transporting anything in the winter usually involved a dog team, and those who could capably drive a team of huskies across the vast empty distances would find employment. Contracting for companies like the Northern Commercial Company, the stage lines running the Valdez to Fairbanks Trail and similar routes, or the U.S. Post Office ("neither rain, nor sleet, nor snow..."), were sought after jobs. Many dog team drivers made good wages in the winter by hauling and stockpiling firewood for the steamships which would ply the great rivers in the summertime. Trappers relied on their teams for access to good trapping grounds. Dog teams served as ambulances, firetrucks, taxicabs, delivery trucks, police cars, and freight trains.

Many have pondered how different the history of the north might have been without the thousands of dogs pressed into service in various ways. We'll never know what might have been, but we have a clear and compelling picture of how it was, and how tens of thousands of dog teams wrote their enduring legacy into our history. ~•~

Alaskan Sled Dog Tales

*"Passenger and freight teams meeting the S.S. 'Corwin.'
Roadstead, Nome, Alaska. June 1, 1914, 11 p.m."* [Lomen Brothers photo]

Alaskan Sled Dog Tales

Ed Crouch's dog team on the Yukon River. [From Wickersham's book, Old Yukon]

Alaskan Sled Dog Tales

RIDING THE ARCTIC CIRCUIT
Excerpted from Judge James Wickersham's *Old Yukon: Tales, Trails, and Trials*

"When the mail team reaches the station or the roadhouse at the end of the day's run, the driver unhitches the team and turns all dogs, except the leader, loose to rustle for themselves. His leader, his parka, gloves, and whip, he brings into the roadhouse; puts the leader under his bunk, hangs his wet garments on the best wires around the stovepipe–and woe unto him who complains about the leader under the bunk!" -James Wickersham in Tales, Trails, and Trials

James Wickersham's classic book, *Old Yukon: Tales, Trails, and Trials* (Washington, D.C. : Washington Law Book Co., 1938), is an account of his years as a pioneer District Court Judge in Alaska. Judge Wickersham was appointed by President McKinley in the summer of 1900 to head the newly created Third Judicial District of the Alaska territorial court. He brought the first law to interior Alaska, a district that covered 300,000 square miles.

After building a modest log home in Eagle City, on the Yukon River, Wickersham began settling mining claim disputes, collecting saloon license fees, and presiding over judicial proceedings across a vast area, traveling by foot, steamer, dog team and revenue cutter.

Alaskan Sled Dog Tales

During the forty years he spent in Alaska, from his public battle against the corporate power of J. P. Morgan and the Guggenheims, who were trying to dominate mining and transportation in Alaska, to the statehood foundations which he helped to lay–he introduced the first statehood bill in Congress in March 1916, the 49th anniversary of the 1867 Purchase of Alaska–Judge James Wickersham's work transformed the territory from a lawless frontier to a shining northern star on our flag.

In his travels across the broad northern land the Judge kept detailed diaries, explaining why in chapter five of his book, titled *Riding the Arctic Circuit*: "It was my practice to keep a dairy of my journeys on the Alaska trails, in the hope that the details of daily travel, trails, temperature, weather conditions, and lodgings may be of interest."

Wickersham begins chapter five by explaining, "Due to the lack of litigation in Eagle in the winter of 1900-1901, I determined to make a winter trip down the Yukon River to hold court at Rampart. Mine owners there were aroused because alleged jumpers had intruded upon placer claims and threatened expensive litigation over their ownership."

The trip downriver would be made by dog team, stopping nightly at roadhouses spaced along the route. Wickersham's writing gives us an excellent first-hand example of typical dog team travel of the day.

"Every dog in our team was quivering with excitement and plunging in the collar anxious to be gone. With a highly developed dog team sense they knew that another journey over snowy trails was to be taken and they were ready to start. On the trail there is change and exercise, long and exciting races with other teams along the icy surfaces of the river trails, bells jingling sweet music in the clear and frosty air, warm rations of rice and bacon deliciously boiled over the evening campfire, with every canine eye on the cook and the steaming kettle. Mouths water while waiting for the savory supper served hot in separate pans at the evening meal–the one meal of the day. Then, too, there are the friendly meetings with strange teams and sometimes jolly good fighting at the overnight roadhouses, and more often with passing teams crowding in narrow trails. Dogs and boys, be they young or old, love Alaskan winter snow trails and the joy of their travel.

"Our friends gathered round the official sled to wish us a safe journey and a dry trail. Many of them looked upon the trip as hard and unpleasant, not without danger from overflow and freezing. Often a deep carpet of snow is insidiously invaded from underneath by the constantly flowing water, and the unwary traveler may find himself suddenly floundering knee-deep in water, far from fire or fuel, in a temperature of thirty degrees below zero, or lower. Unless he can quickly start a fire and change his footwear he will freeze, and he will be helpless to save himself. Most of the cases resulting in the death of travelers in this region are caused by accidents of this kind. We carried on our sled a dozen or more flour sacks of heavy drilling, and when we saw indications of water under the snow or crossing the trail, we pulled a sack over each foot and tied them closely about our feet and legs. This enabled us to wade water for a reasonable distance in safety.

"Our long, Indian-made spruce-basket sled was filled with dunnage bags, and dog feed, generally rice and bacon, sometimes dried fish; with blankets, dry socks, and warm clothing; with Alaska Code and blank court records for law and order purposes; with a well-stuffed grub box, extra dog harness, and soft caribou-skin moccasins for trail-sore dog feet. The load was well wrapped in waterproof tarpaulin and lashed down with the diamond hitch. The dogs were hitched tandem, with the wise old leader ahead. On the right side of the front end of the sled the gee-pole extended forward; the driver ran astride the low hanging rope which attached the dogs to the sled; he guided the team with his whip and voice, and the sled with the gee-pole. At the rear of the sled a pair of handlebars, similar to those of a common plow, enabled the rear guide to manage the sled and keep it in an upright position on sloping ice ways.

"Our lead dog was a heavily-thewed female husky, with fine team sense, and a faculty for finding the hard and beaten trail even when covered with many inches of new-fallen snow. Neither a strong wind carrying clouds of snow or sand, nor water, nor hidden under overflow could drive her astray. When the danger of overflow and water was met she dragged the team through to dry snow and immediately stopped and lay down, as every native dog will do. An inexperienced outside dog under such conditions will stand and shiver while the wet snow freezes around its feet and legs, but the native or husky dog will instantly lie down in the snow and apply first aid to its feet by licking the snow and ice off, and then drying them with his tongue, as his cousins the timber wolves do, thereby escaping all harmful effects.

"All Ready! At this warning the leader sprang into her collar and started the load; every dog barked a joyful farewell. Ed Crouch, the manipulator of the gee-pole, guided the heavy equipage down the steep riverbank and lined it up along the northbound trail on the icy bosom of the mighty Yukon River, and I, the wilderness magistrate, clad overall in blue denim parka, ran behind, hanging to the handlebars."

Judge Wickersham then gives a day-by-day report of his party's travels down the Yukon River: "February 9, 1901. It was a beautiful bright morning when we left Eagle at ten o'clock, thermometer 30 degrees below zero. Trail along the sloping shore ice, broken and bad, but well marked. Reached the Star roadhouse at four PM, five dogs with three hundred pounds on the sled. I had a bad fall when the sled turned over on broken ice near Star. Ed Jesson keeps the roadhouse, good meals; distance covered twenty miles; forty below zero tonight.

"February 10. Fifty-two below zero when we left Star roadhouse this morning early; at noon forty-two below, and tonight forty-three

Alaskan Sled Dog Tales

below. Bad trail today. It had not been traveled since last fall of snow, and one of us walked ahead on snowshoes and broke trail while the other straddled the line and managed the gee-pole. Much sloping ice in places and we had to lift the sled up and down shelf ice. Distance to Montauk roadhouse twenty miles.

"February 11. We determined last night not to leave Montauk roadhouse until late this morning, on account of sore feet and to go only as far as Nation River roadhouse, fourteen miles. The trail is very bad, heavy with snow, and much snowshoeing done to help the dogs. Forty below all day and tonight it is fifty-two below.

"February 12. Fifty-six below zero this morning and the trail covered with new snow, no track to follow, so we remained in camp all day. Tonight it is warmer, thirty-five below and we hope for better conditions tomorrow. Trapper here has 150 marten skins, several black and some gray wolf pelts.

"February 13. It was forty-five below zero this morning when we left Nation, but with an hour it had gone down to fifty. It was thirty-five below at noon on the river trail and forty below when we came into the Charley River Indian roadhouse tonight. There was no sign of a trail during the forenoon and one of us had to go ahead of the dogs and snowshoe to get the team along–then we happily met the bound-up mail team at our noon camp. The forenoon trails made a good afternoon trail for each of us and we traveled much faster in consequence. Traveled thirty-four miles today, according to Ben Downing's mail route distance table. Gave fourteen little Indian children, less than ten years of age, ten cents each and made them happy. Chief Charley was glad to see me, for he remembered that I was the just judge who recovered his stolen dog.

"February 14. It was forty-two below zero when we left the Indian camp this morning, only twenty-five below at noon, but forty below tonight. Good trail today. Coal Creek roadhouse tonight–twenty-four miles. My ankle hurt by fall the first day out is paining me badly and is very much swollen. Raised a bad blister on my other foot trying to shield the bad ankle; opened it and filled the hole with coal oil.

"February 15. Fifty below zero this morning and we did not leave the roadhouse until ten AM. A prospector here reports he has located a good bituminous coal mine miles back from the Yukon. I left the roadhouse half an hour ahead of the dog team and walked twelve miles before they caught up with me. Had noon lunch with 'Pete the Pig' at the mouth of Woodchopper Creek. Warmer this afternoon but a bad wind made it more uncomfortable than an extra ten degrees of cold. Came to Webber's roadhouse at two o'clock and, owing to the bitter wind and distance to the next roadhouse, put up for the night."

In a later chapter of the book Judge Wickersham gave a colorful description of Webber's roadhouse: "Webber's one-room log tavern with a dirt floor stood at the edge of a dense forest. The side walls of the cabin, built of small round logs, were head high, and the central roof log was just above the outstretched fingertips. The tavern was about ten by sixteen feet square inside. It was finished with one clapboard door hung on wooden pins, and one window sash.

"The dining table consisted of boards nailed to poles, about three feet long, driven into auger-holes about four feet apart just below the window. Two pole bunks of similar design adorned the back wall. The dirt floor was spattered with grease from the stove. There was one chair of riven slab set on three pole legs. The two other chairs were boxes, one marked in large letters, 'Hunter's Old Rye,' and the other, 'Eagle Brand Milk.' A dog stable, much smaller than the tavern, stood alongside. These buildings and their accommodations for travelers were typical of those along the Yukon River Trail."

"February 16. Left Webber's late, thermometer thirty-eight below and the wind blowing a gale. Luckily it blew downstream and pushed us

Alaskan Sled Dog Tales

along. We made a mistake in not starting early for we could have reached Circle tonight. We stopped at Johnson's roadhouse–twenty-two miles out of Circle. Weather tonight much warmer–only twenty-two below. The trails are good now and well marked; my feet are getting well; and we travel more rapidly.

"February 17. Left Johnson's early, thirty below, and reached Circle City an hour after noon–distance twenty-two miles. Visited with my brother Edgar and family. Attended Bishop Rowe's services tonight at the cabin church. Public matters here seem in good shape; two foreigners declared their intentions to become citizens; the delinquent miners' meeting recorder came in to talk things over and went away agreeing to surrender the old records to the new United States recorder.

"February 18. Left Circle this morning early, about an hour ahead of the dog team, which overtook us at the 20 Mile roadhouse where we had lunch. We left them there at one o'clock and reached the Half-Way roadhouse after six o'clock, distance traveled forty-five miles. Sun rose at eight and set at four, magnificent day, clear, cloudless, and cold; twenty below zero; trails rough but solid and dry.

"February 19. Thirty-five below zero this morning. Left Half-Way roadhouse at seven o'clock and came to Seventeen Mile Cabin at two o'clock. We could have made Fort Yukon but our feet are sore again and we can get in tomorrow before noon anyway. My right food is badly blistered on the sole. We open the blisters, fill them with coal oil out of our lantern which seems to effect a rapid cure. We have seen wonderful mirages to the westward both yesterday and today. Yesterday the objects seemed to be houses, churches and mills, high, square, and upright. Today the reverse–the objects are elongated–a long flat bridge-like structure with wide arches standing on low piers, a low flat battleship with cannons thrust out at each deck end, and other similar objects. They were so astonishingly like the objects mentioned that we stood gazing at them in amazement. They seemed miles away, and yet connected with the nearby foreground. We passed much open water in the river today, the main river channel is open, running fast and deep; the ice is breaking and falling in and crossings are dangerous. Twenty below tonight.

"February 20. We reached Fort Yukon early, thirty-five below, and walked ahead of the dog team to Britt's cabin at Willow Creek, thirty-five miles in nine hours; crippled by my ankle. Good trail and clear weather.

"February 22. Left Britt's early, thirty below. Fine sunup; walked twenty miles before dog team overtook me; feel better than any day since we left Eagle. Met the Alaska Commercial Co. party on their way from St. Michael to Dawson–Menzies, the auditor, Hill, Marion, and Trump. They had three dog teams with six dogs in each team. The court seems rather shabby in comparison with its one sled and five dogs. Two mail carriers and teams at Britt's with us last night; distance Britt's to Julius cabin, twenty-five miles.

"February 23. Left Julius cabin early, an hour ahead of my team and walked twenty-five miles before they caught up near Victor's cabin' thirty miles to Victors. From running astride the rope and handling the gee-pole Ed is about worn out; his ankle is badly swollen. I have walked all the way so far, but swinging freely along the trail is much easier than running astride the rope and managing the dogs, sled and gee-pole. Thirty below.

"February 24. Walked twenty-two miles today, from Victor's to Smith's cabin and reached the latter an hour ahead of the team. Thirty degrees below this morning but much warmer tonight; looks like snow. Sent mail back to Eagle by every mail carrier we met, going up the river.

"February 25. Snow fell last night and this morning when we left Smith's cabin a keen wind came down out of the north woods. The trail was generally obliterated and traveling very bad. Came to Carsh's cabin–woodchopper, fifteen miles, but as the next cabin is twenty-two miles

Alaskan Sled Dog Tales

away we remained with Carsh for the night. Walked fifteen miles and came in an hour ahead of the dog team. Five above zero this morning, the warmest weather so far on the trip, but a bitter north wind is blowing which is in many ways worse than thirty below with no wind. Carsh and his partner cut cordwood for the A.C. Co. steamboats. The contract is signed by both partners and brings in good wages. They live in a good-sized cabin with two front doors. Carsh goes in one door and his partner in the other. Carsh lives on one side of a line drawn across the middle of the floor, his partner on the other. They do not speak to each other; each has a sheet iron stove and his own dishes. The grub pile is divided and each cooks his own food and eats it alone on his own board table. Each cuts the same amount of wood and the purser on the steamboat divides the money equally between them. We talked to both and found them pleasant fellows–to us–but on account of some misunderstanding, live solitary and speechless.

"February 26. Left Carsh's at eight o'clock; broke trail through badly drifted snow, high wind and clouds of flying snow. Traveled all day with Salmon, the mail carrier, who drove ahead and broke trail. Met a band of Indians going out on their regular spring moose hunt. Reached Ross' cabin, twenty-two miles from Carsh's, for the night; seventeen below.

"February 27. Left Ross's cabin in company with Salmon and his mail team and came into Fort Hamlin at two o'clock–thirty miles in seven hours. Hurricane of wind and snow at our backs all day, coming off the flats into the ramparts through which the Yukon breaks its way. Schidel, a trader who keeps a store here, gave us good food and a bed.

"February 28. Left Hamlin early in a frightful blizzard, wind coming into the water gap off the flats behind us accompanied by dense clouds of fine snow. Five miles down the river we found better shelter behind the bluffs, but a hurricane of wind and snow at our backs pushed

Alaskan Sled Dog Tales

us along all day. Met Jim Oldfield, mail carrier, going upriver accompanied by one of the litigants in a mining case awaiting my arrival in Rampart. He is on his way to meet my party expecting his attorney who was reported to be coming with us. He remained at Fort Hamlin hoping his attorney was yet on the trail, but he was finally disappointed. Distance traveled twenty-three miles.

"March 1. We remained last night in an old abandoned cabin, minus doors and windows, at a place called Salt Creek–a fitting name for the frightfully cold and uncomfortable place it was. No landlord, no stove, no bed–we slept in the most sheltered corner on the packs and dog harness, while the dogs huddled on our feet and at our sides for such comfort as our bodily heat gave them. Left there early ahead of the team to get warm by exercise.

"Ten miles down the river we met the whole band of Rampart Indians going on a moose hunt. Nine large sleds hauled slowly along by a pack of poor dogs hitched to each sled, carried their beds, children, old persons, and such supplies as they have left after a long hard winter in their village cabins. Counted thirty adults. They moved across the north bank of the river and camped intending to send their hunters out from that camp to kill a much-needed moose.

"Reached Tucker's cabin for the night, distance twenty-five miles. Oldfield, the mail carrier, and the litigant looking for a lawyer, came back and remained for the night.

"March 2. Left Tucker's early; passed Drew's coal mine opposite the mouth of Mike Hess Creek. Here the team caught up and we came into Rampart early in the afternoon; distance thirty miles (people are surprised to see me–say that they had no idea I would come–that I made a very quick trip, & etc.).

"Secured a room in the rear of the NAT&T Co. store, while Ed and his dogs got into an outside cabin.

Alaskan Sled Dog Tales

"March 3. A day of rest, in bed until noon; swollen ankles and blistered heels afflict us both. The dogs' feet are equally sore but there is nothing the matter with our trail appetites.

"March 4. Pursuant to public notice, a special term of the United States District Court convened at eleven o'clock today–the first court ever held in Rampart."

James Wickersham described the legal proceedings of his Rampart court, and then detailed the trip back up the Yukon River to his home in Eagle, noting "Met many stampeders from Dawson en route to Nome passing down the river with dog teams."

Also notable was this comment at Nation River roadhouse: "The roadhouse keeper reports a rich strike on Fourth of July Creek; exhibited a glass jar with fifty ounces, about eight hundred dollars, in coarse gold dust which he says came from that creek. Ran into Montauk roadhouse for the night, thirty-four miles. The dogs know we are getting home and travel better."

And the final entry in this chapter: "Left Montauk early; had lunch at Star at the mouth of Seventy-Mile River. Bought a handsome Navajo Indian blanket from Mrs. Matthews; reached Eagle and home at three o'clock; distance thirty-six miles. We were twenty-two days in going from Eagle to Rampart, less than one day and two half days not traveling–full time twenty days, a distance of 520 miles one way and an average of twenty-six miles per day. Returning in 17 days, one day at Nunivak, and one at Circle, which left us fifteen days for the return trip–an average of thirty-four miles per traveling day. We were gone forty-five days and traveled more than one thousand miles. The total expense of the trip for dog team, driver, roadhouse expenses, meals, and beds, amounted to $705. Paid driver and sent my vouchers to Washington with report, paid. Found everyone at home well and happy." ~•~

Leonhard Seppala and Togo [Lomen Bros. photo]

Alaskan Sled Dog Tales

THE 1925 SERUM RUN TO NOME
with an excerpt from Leonhard Seppala's
Seppala: Alaskan Dog Driver

"In the vast silence, Seppala could hear the patter of the dogs' feet on the crusted snow and their steady pant as they pulled ahead in the cold. There was something soothing about the sound of the sled in motion: the creak of the wood like the rigging of a schooner under full sail, the rub of rawhide lashings, the swish of the runners on the snow."
-Gay and Laney Salisbury, in The Cruelest Miles

The 1925 serum run to Nome, also known as the Great Race of Mercy, was a 675 mile dog team relay of diphtheria antitoxin across the U.S. territory of Alaska, accomplished by 20 mushers and about 150 sled dogs in only five and a half days, saving the community of Nome from a deadly epidemic. The race became both the most famous event in the history of mushing and the last hurrah for a means of transportation which had opened the vast northern territory of Alaska.

The gold rush town of Nome was still the largest town in the northern half of Alaska in 1925, with a population of around 1,500 souls. When the Bering Sea froze over the only link to the rest of the world was the Iditarod Trail, which ran 938 miles from the port of Seward, across several

Alaskan Sled Dog Tales

mountain ranges and through the vast Interior of the territory before reaching Nome. Mail and supplies were customarily transported by train to Nenana, and then freighted by dog team 675 miles from Nenana to Nome, a journey which normally took 25 days.

In January, 1925, the town's only doctor, Dr. Curtis Welch, witnessed a series of alarming deaths among his young patients, and on January 22 he sent the following telegram to Governor Bone in Juneau, and to all the major towns in Alaska:

"An epidemic of diphtheria is almost inevitable here STOP I am in urgent need of one million units of diphtheria antitoxin STOP Mail is only form of transportation STOP I have made application to Commissioner of Health of the Territories for antitoxin already STOP There are about 3000 white natives in the district."

By January 24 there were two more fatalities, and at a meeting of the board of health that same day, superintendent Mark Summers of the Hammon Consolidated Gold Fields proposed a dogsled relay, using two fast teams. One would start at Nenana and the other at Nome, and they would meet at Nulato. The trip from Nulato to Nome normally took 30 days, although the record was nine. Welch calculated that the serum would only last six days under the brutal conditions of the trail. Summers' employee, the Norwegian Leonhard Seppala, was chosen for the 630-mile round trip from Nome to Nulato and back. He had previously made the run from Nome to Nulato in a record-breaking four days, won the All-Alaska Sweepstakes three times, and had become something of a legend for his athletic ability and rapport with his Siberian huskies. His lead dog, the 12-year-old Togo, was equally famous for his leadership, intelligence, and ability to sense danger.

Nome Mayor Maynard proposed flying the antitoxin by aircraft, but the only planes operating in Alaska in 1925 were three vintage biplanes which were dismantled for the winter, had open cockpits, and had water-cooled engines that were unreliable in cold weather. While potentially quicker, the board of health rejected the aircraft option and voted unanimously for the dogsled relay. Seppala was notified that evening and immediately started preparations for the trip.

While the first batch of serum was traveling to Nenana, Governor Bone gave final authorization to the plan, but ordered Edward Wetzler, the U.S. Post Office inspector, to arrange a more encompassing relay of multiple drivers and teams across the Interior; the majority of the relay mushers selected were native Athabaskan U.S. mail carriers, widely acknowledged to be the best dog mushers in Alaska. The teams would travel day and night until they handed off the package to Seppala at Nulato.

The mail route from Nenana to Nome followed the Tanana River for 137 miles to the junction with the Yukon River, and then followed the Yukon for 230 miles to Kaltag. The route turned west, 90 miles over the Kaltag Portage to Unalakleet on the shore of Norton Sound, then continued for 208 miles northwest around the southern shore of the Seward Peninsula and 42 harrowing miles across the shifting ice of the Bering Sea.

The serum transfer points were Tolovana, Manley Hot Springs, Fish Lake, Tanana, Kallands, Nine Mile Cabin, Kokrines, Ruby, Whiskey Creek, Galena, Bishop Mountain, Nulato, Kaltag, Old Woman Shelter, Unalakleet, Shaktoolik, Golovin, Bluff, and Nome. And all along the trail were roadhouses which gave the drivers brief opportunity to warm the serum and themselves: the Tolovana Roadhouse, the Minto roadhouse, the Manley Roadhouse, the Eskimo Roadhouse at Isaac's Point, Shaktoolik Roadhouse, Dexter's Roadhouse, the Olson Roadhouse, the Solomon Roadhouse, the Bluff Roadhouse, the Port Safety Roadhouse. Links in a thin chain winding across northwestern Alaska, providing brief intervals of safety and protection to the mushers and their dogs.

Alaskan Sled Dog Tales

The story of the 1925 Serum Run was detailed in a bestselling book by cousins Gay and Laney Salisbury, *The Cruelest Miles* (W.W. Norton & Co., 2003), but the most compelling recounting was given in a book written 73 years earlier, by the famous Alaskan musher Leonhard Seppala, who carried the serum over the treacherous ice of Norton Sound. This is an excerpt from the final chapter of *Seppala: Alaskan Dog Driver*, by Elizabeth Ricker (Little, Brown & Co., 1930), about Seppala's intrepid lead dog, Togo:

The Commissioner had asked me to get off without delay. He explained that such serum as they had was several years old, and with the epidemic steadily increasing they were in dire need of a new supply. I singled the dogs out one by one; naturally not one wanted to be left behind. Twenty were chosen. I planned to drop some of them off along the way, to be cared for at Eskimo igloos until the return trip, when we could substitute the fresh dogs for the tired ones. Also, if any of them showed any signs of weakness or sore feet, they would have a chance to rest up and be in good condition for the home stretch. I intended to leave twelve dogs by the way, arriving in Nulato with a team of eight. I should hardly need more, as I was told the package containing the serum was very light. With fresh reinforcement on the way back I should be able to drive day and night. Thus I picked out the twenty best dogs, though at the time all were on their best behavior, raising their paws politely and pleading to be taken. A dog named Fox was left as leader for the cull team, which was to continue hauling supplies during our absence and was composed of dogs too slow to be of much use in a fast run.

The people of Nome gave us a great send-off. They knew it was a long, hazardous trip, and they realized what a word of encouragement would mean. The first day we made about thirty-three miles, and from then on the team warmed up to the work and averaged fifty miles and over every day. We passed two villages where there were government

Alaskan Sled Dog Tales

schools for Eskimo children, and I told the teachers about the epidemic, advising them to close the school, to keep the children in quarantine, and away from people passing from Nome.

We were lucky in having favorable weather, and the trails were at their best. According to plan, some of the dogs were left along the way to be cared for while the rest of us pushed on. On the third day we arrived at Isaac's Point, where we stopped with an Eskimo family, having covered a hundred and thirty miles since leaving Nome. The next day we started off for Shaktoolik, a native village on the south side of the Bay. It was late by the time we set out over the ice of Norton Bay. We could see it was blowing hard out on the Bay, and with the north wind at our backs we were sure to make good time. The team would deserve a good rest at the end of the day, and surely I should welcome it as well as the dogs. Having crossed the ice, and being just in sight of our destination for the day, we scented another dog team and struck out with a great spurt. As we came up I could see that the driver was busy refereeing a dog fight. With a word of greeting to the man, I was about to pass by when he called to me. In the wind, and with my parka hood up over my ears, I got only three words" "serum–turn back." I thought I must have misunderstood, but when I looked back over my shoulder I saw the other driver waving his arm. I called to Togo to "gee," but he couldn't. The other dogs were still on the spurt, and I had to run about a mile further on before I could slow the team down and turn them. We came to a stretch of hard snow, where I was able to get the dogs under control. Though they hated to, they followed Togo. When we reached the other team a package was tossed into my sled and the stranger handed me a paper which proved to be the instructions accompanying the serum. The young dogs in my team began acting disgracefully, wanting to pick a quarrel with the strange team. Their driver explained that after I had passed out of telephone communication the epidemic had increased so

Alaskan Sled Dog Tales

alarmingly that the officials had decided to speed the serum by short relays running night and day. Thus I had reached the serum after traveling only a hundred and seventy miles, instead of the three hundred for which I had originally planned.

We had had a hard day, covering forty-three miles with the wind at our backs. But the return was even harder.

The gale was in our faces, the temperature was thirty below, and we had the forty-three miles to do over again in the dark. There was nothing for it but to face the music. The dogs did their best, and I drove as if we were in a race. The ice of Norton Sound is notoriously treacherous: it has a habit of shifting and breaking up, so that before travelers know it they have gone for miles on a loose ice-cake with open water on all sides, slowly but surely being blown out into the Bering Sea.

In spite of these unpleasant prospects, we managed to reach Isaac's Point, and after a drive of nearly ninety miles the team were grateful for a brief rest in a comfortable kennel. They were wild for their rations of salmon and seal blubber. After they were fed I went into the igloo and read over the instructions. They called for the serum to be warmed up at each station. Accordingly I pulled the sled inside, and undid the fur and canvas wrapped around the package. I found the serum was sealed up in paper cartons, and as I saw nothing about breaking the seals I instructed the Eskimo to make the igloo good and hot and left the package exposed to the heat. As I looked it over and felt of it I was convinced that if it was a liquid it must have been frozen in the severe cold, though we had protected it as well as possible. I doubted if the heat could penetrate the paper cartons, but I had taken off the last wrapping which I was authorized to touch.

When I had allowed as much time as we could spare I came out to the dogs and began putting them back on the line. An old Eskimo stood by as we hitched up, and observing the increase in the wind he cautioned me:

Alaskan Sled Dog Tales

"Maybe ice not much good. Maybe breaking off and go out. Old trail plenty no good. Maybe you go more closer shore." I thanked him and followed his suggestion, taking a trail further in. At that, we came within a few feet of open water, as the trail over which we had traveled only the day before had broken off and drifted far out into the Bering Sea.

During the afternoon we pulled into Cheenik Village, where another driver was waiting with his relay team. We had traveled in all three hundred and forty miles in the interest of the serum. No other relay made more than fifty-three miles. After delivering the package to the driver at Cheenik, a tired driver and dogs all had a good rest until the next day, when we drove to Solomon and then on into Nome. When we arrived there the whole town seemed to be out to meet us. It was like the winner's reception after a Sweepstakes race.

News of the diphtheria had found its way to the outside papers, and in the States the teams were being followed from day to day by the press. They had become heroes while they were peacefully going on their way, totally unconscious that they were headliners in the press. The last relay team landed the serum in Nome at six o-clock on the morning of the second of February, 1925.

The Serum Drive was Togo's last long run. In that drive he had worked the hardest and best. I appreciated this, and tried to take the best possible care of the old dog. Togo, in his sixteenth year, seemed content to rest on his laurels. He even posed without fuss for a photograph with his cups and trophies, perhaps imagining himself as he was in the old days. It seemed best to leave him where he could be pensioned and enjoy a well-earned rest. But it was a sad parting on a cold gray March morning when Togo raised a small paw to my knee as if questioning why he was not going along with me. For the first time in twelve years I hit the trail without Togo. ~•~

Eli A. Smith, U.S.M. Carrier
Left Nome Alaska Nov. 14, 1905. Arrived Washington D.C. Feb. 25, 1907

FROM NOME TO WASHINGTON, D.C.
The Story of Eli A. Smith

In 1905 Frank and Brownie Caldwell of Indianapolis, Indiana traveled to Alaska and the Yukon on their honeymoon, from Ketchikan to Juneau, Sitka, and Skagway; over the White Pass Route to Whitehorse and and then by river steamer to Dawson City, Yukon, and down the Yukon River to Circle City and finally Nome. Mr. Caldwell was an advance manager for Reverend John P. D. John, a Methodist minister who wanted to bring religion to the gold camps, and the Caldwells also gathered stories, photographs and information for a travelogue series. Mrs. Caldwell's photos, taken with a small box camera, which were used to make hand-colored glass projection slides for the travelogue, and their adventurous stories were published in extensive newspaper accounts of the day.

Alaskan Sled Dog Tales

In December of 1906, after the Caldwells had been on the lecture circuit for several months when Frank met Eli Smith, an Alaskan mail carrier about two-thirds his way from Nome, Alaska to Washington, D.C. Eli Smith was a native of Wisconsin, who for many years had been carrying the U.S. Mail by dogsled along the Alaskan trails out of Nome. One cold nite, while drinking (tea) in the Malamute saloon, Eli entered into a wager of $10,000.00 that he could deliver, within a certain number of months, a letter from the Postmaster of Nome to the Postmaster General in Washington, D.C. The only means of carrying this letter was to be with Eli's dogteam and sled, although he could take a boat from Valdez to Seattle as there were no roads or trails over that route.

Eli left Nome on November 14, 1905 and made the 1,530 miles to Valdez in 37 days. In a paper he prepared when his father's papers were donated to the Library of Congress in 1985, Frank Caldwell's son, Fenton Caldwell, included a few excerpts from Eli's diary; "Dec. 6, 1905 – On Yukon ice, thermometer about 60 below. Ran across two men fetching badly frozen man in to Tanana, and bad trail, men and dogs played out.

Eli Smith and his team shortly after arrival in Washington D.C., Feb. 20, 1907. The boy on the dogsled is President Theodore Roosevelt's son, Quentin Roosevelt.

Alaskan Sled Dog Tales

Sleded frozen man into Tanana and sent back fresh team for others. Frozen man and Gus Brown died next day." "Dec. 9 – On Tanana ice about 50 below. Overtook man dragging sled by yoke. When made camp found both his hands frozen; he didn't know it before. Thawed them out with snow and warm water; they didn't blister, but turned brown. Knew they were gone, so roped him around waste to the back of my sled to hold him up and keep him moving - **** headed for the fort. Sugeon chopped his hands off for him". – Dec. 19 – Met Sourdough Mary going into Dawson from her Copper River placers. Fine team. Said she'd been delayed a week thawing out four men she'd found freezing on the trail and there dogs played out. Gave her some dog moccasins."

After arriving in Valdez, the boat trip to Seattle was made without incident, and Eli and his team of nine dogs headed east, toward Washington, 3,000 miles away, and met Frank Caldwell in St. Louis. Fenton Caldwell wrote about what happened next:

"Three lectures were scheduled for Dec. 7th and 8th in Tomlinson Hall, Indianapolis and Eli agreed to be there to go on stage with his outfit but he must go overland. I feel sure that, from reading Dads scrap book he must have had some rather nervous moments wondering if Eli would make this first appearance on time. I quote a letter written by Eli on hotel stationery bearing pictures of the St Louis fair dated Nov. 22, 1906. 'Mr. Frank Caldwell, Dear Sir; I take the pleasure of wrighting to you with reguards to what we ware talking about wile you were in St. Louis in giving that lecture in Indianapolis on Alaska and what you could do with the dogs. I have arrived in Springfield and if you make arrangements wright to me and let me know. I will bee hear until next Thursday hoping to hear by return mail, Yours ever, Eli. A. Smith, U.S. Mail carrier, from Nome, Alaska, address Springfield, Gen. Delivery.'"

"Also a telegram dated Dec. 4th from Decatur, Ill. reads; - 'Mr. Frank Caldwell, Indpls, Ind. Roads are bad will leave today, Eli A. Smith, 1220 PM.'

"It also appears, from press reports, that Eli made it from Decatur to Indianapolis in three days and, before a large audience, during an

Alaskan Sled Dog Tales

intermission of Dads lecture the lights came on in Tomlinson Hall and from the wing of the stage seven Alaskan dogs came lunging out with the loaded sled and Eli in all his furs at the pole yelling 'Mush-Wolf! Hya Sport! Mush-On, Pasco!'"

For the next several months Frank Caldwell and Eli Smith traveled parallel paths, with Mr. Caldwell going by train with his considerable load of slide show equipment, and Eli Smith mushing his seven-dog team to meet him at the selected rendezvous and speaking places en route, all the way to the Capitol in Washington D.C.

Upon his arrival in Washington, Eli was greeted at the White House by President Teddy Roosevelt, posed for photos with the President's son Quentin in his dogsled, and then went on to the Post Office Department with his team to deliver the letter from Nome to the Postmaster General, Mr. Cortelyou. Fenton Caldwell wrote, "I have a rather vivid memory of

When the snow gave out Eli Smith put wheels on his dogsled.

Alaskan Sled Dog Tales

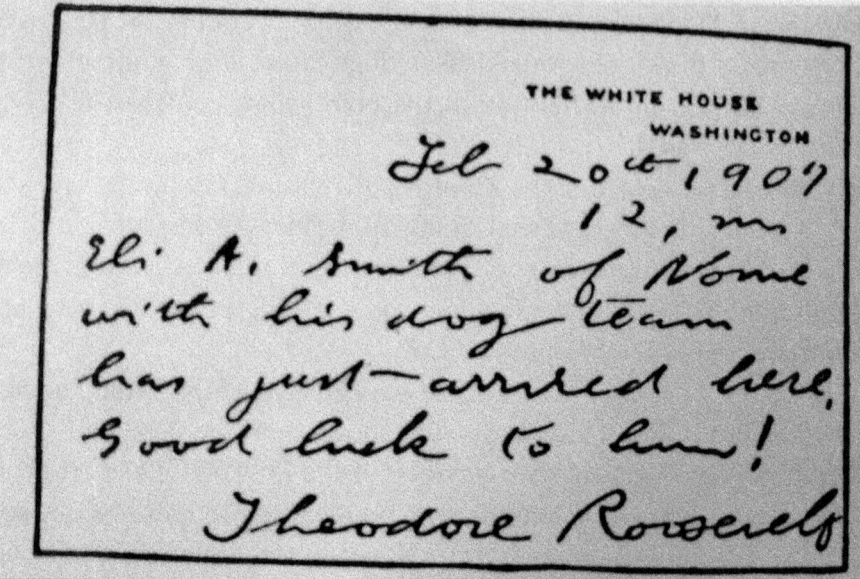

Feb. 20th, 1907. Eli A. Smith of Nome with his dog team has just arrived here. Good luck to him! Theodore Rooevelt

Eli because he came out to our house at 929 Udell St. with his dog team and sled and spent Friday nite Dec. 7, 1906, putting his dogs to bed in our back yard. Eli was not a large man but seemed to be all muscle and sinew. His face was like Cordaven leather, his hands were rough and bony and his voice was rasping. I never felt at ease in his presense and those dogs terrified me."

The collaboration of Frank Caldwell and Eli Smith resulted in a book, *Wolf the Storm Leader*, published by Dodd Mead & Co. in 1910 and reprinted in 1937. Told from the perspective of a wolf in Smith's team, the book became a popular one with a readership which loved northland dog stories such as *Balto*, *White Fang*, and *The Call of the Wild*.

Eli Smith's epic trip began, as noted, with a wager of $10,000 if the 8,000-mile journey could be made in 18 months. As an accomplished mail team driver Eli Smith had a good foundation for starting the trip, and he chose ten good dogs to haul his 450 pounds of food, gear, and letters for President Theodore Roosevelt. He left Nome on Nov. 14, 1905, following

Alaskan Sled Dog Tales

the Iditarod Trail south out of Nome, and he didn't see another human for the first eight days of his trip. He would win his bet and return to Nome on the same sled, but not until almost five years had passed.

In a 2012 article for the Washington, Pennsylvania newspaper, the *Observer-Reporter*, writer Park Burroughs told of Eli Smith's visit to his area a century before: "Smith was a Wisconsin native who had gone to Alaska to search for gold. He returned home in May in the most novel fashion and settled in for a long visit in Milwaukee. But while there, three of his dogs died from poisoning. On Sept. 8, Smith resumed his journey with the remaining seven of his team.

"Smith passed through West Alexander and arrived in Claysville on Feb. 8, spending the night at the Central Hotel. The next day, he arrived in Washington [PA]. 'His dog team came down the west Washington Hill on the jump and it was a novel sight,' *The Washington Reporter* noted.

"Residents were infatuated by Smith's 'wolf dogs,' which were boarded at the Hoxworth livery stables on East Wheeling Street. Smith told them that he knew Jack London when the author was in Alaska, and that one of his dogs was inspiration for the principal character in *'The Call of the Wild.'*

"On the night of Sunday, Feb. 11, Smith lectured at Town Hall about his adventures, introduced his dogs – the leader Pasco, Wolf, Frank, Sport, Jim, Spot and Jack – and demonstrated the use of snowshoes.

"A photograph of a crowd surrounding the sled and team appeared in Monday's newspaper with another article: 'The animals were hitched up Sunday and took a little run about town. It is likely that the weather had something to do with the interest here, as the dogs were seen under almost their native conditions of cold and snow. When they started out Monday morning to resume their track toward the national capital, they were waving their bushy tails and seemed as eager for the road as a hunting dog is for the field of chase.'

"It's probable that the photographer who captured that image was Dan Harbaugh, who was so taken with Smith's endeavor that he followed him to Cumberland, Md., and proceeded ahead of him to

Alaskan Sled Dog Tales

Washington, D.C., to serve as a volunteer advance publicity agent. When the mailman visited the White House, gave President Roosevelt's sons a ride on the sled and was given a handwritten note from the president as proof of his accomplishment, Harbaugh was with him and shook Teddy's hand. 'This trip is the trip of my life,' he wrote to his boss, E.K. Weller, who operated a photo studio on North Main Street in Washington.

"Smith did not leave the nation's capital until Jan. 5, 1908. He had planned to travel back to Nome by train and by boat, but driving the sled must have become too comfortable to abandon and the lecture fees too necessary to pass up. He did not make it back to Nome until 1910. He died in 1948 at the age of 93."

Frank Caldwell's book, *Wolf the Storm Leader*, which included the story of Smith's epic journey, would remain popular and be kept in print for half a century, becoming a beloved classic in northland literature. ~•~

Eli A. Smith's dogteam, with Wolf, the Storm Leader, identified.

Alaskan Sled Dog Tales

Col. Goodwin's 1910 expedition measuring the Seward to Nome route with a cyclometer attached to dogsled. [BLM photograph]

Col. Goodwin, 1908 Iditarod Trail

The first chapter of another book from Northern Light Media, *The First Iditarod: Mushers' Tales from the 1973 Race,* by Helen Hegener, shares the history of the Iditarod Trail: "Before there was an Iditarod Trail there were shorter routes and trails used by the Native peoples of the land; the *Dena'ina* and *Deg Hit'an* Athabaskan Indians of south-central Alaska, and the *Inupiaq* and *Yup'ik* Eskimos farther north. They were not mushing trails, however. The early peoples viewed dogs as useful for tracking game and sometimes hauling travois-like sleds, but mushing teams of dogs as we know it came later, during the gold rush of the late 1800s, when the prospectors and miners needed a reliable mode of transportation and freight hauling."

The book details how gold was discovered in Nome, Fairbanks, and near Ruby, recounts the first official scouting of the trail in the winter of 1908 by a four-person crew headed by Colonel Walter L. Goodwin, and

Alaskan Sled Dog Tales

then reports a strike was made at Iditarod: "On Christmas day, 1908, two prospectors, William A. Dikeman and John Beaton, both veterans of the Klondike gold rush, discovered gold near the Iditarod River. The last great gold rush was on, and between 1910 and 1912, 10,000 gold seekers came to Alaska's 'Inland Empire,' taking $30 million worth of gold from the ground."

"In 1910 the Alaska Road Commission once again sent Colonel Walter L. Goodwin to follow the Iditarod Trail, this time brushing and mapping the route with ten men and 42 dogs in six dog teams. Starting from Nome on November 9, 1910, they surveyed and recorded the trail, and located potential sites for roadhouses, keeping a log of the distances covered with cyclometers attached to the sides of their dogsleds. Goodwin and his men reached Seward on February 25, 1911, having blazed the Seward to Nome Mail Trail, as it was then known."

That initial exploration of the Iditarod Trail by Colonel Goodwin two years previously, in 1908, resulted in a detailed report he sent to the office of the Alaska Road Commission in Skagway, dated April 16, 1908: "Sirs: I have the honor to report of the Winter Reconnaissance, Seward to Nome, just completed, under written and verbal instructions of Captain Pillsbury, dated January 4th, 1908, as follows:

"After having two basket sleds and 18 sets of dog harness made and assembling provisions and camp outfit at Seattle, I sailed accompanied by Ross J. Kinney and three dogs purchased at Seattle, on S.S. Northwestern on Jan. 16th and reached Seward on Jan. 25th. At Seward we spent five days in arranging equipment, 'tyring out' dogs and repacking the outfit ready for the trip, and the party composed of myself, Geo E. Pulham, R.J. Kinney and Frank Jackson left Seward on Jan 31st.

"The route traversed, briefly described was as follows: The Alaska Central Railway was followed to its end at Mile 54, thence via Turnagain Arm, Glacier Creek, Crow Creek Pass, Eagle River, across country to Old

Alaskan Sled Dog Tales

Knik, across Knik Arm to New Knik, across country to Susitna Station, up the Susitna three miles, up the Yentna, Skwentna and Happy Rivers, Pass Creek to Rainy Pass, down the Dalzell, Rohn and Kuskokwim Rivers to near the Tonzona, across country to the mouth of the Tacotna at McGrath's, up the Tacotna and across country to the Tacotna Slough, over rolling hills to Gane Creek, down Gane and across country to Ophir Creek (the Innoko district), across country to Dishakaket and thence across country to the Kaiyuk Slough to the Yukon, and up the Yukon to Kaltag, and by the Overland Mail Trail via Unalaklik to Nome.

Col. Goodwin provided good descriptions of their travels, and he includes a listing of the many roadhouses along the trail from Seward to Iditarod, approximately 10 to 20 miles apart, (following page). ~•~

View of the town of Iditarod, mountains and streams [between ca. 1900 and ca. 1930] - From: Frank and Frances Carpenter collection (Library of Congress). Gift; Mrs. W. Chapin Huntington; 1951. Library of Congress Prints and Photographs Division, Washington, D.C.

Alaskan Sled Dog Tales

Revised Distance Table
Seward-----to------Iditarod.

Seward to Kern Creek	72 Miles
Glacier Creek Road House	74
Crow Creek Mining Co.	81
Raven Creek Road House	92
Eagle River R.H.	110
Old Knik R.H.	127
New Knik (Settlement)	145
Little Susitna R.H.	167
Susitna (Settlement)	181
Alexander Creek R.H.	189
Lake View R.H.	199
Skwentna R.H.	219
Half Way R.H.	240
Mouth Happy River R.H.	260
Road House	264
Road House	275
Pass Creek R.H.	289
Summit R. Pass (R.H.)	297
Rainy Pass R.H.	302
Rohn River R.H.	311
Farewell Mt. R.H.	330
Peluk Creek R.H.	350
Sullivan Creek R.H.	358
Bear Creek R.H.	367
Salmon Creek R.H.	371
Big River (Berry's) R.H.	387
Crooked Creek R.H.	392
Northern Com. Co. Trading Sta.	410
Kuskokwim Com. Co. Station	411
Tacotna Settlement	427
Big Creek R.H.	441
Half Way R.H.	454
Lincoln Creek R.H.	460
Moore Creek R.H.	476
Ruby Road House	487
Bonanza Creek R.H.	501
Iditarod (Settlement)	520

THE MUSHING PARSON AND HIS TEAM OF DOGS

AN ALASKAN "MUSH" TO PRESBYTERY
BY THE REV. S. HALL YOUNG

"In the summer of 1879 I was stationed at Fort Wrangell in southeastern Alaska, whence I had come the year before, a green young student fresh from college and seminary–very green and very fresh–to do what I could towards establishing the white man's civilization among the Thlinget Indians. I had very many things to learn and many more to unlearn."

These are the opening words of Reverend Samuel Hall Young's classic 1915 book, *Alaska Days with John Muir* (Fleming H. Revell Co., New York 1915). Young paints a vivid picture of the iconic naturalist, arriving on a steamboat with a group of people Young had come down to the dock to meet: "Standing a little apart from them as the steamboat drew to the dock, his peering blue eyes already eagerly scanning the islands and

Alaskan Sled Dog Tales

mountains, was a lean, sinewy man of forty, with waving, reddish-brown hair and beard, and shoulders slightly stooped. He wore a Scotch cap and a long, gray tweed ulster, which I have always since associated with him, and which seemed the same garment, unsoiled and unchanged, that he wore later on his northern trips. He was introduced as Professor Muir, the Naturalist."

Reverend Young and Mr. Muir were destined to become great friends, and Young details their first mountain-climbing jaunt with great relish: "I had been with mountain climbers before, but never one like him. A deer-lope over the smoother slopes, a sure instinct for the easiest way into a rocky fortress, an instant and unerring attack, a serpent-glide up the steep; eye, hand and foot all connected dynamically; with no appearance of weight to his body—as though he had Stockton's negative gravity machine strapped on his back." The book is online to read or download free. The first two chapters are a breathless recitation of the thrilling climb across a glacier and up a sheer mountainside to see the sunset from the peak, and when near-tragedy befalls Reverend Young the story relates Muir's almost unbelievably heroic rescue of his friend.

Reverend Young, the first missionary in Alaska, recounts a six-week voyage through southeastern waters he undertook in a great cedar canoe with Muir and a half-dozen Thlinget Indians as scouts and crew. Visiting villages along the route, Young noted: "I took the census of each village, getting the heads of the families to count their relatives with the aid of beans,—the large brown beans representing men, the large white ones, women, and the small Boston beans, children. In this manner the first census of southeastern Alaska was taken."

One night John Muir stumbled into their Glacier Bay camp with two Indians who'd guided the great explorer off the glacier which would bear his name. Muir had been long overdue when Reverend Young sent them to build a beacon fire, which Muir admitted turned his back in the right direction, but then he excitedly added, "Man, man; you ought to have been with me. You'll never make up what you have lost to-day. I've been

Alaskan Sled Dog Tales

wandering through a thousand rooms of God's crystal temple. I've been a thousand feet down in the crevasses, with matchless domes and sculptured figures and carved ice-work all about me. Solomon's marble and ivory palaces were nothing to it. Such purity, such color, such delicate beauty! I was tempted to stay there and feast my soul, and softly freeze, until I would become part of the glacier. What a great death that would be!"

At the end of the voyage Reverend Young wrote, "I have made many voyages in that great Alexandrian Archipelago since, traveling by canoe over fifteen thousand miles—not one of them a dull one—through its intricate passages; but none compared, in the number and intensity of its thrills, in the variety and excitement of its incidents and in its lasting impressions of beauty and grandeur, with this first voyage when we groped our way northward with only Vancouver's old chart as our guide."

The following spring John Muir returned from his home in the sunny south, determined to visit the glaciers they had not seen on their trip the previous fall, and they once more set out in a cedar canoe with Native guides. Reverend Young wrote: "When we were about to embark I suddenly thought of my little dog Stickeen and made the resolve to take him along. My wife and Muir both protested and I almost yielded to their persuasion. I shudder now to think what the world would have lost had their arguments prevailed! That little, long-haired, brisk, beautiful, but very independent dog, in co-ordination with Muir's genius, was to give to the world one of its greatest dog-classics."

The book which Muir would later write was, of course, the classic *Stickeen: The Story of a Dog* (Riverside Press, Cambridge, MA 1909), which relates one of John Muir's most harrowing adventures, accompanied only by his friend's small dog. Unable to convince the adventure-loving dog to remain behind, Muir set out to explore the face of a great glacier, and reached a dangerous crevasse blocking his way, with only a thin ice-bridge as a crossing and unimaginable black depths below it. He wrote of little Stickeen, showing something of his own nature in telling the story:

Alaskan Sled Dog Tales

"Never before had the daring midget seemed to know that ice was slippery or that there was any such thing as danger anywhere. His looks and tones of voice when he began to complain and speak his fears were so human that I unconsciously talked to him as I would to a frightened boy, and in trying to calm his fears perhaps in some measure moderated my own. 'Hush your fears, my boy,' I said, 'we will get across safe, although it is not going to be easy. No right way is easy in this rough world. We must risk our lives to save them. At the worst we can only slip, and then how grand a grave we will have, and by and by our nice bones will do good in the terminal moraine.'"

Reverend Young and John Muir remained lifelong friends. During the 10 years he lived and worked in Wrangell with his family, Rev. Young established several southeastern missions and became a man of some standing. In 1897 he was strongly considered for appointment as governor of the territory of Alaska by President McKinley. Instead he traveled over Chilkoot Pass and down the Yukon River at the height of the Klondike gold rush, and established the first Presbyterian church in Dawson City in 1898. Continuing down the Yukon River over the next three years, he organized missions at Eagle, Rampart, Nome, and Teller. In 1901 he was appointed superintendent of all Alaska Presbyterian missions. He lived at Skagway in 1902-1903, at Council in 1903-1904, at Fairbanks from 1904-06 and again 1907-08, at Teller in 1907, at Cordova in 1908-10, and Iditarod in 1911-12. During those years he gained a 'Doctor of Divinity' designation and became known as "the mushing parson" because of his many long journeys by dogteam.

In 1913 Dr. Young wrote an article for the church publication *The Continent* in which he shared his story of a journey via dogteam from Iditarod to Seward over the Iditarod Trail, and then by steamer to Cordova, for an important General Assembly of the church. He was accompanied by a young Scotchman and experienced dog musher named Breeze; the few photographs accompanying the article are to treasure, and his colorful first-hand descriptions of the trail are a delight to read.

Alaskan Sled Dog Tales

"The journey is to lead across three high ranges of mountains and two great valleys, the Kuskokwim and the Susitna. The trail has been but recently laid out by the government and is little used, but there are roadhouses here and there at irregular intervals and we will take enough provisions with us for emergencies. As to its being at all a formidable undertaking, why, the prospectors, miners and hunters of Alaska take far harder and longer trips constantly and break the trail for their dogs the whole way in unexplored territory. I anticipate the pleasure of that trip across new country with keen delight."

Dr. Young regaled his readers with wonderful descriptions of the trail, including detailed observations and comments about the many roadhouses visited en route. For this reason, the complete text of his article for *The Continent* is included in this book, beginning on page 77.

The remaining years of Rev. Young's life were detailed in a biography by Alaskan historian Robert DeArmond: "From 1913 until 1921, Young held the title Special Representative of the Presbyterian National Board of Missions, with headquarters in New York, and during that time he made many trips back to Alaska. His wife, Fannie Kellogg Young died in 1915. He was named general missionary for Alaska in 1922 and superintendent of Alaska missions in 1924, with headquarters in Seattle.

"In the summer of 1927, as he approached his 80th birthday, he escorted three different groups of Presbyterians to Alaska; then went east to attend a reunion. He was riding in a friend's car when it had a flat tire. When Young stepped out, he was struck by an inter-urban trolley. He died in the Clarksburg, West Virginia, Hospital September 2, 1927, and was buried beside Mrs. Young at Syracuse, New York.

"His books include *The Klondike Clan, Adventures in Alaska*, and an autobiography, *Hall Young of Alaska*, published shortly after his death. It dwells particularly upon his first decade in Alaska and his work with the Natives. Mount Young in the Chilkat Range, Young Island in Glacier Bay, and Young Rock, which he discovered near Wrangell, were all named for S. Hall Young."

Alaskan Sled Dog Tales

AN ALASKAN "MUSH" TO PRESBYTERY
by the Rev. S. Hall Young, for *The Continent*, Feb. 13, 1913

NOW, IF I am to tell you this story, I hope you will rid your mind of all hardship and hero gush. There are fewer hardships in Alaska than in any other country I know. The people live an exuberant life there with wealth and all that goes to make up the externals of happiness. And as to the heroism, that is all nonsense. I am in Alaska as I write because I like it, because it is the most comfortable, pleasant land to live in and to work in that I know of anywhere and, however insane you may consider the statement, I would rather take a journey like that I am about to describe than go around the world or have a million dollars. I can read all about a journey around the world, and the million dollars would fill my life full of care and trouble; but I cannot read about the region I traversed last spring, and there is no anxious care in simply making your journey day by day, from roadhouse to roadhouse, or to a camp in the snow. Your blood leaps in your veins. The struggle, which Emerson says is the best thing in life, is yours, and the daily victory. Nature sings overhead and underneath and all around you. Pessimism and gloom and homesickness are impossible on the trail.

Alaskan Sled Dog Tales

The time was last March, beginning with the 5th; the occasion was the meeting of presbytery at Cordova, on the coast. It was a very necessary meeting, for we must send a delegate to General Assembly. We must assert ourselves again as the biggest presbytery belonging to that body—in space I mean.

I was at Iditarod, 720 miles from Cordova. Dr. Koonce was at Cordova and Dr. Condit at Fairbanks, 442 miles inland from Cordova. There was no other way for me to get to presbytery but to take my dogs and "mush." To those ignorant people who do not know the meaning of that term, I will condescend to explain that the word "mush" is a corruption of the French marchez, which the coureurs du bois shout at their dogs as they urge them along. It is the word now universally used to describe a journey over the trail, and when we drive our dogs or wish to chase them out of the house, we shout "mush!"

The journey is to lead across three high ranges of mountains and two great valleys, the Kuskokwim and the Susitna. The trail has been but recently laid out by the government and is little used, but there are roadhouses here and there at irregular intervals and we will take enough provisions with us for emergencies. As to its being an at all formidable undertaking, why, the prospectors, miners and hunters of Alaska take far harder and longer trips constantly and break the trail for their dogs the whole way in unexplored territory. I anticipate the pleasure of that trip across new country with keen delight. A young Scotchman from the north of Ireland, William Breeze, known far and wide as an experienced "dog musher," is to be my companion. He is bound for Susitna, 300 miles from Iditarod, on a prospecting trip, and will take care of my dogs, boil their feed at night and do the heaviest part of the work.

And now let me introduce you to my team. It is one of the finest teams in all the North. They are five pups of the same litter now 6 or 7 years old. They are a cross between the MacKenzie River husky and the shepherd dog, and have the long hair and hardy endurance of the former and the sagacity, intelligence and affection of the latter. Being brothers, they know each other and are taught to work together, although this fact

Alaskan Sled Dog Tales

does not hinder them from engaging in a general mixup now and again. However, if attacked by strange dogs, the whole five work together beautifully, centering their forces with Napoleonic strategy and beating the enemy in detail. The leader is black, white and tan. marked like a shepherd dog. He had been named "Nigger," but I have changed his name simply to "Leader." It sounds enough like the original to please him and set him going.

The sled is a basket sleigh with handle bars and brake at the back and a "gee-pole" in front, with an extra rope when we have to "neck it" to help the dogs. My wolf robe, given me by Third church of Pittsburg and my old church at Cedar Falls, Iowa, is spread on the floor of the sleigh for my accommodation in the brief intervals of riding. For "dog mushing" in Alaska does not mean luxuriously riding in your sleigh wrapped up in your fur robe while the dogs haul you along the trail. When Egbert Koonce sledded 1,200 miles from Rampart to Valdez in 1902 on his way to General Assembly, I told the Assembly of his feat. A good old doctor of divinity said: "It must be, after all, a really luxurious way of traveling, wrapped up in your furs and reclining in a comfortable sleigh behind your dogs."

I turned to Koonce and asked him how much of that 1,200 miles he rode. He replied, "About two miles."

I shall ride more than this on my way to Seward, but there will not be many places where I can ride half a mile without getting out and running behind the dogs. The beauty of dog mushing is that you are compelled to work as hard as the dogs. You are not on a beaten boulevard, but are wending your way around trees and stumps, over hummocks, up and down hill, along the sides of the mountains, and must keep your hands on the handle bars, lifting the sled on the trail where it runs off and often breaking the trail ahead with your snowshoes. When the dogs are on fairly good roads, they swing along uninterruptedly and you run your best behind. If there are two of you, one holds the handle bars and the other sprints on alone, either in front or behind the sleigh. You will get pretty tired the first two or three days, but after your muscles become

Alaskan Sled Dog Tales

hardened and you get your second wind you can run at your keenest gait two or three miles at a time.

On the Trail Through the Wilderness

But let us get started. The trail is well beaten from Iditarod to Flat City, seven and a half miles, and I get aboard, Breeze at the handle bars. My huskies leap into the harness at the word and we make a flying start. I ride perhaps half a mile, then jump off without stopping the team and run ahead of the dogs up the hill. 1 soon find my fur "parkie" too heavy and discard it for the lighter one made of drilling, in which I do the rest of my mushing to the end of the trail. Moccasins are on my feet, for the trail must be taken flat-footed if one is to have reasonable comfort. A brief halt at Flat to bid friends there good-by, and off we go again.

After two or three miles we leave the broad road and strike the trail .through the wilderness. We soon begin to labor up the first divide. No more riding now. The trail is hard enough to dispense with snowshoes, but heavy enough to make us both walk and labor. I strike the trail ahead, leaving Breeze to the handle bars. I begin to feel the joy of it. The keen, dry air is like wine. The trail winds through the woods, along the edges of gorges and then up a steep mountain. Now the timber ceases and we have rounded wind-swept summits. I leave the little dogs far behind, for it is heavy pulling up the steep. Their bells twinkle faintly from below. I gain nearly a mile on them before they round the summit. I strike my lope down the farther side, but soon hear the bells as they charge down upon me and pass me swinging on toward the roadhouse.

We make only twenty miles the first day, for it was nearly noon when we started, and we are glad to stop at Bonanza roadhouse when dusk is coming on. How good the moose meat tastes! How sweet the beds of hard boards and blankets! The luxury of rest we enjoy to the full. The dogs are fed, our moccasins and German socks hung up to dry and we crawl into our bunks with sighs of relief. There is no floor in the roadhouse, all the lumber has been whipsawed by hand, the furniture manufactured out of boxes and stumps and the utensils are the rudest.

Alaskan Sled Dog Tales

But the luxury of splendid meat and good sour-dough bread and coffee makes us feel that we have all that goes to make life desirable.

An early start is necessary every morning. We eat our breakfast by candle light, fill up our thermos bottle with hot coffee, take a big hunk of roasted meat for lunch and "hit the trail" by daylight.

Twenty-six miles today to Moore Creek roadhouse. Snow begins falling in the morning and soon the trail is obliterated by the fast coming feathery flakes. Now the snowshoes must be unstrapped and one must break the trail ahead. We take turns and swing along at a three and a half mile gait. This is real work, and we reach the roadhouse in the middle of the afternoon, really not so tired as on the preceding day.

These are samples of the journey throughout, but, oh, the variety—no two miles alike—and the panorama of beauty that unfolds before us! Notice the beauty of the frost sparkles on the trees. The wonderful law that gives its own distinct varieties of frost crystals to each species of tree; fir, spruce, birch, cottonwood or alder, is exemplified so plainly here that after the first examination you can tell the kind of tree under the frost crystals by the shade of silver. The mountains tower above you, windswept, waving snow banners. The vastness of that white hush awes and thrills you. A rough sound would be blasphemy in the solemn silence. The whole landscape is a poem.

The third day we make a "long leg," as the sailors say, from Moore Creek roadhouse to Big Creek, thirty-six miles, every foot of which we have to break trail with snowshoes. I strike ahead on my light "trailers" and Breeze wallows along behind. The fresh snow is so light and deep that it is difficult for him to keep the sled on the trail, and I often mislead by veering a little to right or left. When this occurs, down goes the sled in the deep snow beside the trail, and it has to be lifted up again and the dogs urged on.

I get far in advance of him again and again. When I get weary snowshoeing, Breeze takes my place and I his at the handle bars. But in spite of the heavy trail and the weary work for dogs and men, we make the thirty-six miles.

Alaskan Sled Dog Tales

The coming day we have but fourteen miles and a half to make to the village of Tacotna, but it is the hardest mush so far and it takes us nearly all day. The poor little dogs burrow through the snow like gophers. Sometimes from my snowshoes ahead or alongside I can see only their ears and the stumps of their tails. It is joy indeed when on approaching the wilderness village an old friend, Dr. Green, who combines the offices of postmaster, magistrate, physician, dentist and miner, comes across the Tacotna river to guide my tottering steps to his hospitable door, and Mrs. Green's roasted wild chickens are the best viands on earth.

Another hard mush of fourteen miles brings us to another dear old friend, or a pair of them, Mr. and Mrs. Elmer Smith. It is a cheering fact that on this trail through the wilderness I only stopped at one roadhouse where the people were all strangers. There is nothing so fine in all the world as the fellowship of the wilderness.

There is a bond between men who have conquered the same mountain difficulties, lain under the same blanket in the snow and helped one another over the trail, that is stronger than death. Elmer Smith used to lead the choir when I preached at Nome, and Mrs. Smith was superintendent of the Sunday school there. They are choice and refined people, fit for any society. Mrs. Smith is the only white woman in a radius of fourteen miles, but the happiest and cheeriest person you ever saw.

We are now in the valley of the Kuskokwim. The snow is deep. With Breeze double-tracking ahead, I work for four hours to get my dogs along seven miles. Then going suddenly across a divide, we strike shallow snow and hard trail and swing gayly into the Berry roadhouse, twenty-three miles from Tacotna. The Indian landlady cooks some grouse and caribou, for by this time we hardly touch bread or potatoes, eating vast quantities of wild meat. To those who have mushed along those trails and eaten this wild game it seems the most desirable food possible. The king of all the game is the *ovis dalli*, the white mountain sheep of Alaska. There is no other meat that compares with this.

From Berry's on, across the McKinley range of mountains 150 miles, we have pretty good roads, fine, clear, sunny weather and no fresh snow.

Alaskan Sled Dog Tales

Through the sparkling woods, along the river beds, we hurry, and over rounded and jumbled foothills covered with scraggly trees, the range of the caribou, up deep gorges where moose tracks are plentiful. We always steer a little to the right of majestic Mount McKinley, which lifts its mighty shoulder 20,350 feet in the sky, and the nearer Mount Foraker. We bend after three days down to the South Fork of the Kuskokwim, right under the twin mountains Egypt and Pyramid. Here we stop with a typical man of the wilderness, "French Joe."

He has built his log roadhouse with his own hands, whipsawing the lumber for the floor and for his tables. He is a hunter and trapper, and his walls are hung thick with pelts, all perfect and beautiful; silver, red and cross fox; lynx, wolverine, gray wolf, marten, mink and other furs. He is king of the wilderness and independent of the whole world. Native jams, cranberries and blueberries put up in sugar, currant wine, home-grown potatoes and turnips and a great variety of choice meat were spread in profusion before us. The banks of the world might all break, and its governments go to smash and its crops fail, but Joe would live at the foot of Mount Egypt his cheery, independent, carefree life. In spite of the strenuous mushing, I am gaining in flesh, my muscles hard as nails, my spirit buoyant.

Seized by Lumbago on the Trail

The day out from Joe's I meet with my first disaster. We have nineteen miles of absolutely clear ice on the south fork of the Kuskokwim. The river is full of air holes and open riffles. The dogs swing along at a ripping pace, digging their toenails into the hard ice, the sled slipping sideways and sliding dangerously near to open places. Breeze often has to run ahead at full speed to choose a route, for there is no trail on the ice. Half way up the river I "get gay," as Breeze says. I leave the handle bars to find a route, and fall down hard on the smooth ice. A sharp pang strikes through the small of my back as if from a spear thrust. I get up and go along, thinking the pain will cease, but soon I realize that I am in the grip of an old enemy—lumbago.

Alaskan Sled Dog Tales

From this point on to Seward I cannot make a move without pain, sometimes so great that I gasp for breath. At night in the roadhouse I have great trouble getting into my bunk, and sometimes Breeze has to lift me out in the morning. Were I at home I would be in bed for a couple of weeks, with doctors and nurses fussing over me, but it is just as well that I cannot stop. I take the philosophy of an old fellow in the Rainy Pass roadhouse, near the summit of the range, who says the best cure for a lame back is to "keep on a-mushin'!" I think of Edmund Vance Cook's verse, and it does me more good than all the horse liniments they rub on me.

> *Did you tackle the trouble that came your way*
> *With a resolute heart and cheerful?*
> *Or hide your face from the light of day,*
> *With a craven heart and fearful?*
> *Oh! A trouble's a-ton or a trouble's an ounce,*
> *Or a trouble is what you make it,*
> *And it isn't the fact that you're hurt that counts,*
> *But only, how did you take it?*

We drop into the canon of Happy River and here we have our famous moose hunt. Soon after we enter this gorge, we come upon its track—a big bull moose. Now here comes this big. blundering beast to poke our trail full of deep holes and excite our dogs. He is running ahead of us. The snow is five or six feet deep and he goes in almost to his back every step. The walls of the canon are sheer and he cannot escape up its side. The river turns and winds and here and there are little patches of level ground thick with large spruce trees.

For three miles we do not catch sight of the moose, but our dogs show that he is close ahead. In spite of my lame back I have to struggle ahead of them and bat Leader in the face with my cap. Breeze is standing on the brake to keep them from running away. The moose tracks fill our trail for a while, smashing it all to pieces, and then veer sideways to a little patch of woods, and the dogs will go pell mell in the moose's track, burying our sled out of sight in the deep snow. Then we have to haul them around and lift the sled on the track again and try to get them along the trail.

Trying to Overtake a Bull Moose

Three miles down the river we catch sight of the big moose and the dogs go wild. Being from Pennsylvania, I have the kindliest feeling toward this moose; I do not want to hurt him at all, but only, like Taft, wish he would keep out of the running, and like Woodrow Wilson, want to go by him. But our bells are jingling and our dogs barking and we are shouting at them and it is a fearsome thing to the bull moose, this animated machine that is charging down the river at him. So on he struggles through the deep snow, spoiling our trail and filling my companion's mind with blasphemous thoughts that occasionally break out in spite of his self-restraint.

Four miles of this moose hunt, with the big brute growing more tired and we more anxious to pass him. Instead of our hunting the moose, he is haunting us. At last, around a little point of woods we see him lying down in the middle of the river right ahead of us. The dogs break bounds and almost upset me as they dash down the trail, with Breeze standing on the brake and yelling "Whoa!" The weary bull moose staggers to his feet again and makes the edge of the woods, but there lies down again. The trail veers right up to him. I run ahead and take Leader and Ring, one in each hand, and Breeze does the same with Teddy and Sheep. Mose is more tractable and we can control him with our voices. We drag the dogs, with the sled behind, pass the big brute, his long face not a rod from us, and then, setting Leader on the trail again, we urge them down five miles farther to the Happy River roadhouse.

Ben Atwater and the Wilderness Brotherhood

At Halfway roadhouse we catch up with old Ben Atwater. We have been hearing of poor old Ben all along the trail. He is an old miner and prospector whom I had known thirty-four years ago at Wrangell. He had been living on the Kuskokwim river not far from Tacotna.

Alaskan Sled Dog Tales

Three months before we found him Ben did a very foolish thing. He was hunting wild chickens and got up on a log to "view the landscape o'er." He rested his double barrel shotgun on the log, put the palm of his left hand over the muzzle and rested the wrist of his right hand over that. The butt of the gun slipped on the slippery log, the hammers caught, the gun went off and blew both poor Ben's hands off. At Iditarod, a hundred miles distant, we heard the news and promptly sent $100 to Ben's aid. Soon other streams of money began to pursue him. The Yukon pioneers at Dawson heard of it and sent an order by wireless for another hundred. Then $200 came from the Alaska pioneers of Fairbanks. But Ben had struck the trail before any but the sum from Iditarod could reach him. He could not dress himself or feed himself. He was helpless as a baby, but these rough men of the wilderness were caring for him. At one roadhouse and another they had fed and sheltered him, sometimes for days, and then hitching up their dogs, they would haul him on to the next roadhouse, fifteen to forty miles along the trail. Then another would pass him on. When I found him he was chipper as a cricket and told me that he had gained twenty pounds since striking the trail. He had still 150 miles to go, but was in the best hands in all the world. The kindly brotherhood of these men of the wilderness excels that of all other people, I think.

At Knik we find another warm welcome. We hoped to find a boat here that would take us to Seward. Knik is on a so-called arm of Cook's inlet, but it is only an arm of the sea for two or three hours twice a day, for the tides here are tremendous. A boat is daily expected, but it disappoints us. The second night here I gather all the people of the village into the roadhouse and have "church." I do not think that I ever took greater pleasure in a service than in this one. Knik has been a town since 1895. There are a number of families here and some interesting children among them, but they have never had a school, and I preached the first sermon that has ever been heard in all that region. There are eight or nine other towns and villages scattered around the head of Cook's inlet and many mining camps, but no preacher of the gospel has ever come to bring these strong people of the wilderness the word of life. Everybody turned out to the service. There were two Christian women in attendance, one of whom has been there fifteen years and the other ten, without having a chance to hear the gospel preached.

Finding that no boat is coming and the time for presbytery approaching, I must mush on. The worst mountain pass of all is before us: Crow Creek pass over the high Alaska range. Fearsome tales are told me of this pass, but there is nothing to do but to try it. Breeze leaves me here and I hire a young prospector. Fred Taulnian, to take me to Seward. Were it not for my lame back I would go alone, but they all say that the pass is too dangerous to be traveled singly even by a strong and vigorous person. So on March 21 we hitched up our eager dogs, whose three days' rest has put them in high spirits, and hit the trail again around the head of Knik Arm. Over dangerous ice, sometimes through the salt water that covers it, with now and then a stretch of good trail, we come to Old Knik. It is only a seventeen mile stretch, but my back is so bad that when I arrive at the roadhouse I am in convulsions of pain. A hot drink and hot applications soothe me, but there is little sleep for me that night.

A Five-Mile Advance in Six Hours

Now hard climbing up a steep road to the base of the pass at Raven Creek roadhouse. A storm is blowing. The snow banners on the mountains that overlook the pass and the fast falling snow make it impossible for us to go on, so we spend a day at this fine roadhouse, kept by three men who are hunters, prospectors and hotel keepers as occasion requires. The second morning they hitch up four big dogs as large as Shetland ponies to supplement our five smaller ones, and a sturdy mountaineer with "creepers" on his feet comes to pilot us over the summit. From daylight until noon we struggle before reaching the summit, making only five miles in six hours. The descent from the summit is almost sheer for 2,000 feet.

I have vivid recollections of the trip down that steep place. We turned the dogs loose to follow after the sled. Then two men tied ropes to the back of the sled, and with their creepers hung on behind to let the sled down. They started it gingerly over the edge of the summit, and I, looking on from above, saw a confused jumble of men, dogs and sled rolling and tumbling down that path, the snow gathering around and on top of them until when they reached a more level spot they were out of sight in the body of the avalanche, not so deep but that the men emerged laughing and waving their hands.

For myself, it took me an hour to get down to them. I would take my snowshoe, strike the end into the snow ahead of me, and slide down against it, a foot at a time, repeating the operation again and again. Sometimes coming to too steep a place, I would have to edge along some distance with great care for fear of stumbling over the precipice and wrenching my poor back. But when at last I got to the sled, it was righted and we went gayly on our journey. Not long before we passed this summit two men had lost their lives there, taking chances on a stormy day. One avalanche that would have buried us under fifty feet of snow had it got us thundered into our trail an eighth of a mile behind us.

Down to the town of Glacier on Turnagain Arm we come at nightfall. Here we bargain with a boatman to set us across the next morning to the old town of Sunrise City, twelve miles away, on Kenai peninsula. Another hard day's work brings us to a roadhouse up this river, and then, a cold night hardening the crust of the snow, we swing gayly over another high summit, that of the Kenai range, and down to the Seward railroad and along it to » roadhouse twelve miles from Seward. I had telephoned from Glacier to Rev. Mr. Pederson, the Methodist pastor at Seward. At 9 o'clock in the morning of the 28th Brother Pederson, just starting out to meet us, greeted us with a shout as we swung up in front of his house.

The trip of 520 miles had taken me twenty-three days, but four of those I was lying in camp. I had broken trail with snowshoes over a hundred miles. I had tested my mushing powers and had not found them wanting. I had seen two great valleys for the first time and had prospected them for agricultural possibilities, game, lumber, mining resources and human souls. In spite of my lame back, I never took a

Alaskan Sled Dog Tales

journey that afforded more of instruction and inspiration or more of true enjoyment than this one.

A few days' rest and I took a steamer 200 miles farther to Cordova, where Brothers Koonce and Condit were awaiting me with their wives, and we had a joyful meeting of presbytery.

Mrs. Young, whom I had left a year before at Seattle, greeted me at Cordova, having traveled 1,500 miles to have a five days' visit with me. For I must hit the trail again the Monday after my arrival and mush on to Fairbanks, 442 miles inland, holding the fort there until Dr. Condit returned from the General Assembly.

The Joy of Service in the Big, Broad Land

If the Presbyterian ministry could see Alaska as I have seen it, and know it as I know it and the joy of service there, the Home Mission Board would be besieged by applications for that service. We are not to be commiserated but to be congratulated. With joy I again turn my steps back to—

The great, big, broad land 'way up yonder,
The forests where silence has lease,
The beauty that thrills me with wonder,
The stillness that fills me with peace.

~•~

Mary Joyce with her sled dogs, ca. 1936. Photo by Harry T. Becker. Harry T. Becker Photograph Collection P67-0246 Alaska State Library

MARY JOYCE, ADVENTURER
Mushing from Juneau to Fairbanks

Mary Joyce was an Alaskan adventurer of the highest caliber, and when Alaska was still just a territory she owned and operated a remote lodge near Juneau, became the first woman radio operator in the territory, and flew her own bush plane. In later years, after selling her lodge, she joined Pan Alaska Airways as a stewardess, and then settled in Juneau, where she worked as a nurse and bought two popular local bars.

Mary Joyce's biggest claim to fame, besides her dauntless courage in trying new adventures, was her 1936 dogsled trip from her Taku Lodge near Juneau to Fairbanks, 1,000 miles away.

Alaskan Sled Dog Tales

Mary was invited to participate in the 1936 Fairbanks Ice Carnival as a representative for the City and Borough of Juneau. Always ready for an adventure, Mary decided to drive her dogs on the thousand-mile journey. Leaving in late December for the March event, she hitched five dogs to her sled and joined a group of Natives headed for Atlin, British Columbia for the initial part of the long trip.

At Tulsequah, the party crossed the nearly frozen Taku River. Journaling as she traveled, Mary wrote about one of her trail guides: "Chocak Lagoose scolded his sons and made them put boughs over holes so I could not see the water underneath while crossing. 'White Lady plenty scared.' Crossed on my hands and knees and dogs followed like soldiers. Crossed upper Taku and another place over rapids on huge cakes of ice three feet apart helped by sweepers and snags. Put chain on Tip (lead dog) and each dog fell into water, pulled them out on another cake of ice. In places, just room for sled on ice cakes with water leaping over and gurgling underneath."

Mary's journey had barely begun with that adventure, and it wasn't until a week later that she reached the most hazardous part of the trip, between Burwash Landing and Tanana Crossing, where she was following the Kluane River in temperatures reaching sixty degrees below zero. A biographical note at the Alaska State Library Historical Collections explains what happened next: "The rate of her progress slowed when she became ill en route, causing the public to fear for her safety and speculate on her whereabouts. She flew to the Winter Carnival after realizing she would not complete the trek in time, but returned to her sled and completed the mush after the event.

"The route Mary traversed followed the path of what eventually became the Alaska Highway. For this effort she was awarded a Silver Cup from the city, a 2-month-old husky pup from friend Don Abel, Sr., and a rare 'Honorary Member' title from the Pioneers of Alaska. Her story attracted national media attention."

Mary kept a journal of her trip which was published in 2007 with the title, *Mary Joyce, Taku to Fairbanks, 1,000 Miles by Dogteam*, by her cousin,

Alaskan Sled Dog Tales

Mary Anne Greiner, who wrote glowingly of Mary for the back cover: "She was the first white person over a portion of the trail which later became part of the Alcan Highway. Her narrative and descriptions of Alaska's people, dogteams, vast landscapes and dangers encountered on the trail are wrapped in her wry humor and perspectives of the 30s..."

After Mary's dogsled adventure she invested and co-starred in a film that was shot on location in the Taku River region, *Orphans of the North* (1940), and in the late 1930s and early '40s she became a flight stewardess on Pan-Alaska Airlines, a subsidiary of Pan-American Airlines.

In the winter of 1939 Mary conducted sled-dog tours of the Sun Valley Resort in Idaho. During the Second World War, after warnings of an impending Japanese invasion of Alaska, she moved into the capitol city of Juneau and worked as a nurse at St. Ann's Hospital until the end of the war. After 14 years and at the conclusion of the war, Mary sold Taku Lodge and purchased the Top Hat Bar in Juneau. Later she purchased the Lucky Lady and lived in an apartment above it.

Mary Joyce ran for the office of Alaskan Territorial Representative in 1950, and was reportedly "an important and well-loved Alaskan figure who was regularly invited to speeches and ceremonies both in Alaska and in the contiguous United States. With the exception of a short stay in Wisconsin during the 1940s, she lived in Juneau the remainder of her life. In 1976 she suffered two heart attacks, the second of which took her life. She is buried at the Evergreen Cemetery in Juneau."

Mary's adventures are also described in *Women Pilots of Alaska: 37 Interviews and Profiles*, by Sandi Sumner; and *TAKU: Four Amazing Individuals-Four Incredible Life Stories and The Alaskan Wilderness Lodge That Brought Them Together*, by Karen Bell and Janet Shelfer. ~•~

Alaskan Sled Dog Tales

Mary Joyce with her sled dogs, ca. 1936. Photo by Harry T. Becker. Harry T. Becker Photograph Collection P67-0246 Alaska State Library

Josephine Crumrine is a young Alaska artist who lives in the State and specializes in painting dogs and animals. The most recent of Miss Crumrine's many exhibits was at the American Museum of Natural History in New York City. In the dog portraits featured in this current series of menus Miss Crumrine has captured the spirit of the Old Alaska when the chief mode of transportation was the husky-drawn sled. Her medium was pastels, here reproduced by four-color lithography.

"WOLF"

A peerless leader of the famous team raced by Mary Joyce in the annual Alaska Dog Derby, Wolf has also made a trip to the States. He spent a season at Sun Valley, Idaho, hauling winter sports enthusiasts on a real Alaskan dog sledge.

Mary's leader, Wolf, was featured on a 1954 menu for the Alaska Steamship Line series by the beloved Alaskan artist Josephine Crumrine. The caption reads: "A peerless leader of the famous team raced by Mary Joyce in the annual Alaska Dog Derby, Wolf has also made a trip to the States. He spent a season at Sun Valley, Idaho, hauling winter sports enthusiasts on a real Alaskan dog sledge."

Alaskan Sled Dog Tales

Father Bernard R. Hubbard, the "Glacier Priest," with his favorite sled dog, Mageik.

Alaskan Sled Dog Tales

MUSH, YOU MALAMUTES!
Father Bernard R. Hubbard

"Half the year the highest-paid lecturer in the world, the other half a wanderer among treacherous craters and glaciers."
~ *Literary Digest, 1931*

In 1931 Father Bernard Rosecrans Hubbard, a Jesuit priest, headed a sled dog expedition which took him 1,600 miles down the frozen Yukon River, visiting missions along the way. Fondly known as "the Glacier Priest," he was the head of the Department of Geology at the University of Santa Clara, California, and at one time not only the highest-paid lecturer in the world, but a seemingly tireless explorer as well, leading 32 scientific expeditions into Alaska and the Arctic between 1927 and 1962.

Described as a riveting lecturer, Father Hubbard was skilled in the creation of early multimedia presentations using still pictures, films and his own dramatic narration based on his first-hand adventures. He would later produce over 50 short films and two feature films: *Aniakchak*, in 1933, about the land which would one day become the remote and

Alaskan Sled Dog Tales

In 1934, Rev. Bernard Hubbard, the "Glacier Priest," explored Alaska's Valley of Ten Thousand Smokes. This is a photograph of Father Hubbard and his lead dog Katma wearing improvised gas masks while standing by a smoking volcanic crater. Photograph provided to the press October 10, 1934.

beautiful Aniakchak National Monument and Preserve on the Alaska Peninsula; and *Alaska's Silver Millions*, a documentary about the territory's canneries and salmon industry, in 1936. The latter film was picked up by Fox Studios and distributed worldwide.

Born in San Francisco, California, on November 24, 1888, Bernard Hubbard spent his childhood on his family's ranch near Santa Cruz, California. He received a Master of Arts degree in philosophy through Gonzaga University in Spokane, Washington in 1921, then studied theology in Innsbruck, Austria, where he was ordained a priest in 1923. During his time in Austria, he became enamored of the Austrian Alps and was given the title "Der Gletscher Pfarrer" ("the Glacier Priest"), for reputedly spending more time in the mountains than in church.

Alaskan Sled Dog Tales

Father Hubbard first went to Alaska in 1927, and his summer expeditions of exploration and photography became an annual event. During the winters, he traveled around the United States giving lectures and showing his films, with the proceeds going to support the Jesuit missions in Alaska. In 1931 he not only made his famous journey down the Yukon River, from Nenana to Nulato, Unalakleet, and Holy Cross, but also flew across the Alaska Peninsula to view the May, 1931 eruption at Aniakchak, and in 1936 he visited Katmai's Valley of 10,000 Smokes. Alaskan author Barrett Willoughby wrote a dramatic article about Father

Father Bernard Hubbard, S. J., With Two of His Huskies

Alaskan Sled Dog Tales

Hubbard's first visit to Aniakchak for *The Saturday Evening Post* in December, 1930. Titled "The Moon Craters of Alaska," the article helped popularize his lectures. Father Hubbard received two honorary doctorate degrees, wrote three books, including *Mush, You Malemutes!* (New York: The American Press, 1932), and published stories in numerous periodicals such as *National Geographic* and *The Saturday Evening Post*.

During and after World War II, Father Hubbard became involved with the U.S. military, both as an adviser on Alaska and as a lecturer and chaplain to the troops. In 1945, he traveled around the world, photographing damaged and destroyed Jesuit institutions as part of a fund-raising campaign. In his later years, Father Hubbard returned to Santa Clara, where he established an educational film production and distribution service. After he died in 1962, his 11,000 photographic negatives and artifacts were given to the Santa Clara University Archives. His 200,000 feet of raw film and 50 film shorts are at the Smithsonian's Museum of Natural History in Washington, D.C.

One obituary notice listed a few of his considerable lifetime achievements and stated he was "a world-renowned authority on arctic phenomena and a recognized explorer, geologist, volcanologist, ichthyologist, oceanographer and paleontologist."

On May 28, 1962, *Newsweek* magazine noted his passing: *"Died: The Rev. Bernard Rosencrantz Hubbard, 73, the Glacier Priest, a tireless Jesuit who led 32 expeditions to Alaska and once listed the requisites of an explorer as 'a strong back, a strong stomach, a dumb head, and a guardian angel.'"*

Alaskan Sled Dog Tales

"...I named him Mageik, after the great volcano that, with Katmai, guards the entrance to the former Valley of Ten Thousand Smokes."

In 1941 the famed Alaskan artist Josephine Crumrine painted Mageik for the Alaska Steamship Company, whose menus featured notable sled dogs of Alaska. The description read: "Father Hubbard's famous sled dog looks like a reincarnation of Buck, Jack London's hero of 'The Call of the Wild.' Like Buck, Mageik is no stranger to California, where he spends some winters with 'the Glacier Priest,' and is the constant companion of the noted geologist."

Alaskan Sled Dog Tales

AN ODE TO MUSHING
BY THE REV. S. HALL YOUNG

Samuel Hall Young, who would come to be known as the "Mushing Parson," was one of the first missionaries in Alaska, and he wrote volumes about his work and travels in the northern lands. The following is from his 1919 book, *Adventures in Alaska* (Fleming H. Revell Co., 1919).

Oh, boys, you'll never know the real joy of living 'til you take a winter trip with dogsled in Alaska. The keen, fine air, lungfilling, invigorating; your dogs yelping with eagerness, their feet twinkling, the sled screaming its delight; frost-diamonds sparkling from every branch, frost-symphonies played by the ice-harps under your feet; your own struggle, achievement, triumph, against and over the cold, the difficulties of the trail, the long miles.

The morning breaks, the stars grow pale,
Your huskies leap, shrill shrieks the sled;
You follow free with flying tread;
A joy to live! What joy! to thread
The fluted ribbon of the trail.

~•~

Alaskan Sled Dog Tales

Artwork by Hattie Longstreet from Esther Birdsall Darling's "Baldy of Nome."

Alaskan Sled Dog Tales

OLYMPIC SLED DOGS
Seppala and St. Godard Competed

". . . one of the most picturesque and interesting events on the program."
~Official Report for the 1932 Winter Olympics

Every so often, usually as the Winter Olympic competitions are once again riveting the world's attention and interest in snow-related adventures, the question arises why sled dog racing is not a recognized Olympic sport. There's no easy answer to the question, but proponents of the idea can take encouragement from history. To the surprise of many mushing enthusiasts, a sled dog race was run as a demonstration sport at the 1932 Winter Olympics in Lake Placid, New York. Held in February, it was the third Winter Olympics event, and the first one held in North America. The Games were opened by New York Governor Franklin D. Roosevelt, who would be elected President of the United States later the same year. Basketball star Wilt Chamberlain carried the Olympic Torch.

The sled dog race, run as a demonstration of a sport indigenous to the United States and North America, was included because, as was noted in The Official Report for the 1932 Winter Olympics: "Winter travel by dog team in the northeastern snow belt of the United States, in Canada, and in Alaska, is both a sport and a measure of necessity when all other means of getting across the frozen wastes of snow fail. In the Far North dog teams carry mail and freight and follow regular routes and schedules."

Alaskan Sled Dog Tales

Site of the 1932 Winter Olympics at Lake Placid, New York

The race was held under the rules of the New England Sled Dog Club over a 25 mile course, run each day for two days for a total of 50 miles. Five contestants from Canada and seven teams from the United States competed with seven dogs per sled, each team leaving at three minute intervals. The Official Report stated "Many American and Canadian sportsmen are interested in the raising or racing of sled dogs, Siberian, Alaskan, or Labrador breeds, the best racing teams usually being crossbred. Dog derbies have for years been a picturesque part of the winter sports-life of Lake Placid, and the Olympic demonstration derby was one of the most picturesque and interesting events on the entire program."

The racers included three-time All Alaska Sweepstakes champion Leonard Seppala, who had gained nationwide attention only a few years before for his role in the lifesaving serum run to Nome. Another well-

Alaskan Sled Dog Tales

Leonhard Seppala's racing team of Siberian Huskies.

known entrant was Colonel Norman D. Vaughan, who had just returned from Antarctic exploration as a dog driver for Admiral Richaed E. Byrd. Also running the race was a woman, Eva "Short" Seeley, who was very influential in the development and recognition of the Alaskan Malemute and the Siberian Husky.

Emile St. Godard, a French Canadian from The Pas, Manitoba, had won The Pas Dog Derby in 1925, which was one of the world's premier sled dog races at the time. He was destined to become Canada's most revered champion musher and the only sled dog musher in Canada's Sports Hall of Fame, dominating the field for so long that fans often commented it would be "St. Godard against the field."

Alaskan Leonhard Seppala and Canadian Emile St. Godard faced each other annually at the Eastern International Dog Derby in Quebec. Over six years, St. Godard would win the race four times, and Seppala twice.

Alaskan Sled Dog Tales

They also faced off in a variety of different races over the years, of which St. Godard won the majority.

Arthur Daley, sportswriter for *The New York Times*, wrote: "Lake Placid, New York, February 8, 1932. In the colorful sled dog race it was a Canadian team that was victorious as Emile St. Godard, the veteran Manitoba musher, emerged as the victor over Leonhard Seppala of the United States… These two keen rivals, less than a minute and a half apart after the first twenty five miles yesterday, again staged a bitter battle on the second twenty five mile route today. St. Godard proved that his Russian Wolfhound-Malamutes were faster dogs when he finished first once more, compiling a total time of 4 hours, 27 minutes, 12.5 seconds. Seppala, famous for his race with death to bring the antitoxin to Nome, was clocked in at 4 hours, 31 minutes, 1.8 seconds for the fifty miles."

Following St. Godard's victory Seppala acknowledged his rival's superiority as a sled dog driver, returned to Alaska and would never compete with him again. St. Godard was inducted to Canada's Sports Hall of Fame in 1952, where his biography reads in part: "St. Godard was known not only for his winning record, but also for his concern for the well-being of his dogs. He once withdrew from a race just after reaching the homestretch because his dogs were cutting their paws on the jagged ice that covered the trail. In the end, he preferred to relinquish a victory than cause harm to his huskies. Legend has it that his dogs derived their incredible speed and stamina from a steady diet of Lake Winnipeg Goldeye fish. Proving that they were more than just a team, St. Godard fondly referred to this canine clan as his 'family.' His lead dog, Toby, who was half-husky, half-greyhound, was such an integral part of this crew that when he was no longer fit for racing, St. Godard retired from competition. St. Godard remains the only dogsled racer to be inducted into Canada's Sports Hall of Fame."

Alaskan Sled Dog Tales

Sled Dog Race, Demonstration

Driver	Country	Owner	First Race	Second Race	Total
St Goddard	Canada	St Goddard	2:12:.5	2:11:7.5	4:23:12.5
Seppala	United States	Seppala	2:13:34.3	2:17:27.5	4:31:1.8
Russick	Canada	Russick	2:26:22.4	2:21:22.2	4:47:44.6
Wheeler	Canada	Wheeler	2:33:19.1	2:29:35	5:02:54.1
Haines	United States	Taylor	2:34:56	2:31:31.3	5:06:27.3
Pouliot	Canada	Marquis	2:53:14.3	2:52:21.5	5:45:39.8
Defako	Canada	Defako	2:53:49.5	2:55:50.1	5:49:39.6
Belknap	United States	Belknap	2:57:14	2:57:8.5	5:54:22.5
Murphy	United States	McIlhenny	2:42:49.4	3:15:24.1	5:58:13.5
Sears	United States	d'Avignon	3:21.7	3:1:49.5	6:02:11.2
Vaughan	United States	Seeley	3:24:10	3:49:46	7:13:56
Seeley (Mrs)	United States	Seeley	3:28:1.7	3:46:45	7:14:46.7

Leaderboard for the 1932 Winter Olympics Demonstration Sled Dog Race

In his landmark essay, "A History of Mushing Before We Knew It," champion musher and sled dog historian Tim White wrote: "Despite the international character of the participants in the race in Lake Placid, there was little activity outside North America except in Norway, where the use of dogs for military supply and ambulance work beginning at the time of the First World War had been transformed into a sport. The influence of Nansen and Amundsen, who used sled dogs in the North and South Polar regions, was also important in establishing a Scandinavian sled dog sport.

"In the 1952 Oslo Olympics sled dogs were featured again as a Demonstration Sport, this time in the form of pulka races where the driver accompanies the dogs on skis behind a toboggan or pulka." ~•~

Alaskan Sled Dog Tales

Champion French Canadian Musher Emilie St. Godard

Emile St. Godard's champion sled dog team, 1929

Alaskan Sled Dog Tales

DOG TEAM DOCTOR
Dr. Joseph Romig

In 1896 Dr. Joseph Romig traveled to Bethel, Alaska, and opened the first doctor's office and hospital west of Sitka, at a time when there were very few non-native people living in remote southwest Alaska.

Joseph H. Romig was born in Illinois in 1872. His parents were descendants of Moravian immigrants, and in exchange for his pledge to serve for seven years as a doctor at a mission, the Moravian Church sponsored his medical training. In 1896, Joseph married a nursing student he met at school, and the couple moved to Bethel to join Joseph's older sister and her husband as missionaries to the Yup'ik people of the Yukon-Kuskokwim Delta. Bethel was barely a village at that time, consisting of only four houses, a chapel, an old Russian-style bath house and a small store. The Romig home was a simple two-room structure, and included the first hospital: one room with two homemade beds.

For a time, Dr. Romig was one of the only physicians in Alaska, and he became expert at dog mushing, as his practice stretched for hundreds of miles. He became known as the "dog team doctor" for traveling by dog sled throughout the Yukon-Kuskokwim Delta in the course of his work.

When his term of missionary service was complete Dr. Romig left Bethel, and in the following decades he played an eventful and important role in the growth of Alaska. He would eventually be, in addition to a missionary and a doctor, a superintendent of schools, U.S. Commissioner, mayor of Anchorage, railway surgeon and chief of the railroad hospital staff, and by the time he retired in 1939, Dr. Romig would see a new state-of-the-art hospital built in Anchorage.

His adventures in southwest Alaska became the subject of a book, *Dog-Team Doctor: The Story of Dr. Romig*, by Eva Greenslit Anderson, published in 1940.

Alaskan Sled Dog Tales

Alaskan Sled Dog Tales

The Suter Trophy from the 1909 All Alaska Sweepstakes race at the Carrie McLain Museum in Nome. [Photo by Helen Hegener/Northern Light Media]

Alaskan Sled Dog Tales

ALL ALASKA SWEEPSTAKES
The oldest organized sled dog race

"On a cold spring day in 1907 a group of us gathered around the stove in a Nome saloon and began talking about dog races. After a few weeks of arguing we worked out the rules of the 'All-Alaska Sweepstakes.' Beginning with the spring of 1908 this great race of dog teams was run every year until the war, the last one in 1917. It became world famous, and has set the pace for every important dog race since."
~A.A. *"Scotty"* Allan, Gold, Men and Dogs (G.P. Putnam's Sons, 1931)

The All Alaska Sweepstakes is the oldest organized sled dog race in the world, with records kept by the Nome Kennel Club dating back to the first race in 1908. The route from Nome, on the south side of Alaska's remote Seward Peninsula, to the small community of Candle on the north side and return, is 408 miles, following the telegraph lines which linked camps, villages and gold mining settlements on the Peninsula. This route's established communication lines allowed those betting on the outcome to track the race more easily from the comfort of saloons like the famed Board of Trade in Nome, where the Nome Kennel Club was founded the previous year.

Scotty Allan describes the trail to Candle in his classic 1931 autobiography about the Nome gold rush and his colorful racing adventures, *Gold, Men and Dogs*: "It was selected because the trail to it from Nome goes over all kinds of country, from sea ice to high

Alaskan Sled Dog Tales

Team No. 1 starting the 5th All Alaska Sweepstakes, April 4, 1912. G.H. Johnson, owner/driver. Photo by H.G. Kaiser.
[Dr. Daniel S. Neuman Photographs P307-0313 Alaska State Library]

mountains, with rivers, tundra, timber, glaciers, and everything else in the way of mental and physical hardships en route. We knew there wouldn't be any doubt about the excellence of a dog or driver that covered it."

In her booklet and official souvenir history of the race, titled *The Great Dog Races of Nome Held Under the Auspices of the Nome Kennel Club, Nome, Alaska*, author and 1916 Nome Kennel Club President Esther Birdsall Darling described the "why" of the race: "It was early seen that not only would the races furnish much of the winter entertainment. but that there would also be a consistent effort on the part of the dog owners and dog drivers to improve the breed of sled dogs, which up to this time had been but little considered; an effort to instill into all dog users an intelligent

Alaskan Sled Dog Tales

understanding of the accepted fact that care and kindness to their dogs bring the quickest and surest returns from all standpoints. This has resulted in the development of such a high standard for dogs that not alone is their worth acknowledged throughout Alaska, but their supremacy is conceded the world over."

One of the race's most popular dog drivers was a likable Scotsman named Allan Alexander Allan, known as Scotty. Perhaps the most famous musher of his time, Scotty Allan had prospected in the Klondike, following adventure trails from there to Nome, where he quickly joined forces with the aforementioned Esther Birdsall Darling to create the Allan and Darling kennel, historically one of the best known racing kennels in Alaska.

Scotty Allan's venerable leader was a dog named Baldy, and he led Allen to first place in 1909, 1911 and 1912, and to a career total of eight

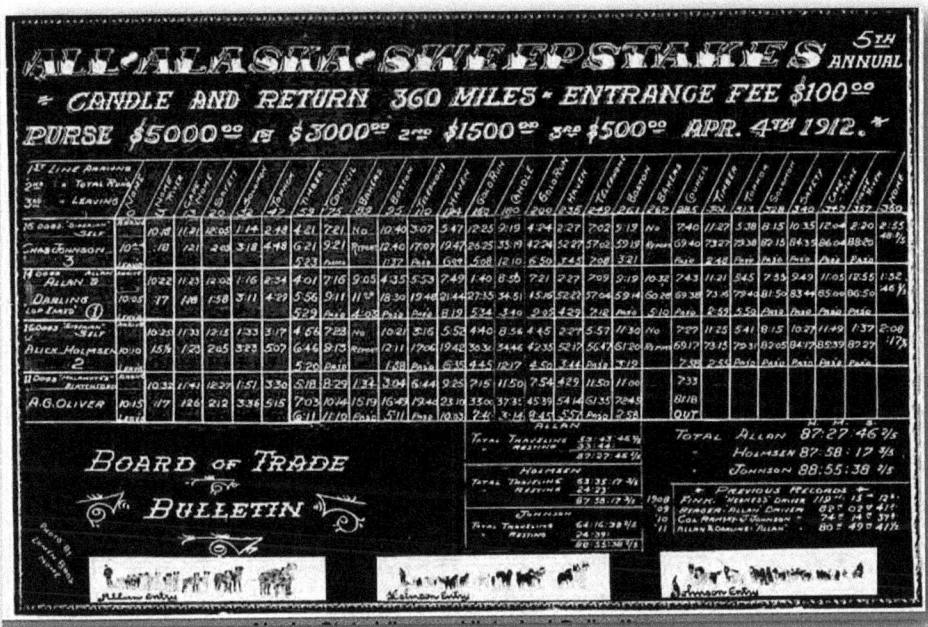

5th Annual All Alaska Sweepstakes, Nome to Candle and return, 360 miles.
[Dr. Daniel S. Neuman Collection P307-0317 Alaska State Library]

Alaskan Sled Dog Tales

top-three finishes in the race. Baldy's exploits were memorialized in a best-selling children's book by Allan's kennel co-owner, Esther Birdsall Darling, titled *Baldy of Nome* and published in 1913. Veteran race judge Al Crane declared the book 'must reading' for anyone seeking to understand the All Alaska Sweepstakes.

Scotty Allan provided dogs for the U.S. government during World War I to haul supplies over the mountains from France to Germany, and his leader Navarre, a grandson of Baldy and also featured in a book by Esther Birdsall Darling, was awarded the French Cross for his heroic duty. Scotty Allan later went on to become a well-respected representative in the Territorial Legislature of Alaska.

Interpretive signs in the Carrie McLain Museum in Nome tell interesting details of the famous race: "At the checkpoints along the trail, handlers aided the drivers with the dogs so they could rest. During the short stops the dogs were given Eagle canned milk which is easily digested and nourishing. Every hundred miles, the teams took a five or six hour rest, and the dogs would be fed raw ptarmigan or ground raw mutton. The drivers wore regulation mushing clothes: an everyday parka, a light fur parka, a stocking cap and a fur cap, plenty of canvas gloves and heavy fur mitts. They used light racing sleds built with hoops instead of straight handles at the back. The hoop was easier to hold onto when riding the runners, and there was less chance of losing your grip and your team."

With colorful drivers like Scotty Allan and Leonhard Seppala, who also won the race three times (1915-1917), the All Alaska Sweepstakes was an eagerly anticipated annual event until the First World War interrupted everything. After the war gold mining dropped off and Nome's population dwindled, along with the local interest in sled dog racing. Finally, in 1983, after several years of planning and preparation, and with the boost in interest brought about by the then-famous Iditarod Trail Sled

Alaskan Sled Dog Tales

John Hegness with his winning team, first All Alaska Sweepstakes, 1908

John "Iron Man" Johnson, winner of the third All Alaska Sweepstakes, 1910

Alaskan Sled Dog Tales

Above: 1910 Race Queen Gladys Curry.
Below: Nome Kennel Club patch.

Dog Race, the Nome Kennel Club was able to bring back the All Alaska Sweepstakes for the 75th Anniversary of the race. Rick Swenson won that year, taking home the $25,000.00 winner-take-all purse.

Twenty-five years later, in 2008, the 100th Anniversary of the event saw the Nome Kennel Club offer the richest purse ever raised for a sled dog race: $100,000.00 winner-take-all!

Sixteen teams entered, with mushers from all across Alaska hoping to have their name engraved on the trophy beside racing legends Scotty Allan and Leonhard Seppala. In total, only four mushers besides Allan and Seppala had ever won the race: John Hegness in 1908, John "Iron Man" Johnson in 1910 and 1914, Fay Delzene in 1913 and Rick Swenson in 2008.

The 1910 time set by "Iron Man" Johnson, driving a team of Siberian huskies which had been imported by Fox Maule Ramsay, had never been broken. He ran the 408-mile trail in 74 hours, 14 minutes, and 37

Alaskan Sled Dog Tales

seconds. For many years Scotty Allan and Leonhard Seppala tried to break "Iron Man" Johnson's record-setting run, but could never do so.

The entrants who gathered in Nome for the Centennial running of the All Alaska Sweepstakes in 2008 were a formidable bunch of mushers, and included the 1983 champion, Rick Swenson, who had also won the 1,000-mile Iditarod five times, more than any other musher. Competitors for the one hundred thousand dollar winner-take-all purse included four-time Iditarod champion Jeff King, 2004 Iditarod champion Mitch Seavey, the reigning Iditarod champion Lance Mackey at the top of his game, and several other mushers who were often at or near the top in mid- and long-distance races. The race was run according to the original race rules, which differed in many aspects from the modern-day races, such as every dog must be brought back to the starting line (no dropped dogs), and handlers could assist their teams on the remote trail.

Fay Delzene, winner of the 1913 All Alaska Sweepstakes

Alaskan Sled Dog Tales

The 2004 Iditarod champion, Mitch Seavey, won the race, and his time, along with the times of fellow Iditarod champions Jeff King and Lance Mackey, who came in second and third respectively, finally broke the 75-year-old record set by "Iron Man" Johnson in 1910.

When the 1983 race champion Rick Swenson was asked how he rated the All Alaska Sweepstakes, he reputedly replied; "It's a historic event, and on a scale of 1 to 10 it's probably an 11. It's an 11 on historical significance, it's an 11 on its difficulty to finish, and it takes an 11 in dog care to win." ~•~

The All Alaska Sweepstakes Records

1908 - John Hegness, driver; Albert Fink, owner
1909 - "Scotty" Allan, Driver; J. Berger, owner
1910 - John "Iron Man" Johnson, driver; Col. Charles Ramsay, owner
1911 - "Scotty" Allan, driver; Allan & Darling, owners
1912 - "Scotty" Allan, driver; Allan & Darling, owners
1913 - Fay Delzene, driver; Bowen & Delzene, owners
1914 - John Johnson, driver and owner
1915 - Leonhard Seppala, driver and owner
1916 - Leonhard Seppala, driver and owner
1917 - Leonhard Seppala, driver and owner
1983 - Rick Swenson, driver; Swenson & Lindner, owners
2008 - Mitch Seavey, driver and owner

Alaskan Sled Dog Tales

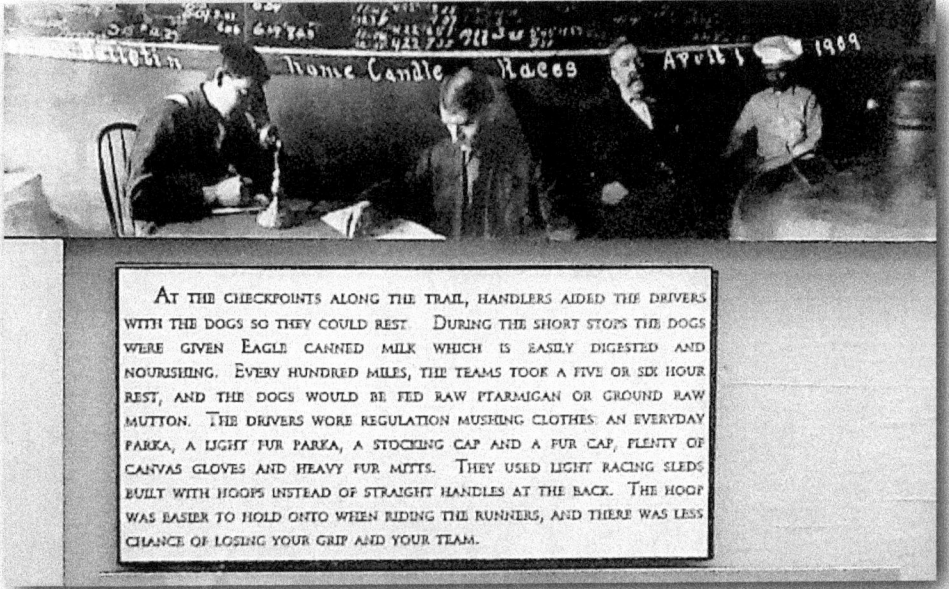

An All Alaska Sweepstakes display at the Carrie McLain Museum in Nome.

Leaderboard for the 1917 All Alaska Sweepstakes.

Alaskan Sled Dog Tales

U.S. Mail being delivered by dogteam. In an online history discussion this photo was identified as being from 1936, at the Doc Pollard house in Kasilof, on the Kenai Peninsula. The mail team driver was identified as "Comer Cole, son of Perry Cole who homesteaded in Kasilof in 1928 to start a fox farm. Comer's lead dog had very unusual markings, almost all white with a black patch on his face, so his team is easy to spot in old photos." [Photo by Harry T. Becker. Harry T. Becker Photograph Collection P67-0376 Alaska State Library]

Alaskan Sled Dog Tales

DOG TEAM DELIVERY
Sled Dog Mail

"So far as there is anything heroic about the Alaskan trail, the mail-carriers are the real heroes. They must start out in all weathers, at all temperatures; they have a certain specified time in which to make their trips and they must keep within that time or there is trouble."
~Episcopal Archdeacon Hudson Stuck

Delivering the mail in Alaska has always presented a formidable challenge to the U.S. Postal Service. Letters, parcels, and supplies from the "lower 48 states" often took weeks or months to reach their destinations.

In 1898 John P. Clum, former mayor of Tombstone, Arizona, and the founder and editor of the *Tombstone Epitaph*, was appointed Postal Inspector for the Alaska Territory, "to examine into postal affairs." During the spring and summer of 1898 alone, Clum traveled 8,000 miles across the Alaska territory by mule and steamboat, carrying postage stamps, mailbags, postal locks, keys and postmarking devices, equipping already-existing post offices and establishing new post offices at Sheep Camp, Pyramid, Canyon City, Eagle City, Star City, Ft. Yukon, Rampart, Tanana, Anvik, Koyukuk, and Valdez. In 1900 John Clum established Nome's first free general delivery service, said to be the largest in the United States.

Alaskan Sled Dog Tales

Circle City mail carrier (no date). Photo by Johnson.

In winter the harsh Arctic weather and limited trail and road system made mail delivery extremely difficult. In the more isolated sections, carrying the mail required methods far different than those traditionally used elsewhere in the United States, and dogs proved superior for the winter transport of mail. Dogs were capable of covering long distances, day or night, and they could travel over the frozen lakes and rivers and follow the sometimes thin trails through mountain passes.

In 1897 Benjamin S. Downing landed a U.S. government-issued contract to deliver mail in the winter, from Dawson City, Yukon Territory 600 miles down the frozen Yukon River to the mouth of the Tanana River. By 1902 Downing had developed a lucrative business delivering mail, freight, and passengers between Dawson City and Eagle, sledding as much as 40 miles a day in temperatures that routinely dropped far below zero. To make the weekly mail runs Downing employed 15 other mail carriers and used 152 dogs, 48 sleds and toboggans, and 252 sets of dog harnesses. He also imported 52 tons of supplies each year to feed both the men and dogs.

Alaskan Sled Dog Tales

By 1901, a network of mail trails throughout Alaska was in use, including a system following almost the entire length of the Yukon River. The historic Iditarod Trail was the main dog trail that carried mail from Seward to Nome, with over-night roadhouses along the route which served mail carriers, freighters, and other travelers who used sled dog teams, horse and wagon teams, or traveled on foot.

Mail dog teams varied in size, with eight to twelve dogs the most common number for pulling a mail sled, which was often heavier and longer than a typical basket-style sled. On average, dog teams pulled sleds containing between 500 – 700 pounds of mail, which meant that each dog had a load of up to 100 pounds (although they hauled less on the more challenging trails). Mail sacks usually weighed 50 pounds each. Rubber-lined waterproof bags were used to protect precious mail from snow, rain, and mud; the dogs often wore moosehide moccasins to protect their feet as much as possible from jagged pieces of ice.

U.S. Mail arriving in Nome, Alaska.

Alaskan Sled Dog Tales

Ben Atwater and his mail team dogs. (no date)

In the 1930s airplanes became the most popular means for mail transport, but dog teams were still used to make "feeder" deliveries to remote locations in bush Alaska. Postmasters were also still allowed to use dogs for emergency mail service to rural points, and the Postmaster General had the authority to build and maintain trails and facilities and to hire contracted mail teams without going through a lengthy bid process.

In the 1940s cachets were produced reading "Alaska Dog Team Post" and depicting artwork of adventurous-looking dog teams in action. These beautifully illustrated cachets, which were fairly common during the WWII years, are prized today by collectors of sled dog memorabilia.

In 1963, the U.S. Post Office Department honored Eskimo dog driver Chester Noongwook of Savoonga, on St. Lawrence Island in the Bering Sea, as the last driver to officially deliver the U.S. Mail via dog team. With his retirement, regular sled dog mail delivery ended in Alaska. In January 1995, Chester Noongwook donated the mail-delivery sled he used on that

Alaskan Sled Dog Tales

historic final run to the National Postal Museum in Washington, D.C. The last official U.S. Mail sled dog driver, Chester Noongwook passed away only one month after making the delivery to the museum.

In 1986 the U.S. Postal System issued a seventeen-cent stamp as part of its transportation series, in recognition of the important role the dogsled played in early mail delivery in the north. A simple image of a basket sled, the type often used for transporting mail across Alaskan trails, is under the words "Dog Sled 1920s." Four-time Iditarod champion Susan Butcher took part in the first-day issue ceremony in Anchorage when the stamp was released.

On January 2, 2009 the U.S. Postal Service issued a new First Class stamp commemorating Alaska's 50th anniversary as a U.S. State (Alaska became an official U.S. territory in 1912 and the 49th state on January 3, 1959). The image selected, which was photographed by official Iditarod

"The last mail team from Gambell to Savoonga, 1963." [photo by Ward Wells]

Alaskan Sled Dog Tales

Mail driver Ben Atwater arrives at Lake Bennett with the mail from Circle City, 1909.

Trail Sled Dog Race photographer Jeff Schultz, depicts veteran sled dog racer Dee Dee Jonrowe on the Iditarod Trail at sunset, near Rainy Pass in the Alaska Range, during the 2000 Iditarod Trail Sled Dog Race. It was a fitting scene for an Alaskan commemorative stamp, evoking images of the dogteams which covered the Iditarod Trail and many others to bring letters, cards, and news of loved ones to those in far away places.

The legacy of mail delivery by sled dog team is remembered today in races such as the Percy DeWolfe Memorial Mail Race, which takes mushers down the Yukon River from Dawson City, Yukon Territory to Eagle, Alaska and return, the route over which famed dog driver Percy DeWolfe courageously carried the mail by dog team and horse and wagon in the winter, and by boat in the summertime, from 1910 to 1949.

Another sled dog race commemorating the history of mail delivery by dog team is the McGrath Mail Trail race, which runs from the gold rush

Alaskan Sled Dog Tales

town of McGrath on the Yukon River, through four official Iditarod Trail Sled Dog Race checkpoint villages to Nulato and then returns to McGrath.

Today it's difficult to imagine the peril and hardships which faced the mail drivers of early Alaska. Winding through endless forests, across frozen lakes and rivers where overflow was a treacherous hazard, across mountain passes where avalanches threatened...

A clear indication of the difficulties facing Alaskan mail drivers was printed in the Bemidji, Minnesota *Daily News* on February 8, 1916, in a brief news item titled 'It's 71 Below In Alaska, So Dogs Go In Where Horses Can't Tread.' "Seward, Alaska, Feb. 1–Mail carriers here from Iditarod said today that when the mail was taken over the trail at Takotna the temperature was 71 degrees below zero. The cold was so intense the carriers had to turn back their horses and set out a second time with dog sleds." ~•~

Eagle, Alaska about 1900, Ben Downing's mail teams ready to go.

Alaskan Sled Dog Tales

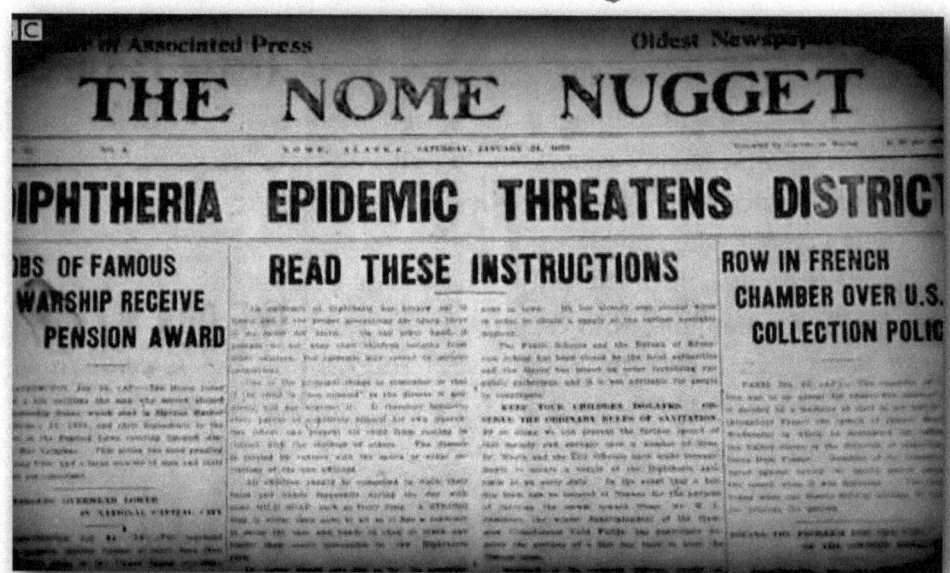

"Diphtheria Epidemic Threatens District." Headline on Nome Nugget, Jan. 24, 1925

The 1908 discovery of gold in the Iditarod district was major news.

Alaskan Sled Dog Tales

SLED DOG NEWS
Reporting History

"From Seward to Knik to Iditarod, from Iditarod to Ruby to Nome, from Nome to Dillingham, from Nome to Ruby to Nenana, from Nome to Cape South Wales, the U.S. mail traveled by dog team."
~Lorna Coppinger in *The World of Sled Dogs*

Alaska's colorful sled dog teams and their courageous drivers were popular topics for newspapers reporting on America's Last Frontier, and editors often selected stories of the north country to headline their evening papers. Sled dog races like the famed All Alaska Sweepstakes were followed from afar; the mushers who won the races were accorded hero worship and their visits reported in detail for curious and appreciative readers.

When the 1925 diphtheria epidemic struck Nome the riveting stories of brave relay drivers and their stalwart teams struggling through fierce blizzards to deliver the antitoxin provided a newspaper editor's fondest wish, an ongoing drama which would guarantee devoted readers searching for updates day after day. Readers could scarcely turn away when faced with headlines such as "Brave Dogs and Men Race for Nome

At the height of the Klondike gold rush in 1898 the news flowed nonstop.

to Save the Children of the City," and the equally urgent and compelling "Time is Running Out as Men and Dogs Race Toward Nome."

The major gold rushes of the Klondike, Fairbanks, Nome, and Iditarod districts kept newspaper boys busily hawking their papers, and when there weren't sufficient reports to run in the evening edition, canny editors either recycled the old news or simply made up stories which sounded viable. Far-off place names were mangled and misspelled, sometimes beyond recognition, and dates could be moving targets when most of the news was several days old anyway.

Many Alaskan towns and communities had their own newspapers, sometimes infrequent and often filled with news which barely fit the description of newsworthy, but in a land where communications of any kind were scarce the smallest publication would find a welcoming and appreciative readership, and would often be passed generously along from person to person until meeting an almost inevitable end as someone's fire-starter. ~•~

Alaskan Sled Dog Tales

"SCOTTY" ALLAN, DOG TRAINER

WINNER OF ALL-ALASKAN SWEEPSTAKES AN OLD TIME RESIDENT OF CHELAN COUNTY AND WELL KNOWN HERE.

The Seattle Post-Intelligencer of Monday night contained an interesting story regarding "Scotty" Allan, who won the All-Alaskan sweepstakes dog team race. The story in itself is an interesting one, but is especially so for the fact that "Scotty" lived in this county for several years, making his home at Leavenworth and is very well known in this

dog harness weighed nine ounces per dog, and his whole outfit of muklucks for himself and dogs, blankets for the animals and tugs and other equipment totaled, sleigh included, only 42 pounds.

There were 14 entries in the race. The pick of human racing machinery was selected for the test of endurance, skill in the handling of dogs, and judgment in the methods of travel. The best dogs of eastern Siberia and Alaska faced the starter's stand on the ice of Bering sea on April 1.

Allan, with Berger's team, made the 408 miles through a blizzard in 82 hours and 2 minutes, and Blatchford in 82 hours and 18 minutes.

The Siberian team, third in the race, made the run in 89 hours.

Cross Breed the Fastest.

Mr. Allan says that after years' experience with dogs he decided that a cross between a setter and the native Alaskan dog proves the best traveler. Each animal for racing purposes should weigh between 70 and 90 pounds.

Mr. Allan has made 17 trips from the interior of Alaska to the coast ports, covering every one that leads to a ship connection and over some of which, in early days, he had to break trail.

So much does Allan love his dogs that they also have the kindest love for him and it is told that during

Scotty Allan's 1909 visit to Seattle and Wenatchee, Washington was well-reported.

WADA IS FORERUNNER

Intrepid Jap Musher to Go to Iditarod Goldfields Via Seward Route, to Carry Mail Matter.

Seattle, Nov. 20—Wada, the famous Japanese musher of Alaska, now in Seattle, will depart on the steamer Yucatan, sailing Wednesday. He will go to Seward, and from thence will make the overland trip to the Iditarod goldfields, carrying letters for Iditarod miners, blazing the trail where necessary and locating sites for roadhouses along the route. Wada is the forerunner of many prospectors who will follow in his wake.

JOE CANNON HAS GROUCH

Chicago, Nov. 20—Speaker Cannon of the house of representatives expresses intense and unconcealed wrath against the so-called insurgent Republicans of the senate and house. He

SEWARD SCHOOL IS HONORED

Mrs. H. P. Wybrant, president, and Mrs. D. C. Brownell, vice-president, of the ladies' auxiliary of Seward, having in charge the local exhibit sent to the Alaska-Yukon-Pacific exposition, have received a letter from Mrs. Mary E.

diameter, good solid roads, raised.

About forty-five head of horses winter in Knik, and hay was cut at Cottonwood and Old Knik for the A. A. Lyden and W. D. Elliott ma hay baler that works by man power and three ton were baled and shipped to Knik for Mrs. E. M. Pure horses. The hay at Old Knik is red top and is equal to the out hay.

Knik has gone dry. G. W. Pa has looked up the saloon, there i not enough business to cover the pense of the license, and it will haps be looked up for some time. Hughes, who attended bar for Palmer for the past two years' half, retires for a long winter's and will live with his wife at hi home in Cottonwood.

Andrew J. Duffy, proprietor o Pioneer restaurant here, has vary ill for some time. Sto troubles is his complaint and th regularity of the mail has cau delay of medicines which he ha for. At present he is feeling what relieved. Should he get again, he will have to be taken to Susitna, or the doctor there over here.

Within the past two months six houses have been built here. Stanton Shafer, one of the

News of the Japanese musher, Jujiro Wada, on the Iditarod Trail, 1909.

Alaskan Sled Dog Tales

"United States reindeer mail team, Nome to Teller route."
[Lomen Brothers Photograph Collection P28-180 Alaska State Library]

"Sled deer hauling reindeer meat to village. Deering herd, 1928. Photographer Clarence Leroy Andrews." [C. L. Andrews Photograph Collection P45-0588 AST]

Alaskan Sled Dog Tales

THE HUSKIES AND THE REINDEER
"reindeer are gentle, timid, and eat little"

". . . [dogs are] treacherous and unreliable beasts . . ."
~Sheldon Jackson

The colorful history of sled dog travel has been well documented over the years, in books ranging from the classic *Gold, Men and Dogs*, by A.A. Scotty Allen (G.P. Putnam Sons, 1931); to Archdeacon of the Yukon Hudson Stuck's *Ten Thousand Miles with a Dogsled* (1914). But one of the most compelling books ever written about sled dog travel in the north country is a newer title, published in 2003 by W.W. Norton & Company. *The Cruelest Miles: The Heroic Story of Dogs and Men in a Race Against an Epidemic*, by cousins Gay Salisbury and Laney Salisbury, details the heroic relay dash of twenty men and more than two hundred dogs who raced across 674 miles of Alaskan backcountry to deliver lifesaving serum and save the citizens of Nome from a diphtheria outbreak.

The book includes some wonderful history of the state, and at one point the Salisbury cousins note the central role of sled dogs in the history and development of the territory of Alaska: "...It was dogs and dog traction, for centuries the mainstay of Eskimo survival, that made

Alaskan Sled Dog Tales

An old photo of reindeer teams leaving Anvik Mission with 1,023 pounds of mail bound for Kaltag, December 27, 1920. Photo: Rev. J.W. Chapman

[Rev. J.W. Chapman Collection P86-004 Alaska State Library]

this new world run. During the gold rushes, dogs brought the modern world to Alaska, hauling food, mining supplies, medicine, passengers, and gold across the network of rivers and trails that Eskimos and Athabaskans had been following for hundreds of years."

Then, in the next paragraph, the Salisburys report a little-known aspect of Alaskan history: "In addition to trade goods, the gold rush brought some strange ideas to Alaska, and the most bizarre may have been the belief of some U.S. government officials that Alaskans would be better off living in Alaska without dogs. Ambitious entrepreneurs tried many alternative forms of transportation and communication that they hoped would be superior to dogs, including horses, goats, hot-air balloons, bicycles, ice skates, ice boats, ice trains. and passenger pigeons. But the favorite choice of several key officials was the reindeer."

Alaskan Sled Dog Tales

Incredibly, the primary proponent for reindeer was Dr. Sheldon Jackson, a Presbyterian minister and the head of Alaska's fledgling education system at the turn of the century. A staunch supporter of reindeer who argued their qualities far and wide, Jackson even testified before Congress that dogs were "treacherous and unreliable beasts," and claimed that they "require considerable food for their support, while reindeer are gentle, timid and eat little, foraging on the moss and spruce of the tundra."

Fortunately for our canine friends, the aforementioned Archdeacon Hudson Stuck challenged Jackson's assertions. He'd written compellingly in Ten Thousand Miles With a Dogsled that the husky dog was prized and called "the Friend of Man," and he observed "There is not a dog the less in Alaska because of the reindeer, nor ever will be..."

When the Canadian government introduced reindeer into Labrador under the direction of Dr. Wilfred

Above: Archdeacon Hudson Stuck
Below: Dr. Sheldon Jackson

Alaskan Sled Dog Tales

Above: Reindeer transportation
Below: Reindeer in harness

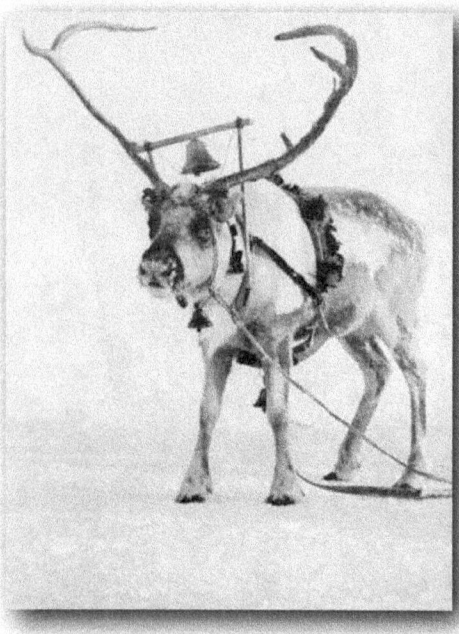

Grenfell, who stated his hope they would "eliminate that scourge of the country, the husky dog," the Archdeacon Stuck responded, "Instead of the reindeer eliminating the dog, there is far greater likelihood of the dog eliminating the reindeer..."

After a few side paragraphs on feeding and caring for reindeer as opposed to dogs, the Archdeacon went on, warming to the argument: "Speaking broadly, the reindeer is a stupid, unwieldy, and intractable brute, not comparing for a moment with the dog in intelligence or adaptability." He did, however, admit to the reindeer's usefulness in one regard: "Wherein lies the success of the reindeer experiment in Alaska? Chiefly in the provision of a regular meat supply..."

But back to the history and how the situation reached such an impasse. During the later half of the 1800's, whaling ships traveled extensively along the Bering Sea coast of Alaska as traders found a native populace willing to exchange their pelts, hides and meat of the

Alaskan Sled Dog Tales

resident marine mammals for guns, ammunition, tobacco, alcohol, and foods like sugar and flour. So great was the impact of these negotiations, when coupled with wildlife populations diminished by poaching and various other reasons, that by 1888 Captains of the U. S. Revenue Cutter Service ships which patrolled the waters of western Alaska became concerned for the well being of the Native Alaskans living along the Bering Sea villages.

Dr. Sheldon Jackson, a Presbyterian minister and the Commissioner of Education in Alaska, joined forces with Captain Michael A. Healy, of the U. S. Revenue Cutter *Bear*, who was essentially the federal government's law enforcement presence in the vast territory of Alaska. In his extensive travels Healy had witnessed the success of the Chukchi people of eastern

Alaska Reindeer, Kotzebue Herd No. 2. Lomen Bros. photo.
[George A. Parks P240-215 Alaska State Library]

Alaskan Sled Dog Tales

Siberia at raising reindeer, and he suggested the idea to Jackson of transporting domestic reindeer from Siberia to western Alaska as a solution to the food shortages among Native Alaskans.

Beginning with a successful trial run of 16 reindeer imported to the Aleutian Islands in 1891, Captain Healy made five trips to Siberia during the summer of 1892 and thus began the establishment of small reindeer herds, which were distributed to mission schools on the Seward Peninsula and throughout western Alaska under the direction of Jackson.

By 1905 the reindeer population was estimated at over 10,000 animals, due in part to the discovery of gold in Nome in 1898, when a large demand for reindeer meat popularized their raising. Reindeer, who could graze freely on native lichen and did not need to be fed, were also used to pull sleds full of gear and supplies for the miners, and in 1899 reindeer were used to deliver mail for the U.S. postal service.

The first route was established by Sheldon Jackson, from St. Michael to Kotzebue, and another early route, managed by William Kjellmann, ran from the Eaton Reindeer Station, near Unalakleet, over what must have been the same route followed by today's Iditarod trail, to Nome. The establishment of reindeer stations throughout western Alaska allowed the use of reindeer relays of from thirty to fifty miles, carrying 200-300 pounds of mail. A photo taken at Anvik Mission by Rev. J.W. Chapman shows multiple reindeer teams being readied to leave from in front of the mission with 1,023 pounds of mail bound for Kaltag.

In 1906, a government investigation found that the majority of the reindeer in Alaska were owned by mission schools and non-Natives, so Dr. Jackson's services were ended and a government policy was established with the goal of placing more reindeer into Native Alaskan ownership. The U. S. Reindeer Service was formed with reindeer distribution largely handled by school superintendents employed by the Bureau of Education, and the reindeer population grew to an estimated

Alaskan Sled Dog Tales

20,000 head by the close of 1908. By 1913 Alaskan Natives owned over 65% of the estimated 47,266 reindeer in Alaska.

The herds grew quickly over the following twenty years and in the 1930s the reindeer population peaked at 640,000. Colorful Alaskan characters became identified with the reindeer industry, such as Carl J. Lomen, known as The Reindeer King of Alaska for his unstinting role in organizing, promoting, marketing, and lobbying for the reindeer industry; and a Native woman, Mary Antisarlook, known as Sinrock Mary the Reindeer Queen, grew famous for her immense herd of reindeer and became one of the richest women in the North.

In 1937 the Reindeer Act was passed and restricted ownership of domestic reindeer to Native Alaskans. For a complexity of reasons the herds were already in decline by that time, and by 1950 there were only 25,000 reindeer reported to be under private ownership.

Above: Sinrock Mary, Reindeer Queen
Below: Carl Lomen, Reindeer King

Alaskan Sled Dog Tales

Reindeer pulling a dogsled.

Meanwhile the sled dog, which had been used as a draft animal for centuries, was gaining popular favor as a practical means of transporting goods, materials, and people over long trails under the most adverse conditions. The Klondike gold rush saw the importation of thousands of dogs to the north country from 1897 to 1899, and the Fairbanks and Nome gold rushes which quickly followed brought even more dogs to Alaska and the Yukon, cementing a legend of dauntless dogs bravely forging through blizzards, over mountains, and down rivers with their masters' loads.

When the Nome Kennel Club, founded in 1906, organized a series of races to encourage the breeding and training of better sled dogs, their place as primary transportation animals was strengthened. The 408-mile All Alaska Sweepstakes, founded in 1908, captured the imagination of an

Alaskan Sled Dog Tales

entire nation with colorful champions such as Scotty Allen and Leonhard Seppala. Their teams blazed across remote and dangerous trails, and their thrilling exploits under the northern lights were immortalized in popular novels such as Esther Birdsall Darling's *Baldy of Nome* and Barrett Willoughby's breathlessly-paced romance based on the famous All Alaska Sweepstakes race, *The Trail Eater*.

In February, 1924 there was an unfortunate incident near Nome when Hans Samuelson was driving three reindeer to the Nome Biological Survey Station. Several sled dogs from a kennel belonging to Fred Ayer had been turned loose to exercise, and when the dogs scented the reindeer they chased and killed two of the animals. In trying to rescue his reindeer, Hans Samuelson shot and killed four of Ayers' sled dogs.

When the Nome diphtheria epidemic struck in 1925, the use of sled dog teams in relaying the life-saving serum once again galvanized public attention and popularized the working sled dog. Leonhard Seppala and Gunnar Kaasen travelled to major cities and exhibited their serum run teams, and a bronze statue of Balto in New York's Central Park was ceremoniously unveiled by the famous lead dog himself.

Sheldon Jackson may have vociferously testified against the sled dog before Congress, but the reign of the reindeer in Alaska was relatively short-lived in the history of the north. They're still being raised in northwestern Alaska, although not in the vast numbers seen during Carl Lomen and Mary Antilarsook's time.

The Reindeer Research Program, established in 1981, has taken an active role in the re-development and promotion of the Alaskan reindeer industry, noting that currently, there are approximately 20 reindeer herders and 20,000 reindeer in western Alaska. An additional 10,000 reindeer exist in herds on Nunivak, St. Paul, Umnak, and other Aleutian Islands, along with a few fenced herds along Alaska's road system. ~•~

Alaskan Sled Dog Tales

Alaskan Sled Dog Tales

SLED DOG MAGAZINE COVER ART
Dashing Through the Snow

"The northern lights dancing over a dog team winding along a frozen river, now there's an image of the north that needs no explaining caption."

The dynamic image of a fast-paced sled dog team dashing through the snow to some unknown destination has always been one to stir the hearts of men–and women, and compelling photos and artwork of dog teams have graced magazine covers for almost as long as magazines have been published. Whether providing an exciting lead-in to a story within the pages, or just drawing the reader's eye with the promise of a colorful tale ahead, a sharp-looking team of huskies being driven by a bold musher has always made enticing cover art.

Over the next few pages some early magazine covers portray the splendid picture which defines the north country, sled dog teams in graceful stride, designed to invite daydreams from those readers who've never been there, and knowing smiles from those who have. ~•~

Alaskan Sled Dog Tales

Alaskan Sled Dog Tales

Alaskan Sled Dog Tales

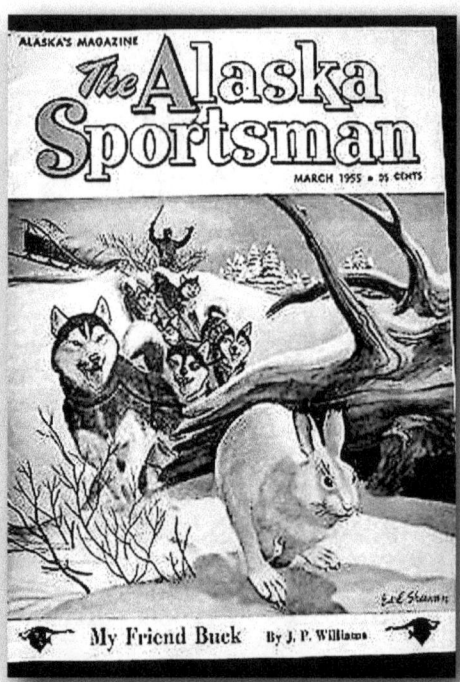

Alaskan Sled Dog Tales

Alaskan Sled Dog Tales

Leonhard Seppala's racing team of Siberian Huskies.

Golovin. Dexter's Roadhouse to the left, his tombstone on right. [HABS 1981]

Alaskan Sled Dog Tales

RACING DOWN TO GOLOVIN
Seppala's Epic Serum Run

> *"With few reserves to call on, the team began to stumble from exhaustion. But they did not stop, and strained up the final ascent, then raced three miles down to Dexter's Roadhouse in Golovin."*
> ~The Cruelest Miles: The Heroic Story of Dogs and Men in a Race Against an Epidemic, by Gay and Laney Salisbury

The Dexter Roadhouse was a key point on the Iditarod Trail in 1925, when men and dogs raced blizzard conditions to bring a life-saving antitoxin to Nome. The local landmark sat at the end of two of the biggest challenges on the trail: the shifting pack ice of Norton Sound and the harrowing climb to the summit of what was known locally as Little McKinley. Both would be crossed in a raging blizzard by champion dog driver Leonhard Seppala and his renowned racing team of Siberian huskies, capably led by the inimitable Togo.

Golovin is located on point of land between Golovnin Bay and Golovnin Lagoon, southeast of White Mountain, about 62 miles east of Nome. The area receives its name from Russian Vice-Admiral Vasily

Alaskan Sled Dog Tales

The Dexter Roadhouse at Golovin. [this photograpg and photo on page 134 are both by Walter Smalling Jr. for the 1981 Historic American Buildings Survey]

Mikhailovich Golovnin, who visited Alaska to inspect the workings of the Russian-American Company in 1807-1809 and ten years later, in 1817-1819. The town name is misspelled while the bay and lagoon retain the original Russian spelling.

Around 1890, John Dexter, one of the employees of the nearby Omalik mines, married an Eskimo woman and established a trading post and roadhouse that became the center for swapping prospecting information for the entire Seward Peninsula. John Dexter was listed as postmaster of both the Cheenik Post Office (est. 1899, discontinued in 1903) and the Golovin Post Office (est. 1906, discontinued in 1958).

Gold was discovered in 1898 at Council and Golovin became a supply point for the gold fields. Supplies were unloaded from ships at Golovin and shipped across Golovnin Lagoon and up the Fish and Niukluk Rivers to Council. When gold was discovered in what is now Nome, much of the mining and shipping activity moved there and Golovin declined in population.

But in February of 1925 the Dexter Roadhouse was the goal of champion dog musher Leonhard Seppala, winner of three All Alaska Sweepstakes races and many smaller contests. His fleet team of Siberian huskies responded to his quiet way with devotion. One race competitor reported, "That man is super-human. I couldn't see that he drove the dogs. He just clucked to them every now and then and they lay into their collars harder than I've ever seen dogs do it before."

Seppala and his team, with his trusted leader Togo, were part of the Serum Relay now, taking on one of the most challenging sections of the trail, across the treacherous shifting ice of Norton Sound in a blizzard. Cousins Gay and Laney Salibury told of his heroic crossing in their classic book, *The Cruelest Miles*: "The wind was howling and the ice on Norton Sound hissed and cracked. While Seppala harnessed the last dogs to the gang line, an old Eskimo

"Togo," Leonhard Seppala's lead dog

Leonhard Seppala and "Togo"

Alaskan Sled Dog Tales

emerged from the roadhouse and headed toward him.

"'Maybe you go more closer shore,' he said quietly. Eskimos did not take unnecessary chances on the trail and this time even Seppala understood that he had to be cautious."

"Much of the trail between Isaac's Point and Golovin was a few miles offshore, bypassing a number of craggy points that jutted out from the coast. Although the trail would be rougher, Seppala decided to stay within a few hundred feet of the land.

"It was about 40 below now and as he edged down the bank at Issac's Bay he could feel the wind building in strength. The Eskimo had been right: this was no time to be out over water. The ice he had crossed a day earlier had already broken up and around him he saw cakes of ice threatening to come loose. The cracks seemed to be getting closer, and in some places open water was just a few feet away. Water spurted up through cracks and the ice heaved. Togo zigzagged around the weak spots and several times put on a burst of speed toward shore. Once the last bay had been crossed, the team turned toward the mainland, putting the ice floes behind them, and Seppala breathed a little easier.

Leonhard Seppala and his Siberian Husky team.

Alaskan Sled Dog Tales

"A few hours later the entire section of ice over which they had come broke up in chunks and blew out to sea."

Seppala had just crossed the most dangerous section of the trail, but he now faced the most challenging: A series of ridges they would have to climb to the 1,200' summit of Little McKinley, which overlooked Golovnin Bay. Many mushers considered it the toughest part of the trail to Nome as ridge after exposed ridge stretched out over eight miles. "The downgrades are steep and the dogs and drivers have little time to recover from one ridge before they have to breathe in deep and charge up the next."

But Seppala's plucky little Siberians, having traveled 260 miles of trail in four and a half days with only five hours of rest, and facing a total climb of about 5,000 feet, steadfastly trudged up the ridges.

"With few reserves to call on, the team began to stumble from exhaustion. But they did not stop, and strained up the final ascent, then raced three miles down to Dexter's Roadhouse in Golovin. Seppala passed the precious bundle of serum to the awaiting relay musher, Charlie Olson, who set off into the blizzard facing a wind chill factor of minus seventy degrees below zero. Charlie would arrive at the roadhouse in Bluff, twenty-five miles distant, with frostbitten hands and exhausted dogs, and he would caution the last driver, Gunnar Kaasen, against setting out in the storm. But knowing the danger of epidemic faced by Nome, Kaasan would put his faith in his lead dog, Balto, and set out.

Leonhard Seppala's part of the Serum Run was over, he and his dogs could enjoy a well-earned rest now. "Since picking up the serum from the last relay musher, Seppala's dogs had traveled 135 miles, more than two and a half times the distance covered by any of the other drivers." ~•~

Alaskan Sled Dog Tales

Natkusiak, Emiu and Karsten Andersen in front of a long expedition sled, Borden Island, Northwest Territories, Canada. Photo by Vilhjalmur Stefansson, May, 1916

Arctic explorer Viljhalmur Stefansson and his fellow expedition members took thousands of photographs of their travels in the Arctic. March, 1914.

Alaskan Sled Dog Tales

SPLIT-THE-WIND
"... the greatest musher..."

"'Twenty-three minutes and eighty-nine seconds flat!"
~Split-the-Wind

The Canadian Arctic Expedition, organized in July, 1913 under the leadership of explorer and anthropologist Vilhjalmur Stefansson, was designed to be the most comprehensive scientific study of the Arctic ever attempted, comprised of a multi-pronged approach to researching and documenting the most northerly reaches of the North American continent.

Scientists of many disciplines, and from several countries, answered the call and joined the expedition, and while many of them lost their lives, most returned almost four years later with thousands of artifacts, specimens, photos, film and sound recordings; scientific data and knowledge which has been used in Arctic science ever since.

Unfortunately in the winter of 1913 the expedition met with fiercer than normal weather, and all of the expedition ships were frozen into the ice before they could reach their initial destination of Herschel Island. The

Alaskan Sled Dog Tales

Dog sleds of the Stefannson-Anderson Canadian-Arctic Expedition, built in Nome, Alaska, 1918. Lomen Bros. photograph.

Karluk, the flagship of the expedition, was eventually crushed by the ice, leading to loss of eleven lives before a famous rescue by the revenue cutter *Bear*.

One of the most compelling books to come out of the Canadian Arctic Expedition was written by Harold Noice, who joined as a sailor and crew member on the schooner *Polar Bear* when she left Seattle in March 1915. Noice maintained a detailed diary during his time with Stefansson's exploration party, and was with the intrepid explorer during the discovery of new lands in 1916 and 1917.

In 1924 Harold Noice published an account of his adventures with the Canadian Arctic Expedition, titled *With Stefansson in the Arctic*. In his book, Noice told of an Eskimo guide for Vilhjalmer Stefannsson's expeditions named Emiu, who was also known as "Split-the-wind" due to his fondness for fast dog teams.

Alaskan Sled Dog Tales

Originally from Nome, and formerly a cabin boy on the schooner *Polar Bear*, Emiu took part in all of the 'New Land' sled trips in the Arctic islands between 1916 and 1918. Emiu had, according to Noice, spent two years in Seattle and most of the rest of his life in Nome, Alaska.

"Split was a game little fellow, like a compact bundle of fine steel wires. He had a habit of pulling his belt tight which made him look even more gaunt than he was, and at camp-time he used to delight in talking about the fine beefsteaks we would order when we finally got back to civilization."

"Split told us… how on such a date he had trained the team of racing dogs that won the All Alaska Sweepstakes in so many hours, 'Twenty-three minutes and eighty-nine seconds flat!'" A search of the All Alaska Sweepstakes race results for the early years of the race does not show a team finishing within that specific time configuration, and the available

Emiu, who came to be known as Split-the-Wind.

finishes do not include a time for 24 minutes and 29 seconds, which is what the adjusted time would be.

Split was one of several former members of the Canadian Arctic Expedition who succumbed to the influenza epidemic of 1918. According to Noice, "Little Split died of influenza a few days after he reached Nome."

For the most part, Split-the-Wind has all but disappeared from the annals of history; references to the speedy little musher are difficult to find, and photos of him are rare. Unfortunately this was not an unusual development in early Alaska, when photographers needed to be selective about how they utilized photographic equipment and materials which were difficult to move and to use in the extreme northern weather conditions.

A passing mention of Split-the-Wind is found at the Iditarod Historic Trail Alliance site, as one of an elite group of Alaskan mushers: "An

The schooner Polar Bear.

Alaskan Sled Dog Tales

assortment of travelers used the Trail. The majority were prospectors, trappers, or Natives who traveled—often without dogs or with one or two to help pull a sledload of supplies—to isolated cabins. A surprising number walked along the Trail. The hero of the Trail, however, was the dogsled team and driver.

"These noteworthies earned nicknames befitting the men who raced along the Trail carrying fresh eggs or oranges, mail or express, or shipments of gold—Frank Tondreau, known from Belfast to Point Barrow as the Malemute Kid; the famous racer John "Iron Man" Johnson and his indefatigable Siberians; Captain Ulysses Grant Norton, the tireless Trojan of the trails; the Eskimo, Split-the-Wind; and the wandering Japanese, Jujira Wada. All were welcomed in the camps and became often interviewed celebrities."

There's another brief mention of this remarkable musher in the book *America's Forgotten Pandemic: the Influenza of 1918,* by Alfred W. Crosby, who is Professor Emeritus in American Studies, History and Geography at the University of Texas at Austin. Crosby explains that between August, 1918 and March, 1919 the Spanish influenza spread worldwide, claiming between 50 and 130 million lives, making it one of the deadliest natural disasters in human history. In a strange twist, nearly half of those affected by the disease were healthy young adults between the ages of 20 and 40, and as the pandemic spread through the Eskimo communities around Nome it had devastating results.

Of the intrepid Emiu, Crosby writes: "One Eskimo who died was a twenty-five-year-old named Split-the-Wind, known as the greatest musher that Alaska had ever produced. He had survived incredible hardships while guiding Vilhjalmer Stefannsson, the great explorer, in the deep Arctic, eating snowshoe lacings when there was nothing better; but now he was dead of Spanish influenza, along with 750 other Eskimos of the Seward Peninsula." ~•~

Nellie Neal Lawing's autobiography, published in 1948.

Alaskan Sled Dog Tales

ALASKA NELLIE'S DOGTEAM ADVENTURES
Rescue in Hell's Acres

"There were possibilities of an extensive business at this place for at least three years, as I saw it, and now I would be needing a dog team and dog kennels, a place for harnesses and a small building in which to cook dog food. On the mountain above the lodge I cut logs for the kennels and the cookhouse."
~Nellie Neal Lawing in her autobiography, *Alaska Nellie*

Alaska Nellie was one of the territory's most colorful and beloved personalities, a larger-than-life adventuress whose exploits would easily fill a number of exciting books, beginning with her own autobiography. She was reportedly quite sweet-natured and ladylike, but she was also a hard-working, sharp-shooting, fearlessly independent entrepreneur who carved a place for herself at a time when that was a difficult challenge for anyone, let alone a diminutive woman with oversized dreams.

Nellie Neal Lawing, familiar to Alaskans as the peerless "Alaska Nellie," arrived in Seward on July 3, 1915, just as construction of the Alaska Railroad was getting underway. Nellie wrote in her autobiography, *Alaska Nellie*, that she set out to seek a contract "to run the eating houses on the southern end of the Alaska Railroad," and she

Alaskan Sled Dog Tales

Railroad tunnel, mile 48.2, and the high trestle at mile 49, near Grandview.

described her effort: "On my first time out on an Alaskan trail, I had walked one hundred fifty miles and as usual was alone. This accomplishment, in itself, might have satisfied some, but I was out here in this great new country to contribute something to others, and I felt this means could best be served by becoming the 'Fred Harvey' of the government railroad in Alaska."

Likely due in part to her plucky approach, she was awarded a lucrative government contract to run a roadhouse at mile 44.9, a scenic location which she promptly named Grandview.

Nellie was the first woman to be awarded such a contract. Her agreement with the Alaska Engineering Commission was to provide food and lodging for the government employees; her skill with a rifle filled out the menu, and her gifted storytelling kept her guests highly entertained. According to the terms of her contract, Nellie could purchase supplies from the government commissary, her freight would be delivered at no charge, and

Alaskan Sled Dog Tales

she would be paid fifty cents per meal and one dollar per night for lodging. The government employees on the railroad paid her with vouchers, which she turned in monthly for payment.

Nellie described the accommodations at Grandview in her book, *Alaska Nellie*, "The house was small but comfortable. A large room with thirteen bunks, used as sleeping quarters for the men, was just above the dining room. A small room above the kitchen served as my quarters. To the rear of the building a stream of clear, cold water flowed down from the mountain and was piped into the kitchen. Nature was surely in a lavish mood when she created the beauty of the surroundings of this place. The timber-clad mountains, the flower-dotted valley, the irresistible charm of the continuous stretches of mountains and valleys was something in which to revel."

Alaska Nellie's Grandview Roadhouse, Alaska Railroad mile 44.9, 1915

Alaskan Sled Dog Tales

One harrowing event Nellie's life occurred in the dark cold of winter. She generally used her dog team for trapping along the corridor which would later become the Seward Highway, but her team would play an important role in one of the major events in Nellie's life. She tells the story in her autobiography, *Alaska Nellie*, setting the stage with a description of a blizzard raging in the mountains, a mail carrier overdue, and the brief daylight passing: "A few hours of daylight was all we had and the Alaskan night settled down by 2 o'clock in the afternoon.

"The telephone rang and I was advised the mail had left Tunnel at 9 a.m. with a seven-mile journey by dog team to Grandview, the summit, and another five miles to Hunter. What a day to be on the trail! And still no sign of the mail carrier and five hours had passed since he left Tunnel.

"Five more hours went by and still no one arrived. During the next hour I decided to hitch up the dogs and go in search of the man, for I judged he must be in trouble.

"I left at 8 p.m., at the height of the storm, after putting a rabbit-skin robe, shovel, lantern and snowshoes on the sled. As I drove the dogs around the mountain where the howling north wind hit us, it was almost unbearable. The dogs refused to go and turned back to the sled. By putting on my snowshoes and breaking trail ahead of them, I urged them on and on.

"As we entered Hell's Acres, we encountered a large snowdrift covering the trail. After working our way over this, the dogs started on a run. They had scented the mail carrier's dogs! They couldn't be far away, but the blinding snow and darkness made it impossible to see but a short distance. After working our way over another drift, we came to the carrier's dogs lying in the snow.

"Henry Collman, the carrier, was near the sled in a stooping position and nearing the point of becoming helpless, with his face, hands and feet frozen. His dogs were nearly exhausted. Hell's Acres had him in its

Alaskan Sled Dog Tales

clutches and nearly claimed his life! I helped him on to my sled, but his dogs were not ready to go, as they were bedded down in the snow. At the approach of my dogs they growled and barked, but I was prepared to end their fight if they had attempted it. I put two of Henry's dogs to my sled and turned the others loose to follow us.

"After arriving at the roadhouse I helped Harry into the house and began rounding up the loose dogs and tying them up. Back in the house, I found Harry in great pain. He was thawing out too rapidly. After filling a washtub with snow, I packed his feet with snow, then applied snow packs to his face and hands, keeping him warm at the same time so the snow would melt fast.

"He took hot drinks and I applied kerosene, which has a healing effect on frozen parts. After several hours be became drowsy and fell asleep.

"Seward and Susitna Mail Team, 1913." Typical of the teams which hauled freight and mail over the Iditarod trail, and past Alaska Nellie's roadhouse at Grandview.

Alaskan Sled Dog Tales

"Erick Johnson's U.S. Mail team at Portage Creek, Alaska."

At 3 a.m. I hitched two of his dogs in with my team of five and went back for his sled and the mail. The wind ceased and the trail was covered with huge snowdrifts, but I made it through with snowshoes and the help of the noble dogs. I hitched the dogs to his sled and trailed my sled behind, working on the gee pole. When I returned to the house, my patient was still sleeping. I decide to take the mail through to Hunter, where they were holding the train for it, when I last heard from them. The wires had since gone down and there had been no news since early evening.

The trail to Hunter was mostly down hill and was made without much difficulty, except for a few drifts. As I was driving up to the train, Lloyd Maitland, the conductor, said: "Here's that damn mail carrier now! Say, dog musher, where have you been? What happened to you? We've been holding this train here all night!"

Alaskan Sled Dog Tales

"Well, what a question to ask at a time like this!" I said. "And besides, who do you think you're talking to?"

As I pulled back the hood of my parka, Maitland said:

"For the love of dog mushers! If it isn't Nellie Neal! How did you happen to get the mail? We've been trying to get you on the 'phone. I guess the wires are down."

"I'm not guessing. I know they're down," I replied. "Henry Collman, the carrier, didn't get to Grandview, so I went after him and found him frozen down in Hell's Acres. I took him to the roadhouse where he is now, and he was sleeping when I left. He was badly frozen."

The mail was put aboard and Mr. Maitland, the conductor on the train, gave me a receipt for the sacks and pouches, which I later learned contained valuable goods.

"It was 7 a.m. when I returned home. Henry was still sleeping. After putting the dogs in the kennels and making a fire in the kitchen range, I sat down to rest. When I attempted to get up, I staggered and nearly fell, but after breakfasting I felt better. I fed my patient and took food to the dogs. Henry's first thought on waking was about the mail and his dogs.

"'You have nothing to worry about,' I said to him. 'Your dogs are in the kennels and the mail is in Seward.'

"'Well, tell me, how did it get there?' he asked.

"'If you must know, I took it. Here are the receipts for it that the conductor gave me.'

"Several days later, he and his dogs were taken to Anchorage where he entered the hospital and received treatment for frost bite. He fully recovered and left for his home in the 'States.'

"Along this same trail where this young man came so near to losing his life, can be seen graves of several trail blazers who lost their lives at this point, where storms do their utmost to try the strength of man and beast. In the summer months a more beautiful place is hard to find. Acres of wild flowers cover the mountain slopes and valleys.

"Toward the end of the year, at the approach of the holiday season and my third Christmas in Alaska, a small package came through the mail, over the trail by dog team, for me. This contained one of the greatest surprises of my life. It was a necklace of solid gold nuggets! A large nugget formed the pendant in which a diamond was set. In the package was a note containing many names and these words:

"To Nellie–from oldtimers

Who on snowshoes broke down the trail;

Who fought the elements to take through the mail.

They struggled on without food or rest–

To rescue the perishing they did their best."

Nellie tells another dog team story in her autobiography, *Alaska Nellie*: "One cold winter day in December when the daylight was only a matter of minutes and the lamps were burning low, two U.S. marshals, Marshals Cavanaugh and Irwin, together with Jack Haley and Bob Griffiths, arrived at the roadhouse. The heavy wooden boxes they were removing from their sleds had been brought from the Iditarod mining district. They contained $750,000 in gold bullion. '"Where do you want to put this, Nellie?' called the men, carrying their precious burden.

"'Right here under the dining room table is as good a place as any,' I answered. And it was as simple as that. There it stayed until the men carried it back to the sleds, next day. They were able to go to sleep, for it was as safe right there in my dining room as it would have been in the United States Mint. No one would dare to touch it."

Alaska Nellie became known far and wide, and the foreword to a 2010 reprinting of her autobiographical book, *Alaska Nellie*, by Patricia A. Heim, sums up her legendary status::

Alaskan Sled Dog Tales

"Nellie Neal Lawing was one of Alaska's most charismatic, admired and famous pioneers. She was the first woman ever hired by the U.S. Government in Alaska in 1916. She was contracted to feed the hungry crews on the long awaited Alaska railroad connecting Seward to Anchorage. The conditions were harsh and supplies were limited. She delivered many of her meals by dogsled, fighting off moose attacks and hazards of the trail, often during below-zero blizzards. She always brought with her a great tale to tell of her adventures along the trail, how she had wrestled grizzlies, fought off wolves and moose, and caught the worlds largest salmon for their dinner, always in the old sourdough tradition. The workers listened and laughed with every bite.

"Nellie was an excellent cook, big game hunter, river guide, trail blazer, gold miner, and a great storyteller! It wasn't long before Nellie became legendary and was known far and wide as the female 'Davy Crockett' of Alaska, her wilderness

Above: Nellie Lawing proudly wearing her gold nugget necklace.

Below: Alaska Nellie in her fur parka.

Alaskan Sled Dog Tales

By the 1940's Alaska Nellie's fame was such that a letter from Ohio addressed to simply "Nellie, Alaska" was delivered to her. This letter is in the Seward Museum.

Nellie's horses, Whitey and Hornet. From a photo in the Seward Museum.

Alaskan Sled Dog Tales

adventures and stories of survival on the trail spread like wildfire. Letters addressed simply 'Nellie, Alaska' were always delivered."

Nellie later operated the Dead Horse Roadhouse near the Susitna River, at a railroad camp known as Curry, and then, in 1923, she bought her final home, the Roosevelt Roadhouse at mile 23.3 of the Alaska Railroad, which she had first admired in 1915. The railroad stop along the blue-green waters of Kenai Lake was renamed Lawing after Nellie Neal married Bill Lawing on the stage of the Liberty Theater in Seward on September 8, 1923.

Working together, Nellie and Bill Lawing built the roadhouse into a popular tourist stop on the Alaska Railroad. Vegetables from Nellie's garden were served with fresh fish from the lake or with game from the nearby hills, and Nellie's stories, often embellished with her rollicking tall tales, kept her audiences delighted. Celebrities, politicians, tourists and even locals came to enjoy the purely Alaskan hospitality at the Lawings' roadhouse on Kenai Lake.

Bill Lawing died of a heart attack in 1936. Heartbroken at losing him, Nellie continued entertaining guests and visitors for another twenty years, cementing her place in Alaska's history by welcoming the humorist Will Rogers, General Simon Bolivar Buckner, and the actress Alice Calhoun into her home.

On May 10, 1956, Nellie died peacefully while sitting in her favorite rocking chair. She was buried next to her beloved husband Bill in the Seward cemetery, under magnificent huge Alaskan spruce trees, and her gravestone bears the image of a pineapple, a symbol of hospitality. ~•~

Alaskan Sled Dog Tales

Leonhard Seppala with his favorite leader, Togo. They traveled almost 60,000 miles of trails, and it was said "you cannot speak of one without mention of the other."

Alaskan Sled Dog Tales

SEPPALA'S DOGS
Togo, Fritz, and Balto

"It is almost impossible to place a price on a good dog, especially if he is a leader." ~Olaf Swenson, who helped Seppala import Siberian huskies to Alaska

Legendary Alaskan dog driver Leonhard Seppala cuts a giant swath across sled dog racing history, often photographed in his signature squirrel-skin parka, with his handsome huskies beside him. Born in Norway, Seppala emigrated to Alaska during the gold rush and learned to drive dogs by hauling freight and supplies for the mines around Nome. His kennel partner in later years, Elizabeth M. Ricker, described Sepp as "a modest, unassuming character," but she also unhesitatingly defines him as "King of the Alaskan Trail."

Seppala entered his first All Alaska Sweepstakes race in 1914, but being unfamiliar with the trail, he made a grave miscalculation and lost. He returned the following year and won, and he won again in 1916 and 1917, equaling the record of another great dog driver, A.A. "Scotty" Allan. When the 1925 diphtheria epidemic threatened Nome -- and Sepp's own daughter -- he and his dauntless team travelled over 260 miles in "The Great Race of Mercy," and thereby secured their place in history.

Alaskan Sled Dog Tales

Balto at the head of Gunnar Kaasen's team at the end of the 1925 Serum Run.

The most famous dog in Seppala's kennel, Balto, was not supposed to be in the Serum Run; in fact, he'd never even led a team before. He was a freighting dog, slower than the racing dogs needed for speedy delivery of the serum, and Seppala had selected against including him in the team when he left Nome. It was only when the Governor of Alaska, in an unexpected move, decided to speed up the relay by authorizing the addition of more teams and drivers to Seppala's leg at the end, that Sepp's young assistant, a Norwegian named Gunnar Kaasen, chose the big black Balto, whom he had long favored and whose merit he wanted to prove, to lead his team in the final leg of the relay.

Seppala's easy choice had been his older, trusted leader, a small, tough husky called Togo, after a Japanese admiral. Togo was a purebred Siberian husky with a black, brown, cream and gray coat, and like most

Alaskan Sled Dog Tales

Siberians of the day, he weighed less than 50 pounds. But what Togo lacked in size he made up for in heart, and Seppala considered Togo his best sled dog, a strong and determined leader. Sepp wrote "I can safely say that he has won more races than any dog in Alaska."

The little husky saved his life more than once, and Seppala often said Togo was "the best dog that ever traveled the Alaskan trail" and "I never had a better dog than Togo."

At the end of Elizabeth Ricker's book, Leonhard Seppala writes about leaving his old friend Togo in her care, and it must have been difficult for him to write the final lines: "It seemed best to leave him ... where he could enjoy a well-earned rest. But it was a sad parting on a cold gray March morning when Togo raised a small paw to my knee as if questioning why he was not going along with me. For the first time in twelve years I hit the trail without Togo."

The largely unsung hero of Seppala's kennel, Togo's half-brother and also a veteran of the Serum Run,

Leonhard Seppala with his leaders. With Fritz above, below with Fritz and Togo.

Alaskan Sled Dog Tales

was Fritz. Born in 1915 and bred by Seppala, Fritz was a cream-colored Siberian husky with a mottled brown and gray saddle, neck and head markings, who became an important foundation sire in early Siberian husky pedigrees. He often led Seppala's team in tandem with Togo in races and on cross-country jaunts, and during the Serum Run he was co-leading with Togo.

In Elizabeth Ricker's biographical book, *Seppala, Alaskan Dog Driver*, Leonhard Seppala called Fritz "a great dog." He proved his greatness by becoming an important foundation sire of the early Siberian husky breed, which was officially recognized by the American Kennel Club in 1930.

In an interesting series of coincidences, Balto, Togo and Fritz were all mounted after they died, and they each travelled long and winding paths to their final resting places. The only one of the three who returned to their birthplace, Fritz was purchased and returned to Nome and is prominently featured in the Carrie McLain museum. Togo is on display at the Iditarod Trail Sled Dog Race headquarters log cabin in Wasilla, Alaska, while Balto remains at the Cleveland Museum of Natural History in Cleveland, Ohio.

Balto, the dog who wasn't even supposed to be in a Serum Run team, went on to become one of the most widely recognized and beloved sled dogs in history. Books, movies, photos, games, toys and much more celebrate the heroic efforts of the dog teams who saved Nome, and for better or worse, Balto became the iconic lead dog whose name would evoke bravery, loyalty and dedication. Generations of schoolkids learned the story of the intrepid sled dog who struggled through a blizzard to deliver the anti-toxin, and while some specific details may not be historically accurate, the legacy is not totally misplaced.

Balto led Kaasen's team through a howling blizzard, along treacherous seaside cliffs and over a trail blown over to the point that Kaasen admitted he didn't know where he was at times. When Balto led

Alaskan Sled Dog Tales

Gunnar Kaasen's leader in the Serum Run, Balto, owned by Leonhard Seppala.

the team into Nome around 5:30 a.m., witnesses said Gunnar Kaasen stumbled off his sled and went to his tired leader, where he said 'Damn fine dog' and collapsed beside him in the street.

On the bronze statue which was erected to honor Balto in New York City's Central Park, a plaque is inscribed with a tribute to all of the Serum Run sled dogs:

> *Dedicated to the indomitable spirit of the sled dogs that relayed antitoxin six hundred miles over rough ice, across treacherous waters, through Arctic blizzards from Nenana to the relief of stricken Nome in the winter of 1925.*
> *Endurance · Fidelity · Intelligence*

~•~

Alaskan Sled Dog Tales

Jujiro Wada with his friend, Captain H.H. Norwood of the whaling ship Balaena, 1903.

Alaskan Sled Dog Tales

JUJIRO WADA
Legendary Alaskan Trailblazer

". . . one of Alaska's best long distance sled dog drivers."
~John Underwood, in *Alaska, An Empire in the Making*

There are many strange and unusual stories in the annals of northern sled dog travel, but one of the most fascinating concerns an enigmatic Japanese explorer and adventurer named Jujiro Wada. Born in Japan in the 1870s, the second son of a lower-class samurai warrior, he traveled to the U.S. in 1890 and worked as a cabin boy for the Pacific Steam Whaling Company and at Barrow for the renowned Charlie Brower, manager of the Cape Smythe Whaling and Trading Company, which was probably where he learned how to handle a sled dog team and to speak Alaska Native languages.

Jujiro Wada was with E.T. Barnette when the businessman landed at what is now the site of Fairbanks. Hearing about the recent gold strikes nearby, Barnette dispatched Wada up the Yukon River with one of Barnette's own dogteams, taking the first news of the strikes to the miners at Dawson City. Wada drove Barnette's team into Dawson City on Dec. 28, 1902, and upon interviewing him the *Yukon Sun* printed a front-page story with the bold headline, "Rich Strike Made in the Tanana."

Alaskan Sled Dog Tales

Several hundred miners quickly left Dawson City for Fairbanks, but most were disappointed to find the best sites were already staked. As the story goes, an angry mob gathered at Barnette's store and threatened violence against both Barnette and Wada. An article in the *Dawson Daily News*, July 8, 1912, mentioned Wada's legendary predicament:

"Jujiro Wada, the mushing Jap who brought the first news of the Fairbanks strike to Dawson, and has made numerous other trips in the North, recently blew into Fairbanks again with a new story about the placer country of Western Alaska. The Times says: Ten years in a placer camp is a long, long time, more than five or ten times that number of years in an older community, where things move more slowly and the population does not come and go with such kaleidoscopic changes. Thus, the return of Jujiro Wada to Fairbanks might be likened almost to the

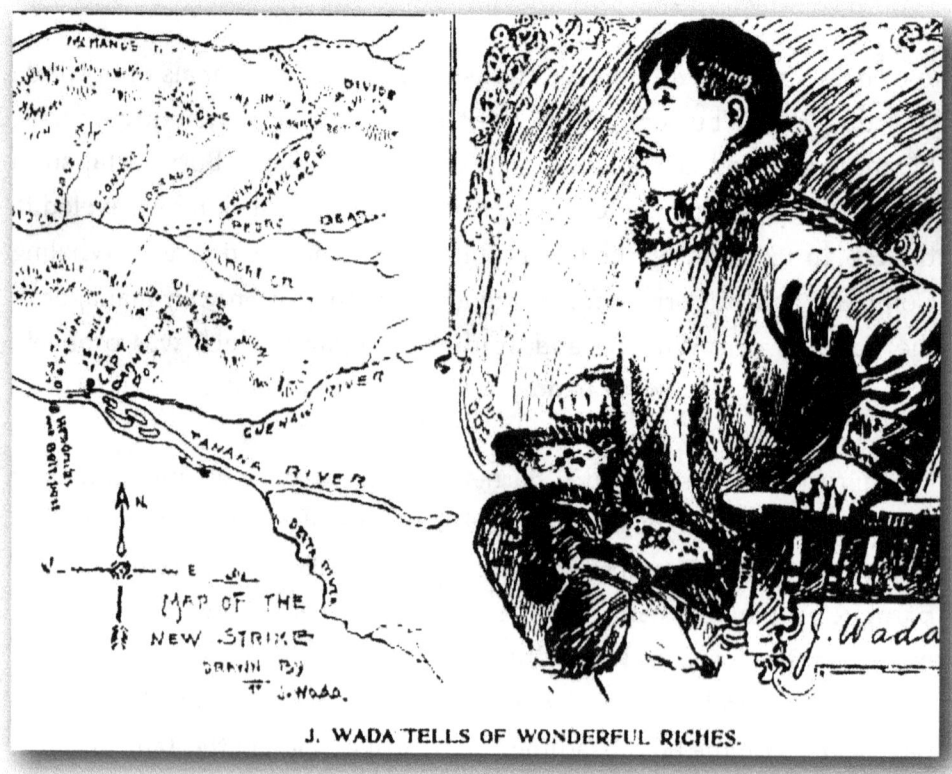

J. WADA TELLS OF WONDERFUL RICHES.

Alaskan Sled Dog Tales

return of one of the Pilgrim fathers to Plymouth, in point of the changes that have taken place in Fairbanks and the generations (placer camp generations) that have come and gone since he first visited the section and then mushed overland to Dawson ten years ago, with the news that caused the Fairbanks stampede. True, when the Dawsonites moved over the winter trail and viewed Felix Pedro's strike the majority of them were in favor of hanging Wada, but the hardy little brown musher has since been vindicated. His estimate of the camp was the correct one, and those of that first stampede who remained have mostly prospered. Thus it always gives him much satisfaction to drop back to Fairbanks and view the progress."

Five years earlier, however, in a *Dawson Daily News* article dated September 1907, Wada had already explained what actually happened:

"The story that I was about to be hanged for causing a thought-to-be-fake stampede was not correct. The fact is that the miners held a meeting

Above: "Jujiro-san"
Below: Jujiro Wada, 1896

Alaskan Sled Dog Tales

Jujiro Wada

to decide as to the price of flour then being offered by one of the trading companies. They thought the price exorbitant. It was rumored that the miners had a rope on my neck, and were about to hoist me. Now that is not true. The other part of the story, that I showed a copy of the (Seattle) *Post-Intelligencer* saying that several years before I had rescued a party of shipwrecked whalers in the Arctic in dead of winter is true. I did show that paper to let some of the boys know I had been up North, but it was not in a plea to save my neck."

For many years Jujiro Wada traveled widely across northern Alaska, the Yukon Territory, and beyond, leading an adventurous life and leaving his mark on the history of the north country. His exploits were the stuff of legend, as he traveled by dog team, hunting, trapping, prospecting, running marathons, and entertaining people wherever he went with his colorful stories. On one of his epic dog mushing trips he travelled from the headwaters of the Chandalar River to the Arctic Ocean, along the shore

Alaskan Sled Dog Tales

of the ocean to the Mackenzie River, and up that river and across the divide to the Porcupine River, taking more than a year, he and his dogs living on game hunted along the way.

Another of Wada's lasting contributions to Alaskan history was helping to pioneer the Iditarod Trail after several gold strikes were made in the Iditarod area, although in most accounts of Wada's travels the trip appears as something of a footnote to his other adventures. In a summary of Yuji Tani's 1995 book, *The Samurai Dog-Musher Under the Northern Lights*, Fumi Torigai, who was documenting Wada's travels for submission to the Historic Sites and Monuments Board of Parks Canada, wrote:

"In December of 1909, at the request of the town, Wada established a route from Seward to the newly discovered gold mine of Iditarod. Acting as the leader of a fleet of dogsled teams, Wada had a relatively uneventful

The whaling ship Balaena.

trip to Iditarod. However, on the return trip to Seward, he and his three companions had to go through prolonged minus 60 F (minus 51 C) weather. Several dogs, including his lead-dog, became too weak to survive the extreme cold and had to be put to sleep. The hardships of Wada and his companions and the ensuing rush of prospectors into the Iditarod area were widely reported in many Alaskan papers."

In early 1912, Wada was in the Kuskokwim area, looking for traces of a Japanese man known locally as Allen, who had disappeared there. On March 11, 1912, Wada was in Iditarod. In July 1912, he and his partner, John Baird, made a gold strike on the Tulasak River. Wada took about $12,000 in gold with him when he went to Seattle to report the findings to his backers, who included Edward Avery McIlhenny of Tabasco sauce fame and the Guggenheim brothers.

Facing pages: "The return of Mr. Wada after a 1,680-mile mush over snow and ice."

Alaskan Sled Dog Tales

Excerpts from an article which appeared in the *Dawson Daily News*, July 8, 1912:

Wada Tells of the Country to the West

"*Jujiro Wada, the mushing Jap who brought the first news of the Fairbanks strike to Dawson, and has made numerous other trips in the North, recently blew into Fairbanks again with a new story about the placer country of Western Alaska, the Times says:*

"*Wada was in Fairbanks a few years ago during the revival of Marathon racing, and figured in several of the big contests, but he left shortly after the great Fourth of July Marathon of 1909 when, before the largest crowd ever gathered at Fairbanks, Jerry Sullivan, of Nome, with his musher's trot, came home with the*

Adams Photo, Dawson City, Yukon Territory, 1908

Alaskan Sled Dog Tales

money. Since that date until Saturday night Wada has found time to cover considerable stretches of Northland, besides spending almost a year in the States.

"One of Wada's Alaskan stunts since leaving Fairbanks was the blazing of the overland trail to the Iditarod from Seward. He was hired to do this by the town of Seward and returning, reported that the route was feasible and that the Iditarod would make a good small camp. The road commission has since followed Wada's route. The next year found Wada down in the States, where almost the first person he met was a now wealthy ex-senator from Texas, whom Wada had known twenty years before up near Point Barrow, just after the Texan had graduated from college. The two held the big talkfest and then they took in the East together, not forgetting the Great White Way at New York. After almost a year in the States under the direction of his old Point Barrow friend, Wada hied himself North once more, backed by the man from Texas whom he now represents and whom he is to meet at New Orleans when he gets outside on his present trip.

"The first point visited last year after leaving San Francisco was Good News Bay, near the mouth of the Kuskokwim. Wada remained there until last November, when he heard of the Aniak river strike, when he moved up river and investigated that country. Still later he stampeded back down river to the Tulasak river and got in on the ground along Bear creek.

"Returning to the Iditarod from the Tulasak, Wada took Jack Baird, formerly of Fairbanks, with him and, moving a prospecting drill, the two crossed over to the Kuskokwim in the spring and proceeded to test some of the ground on Bear creek. The indications were very favourable, hence Wada's trip out to New Orleans to lay his findings before his backer.

"To judge by the bottle of coarse gold that Wada carries with him, taken from Bear creek, some of the nuggets being worth $10, it is evident that the prospectors secured more than indications.

"From the tests made by Baird and Wada the little brown musher is well satisfied that Bear creek will soon be famous as a dredging camp, for there is plenty of gold on bedrock. In fact, the Kuskokwim Commercial company will be

Alaskan Sled Dog Tales

one of the outfits that will put a dredge on Bear creek this summer. Wada does not know who their backers are.

"Referring to the Aniak river, which empties into the Kuskokwim about 75 miles above Tulasak, and which heads back against the same mountain as Bear creek, Wada predicts the men on Marble creek will have a good little camp."

The Seward Museum has a three-part video series online telling the story of the Iditarod Trail expedition of Jujiro Wada, in newspaper articles read by Lee Poleske, president of the Resurrection Bay Historical Society. Recorded as part of the Iditarod Trail Centennial celebration, the free video series, available online, is informative and brings to light some of the history of this little-known Alaskan wanderer.

An article in the Sept. 13, 2009 *Fairbanks News-Miner*, by Ronald Inouye, titled "Jujiro Wada: musher, long distance runner and Fairbanks co-founder?," poses a critical inquiry:

"Why don't we know more about this remarkable individual? His feats and tenacity are exemplary although detractors question some of his motives and willingness to be manipulated by people like E.T. Barnette. Wada wished to become a U.S. citizen so he could own land and stake claims, but his application was denied. Later, during World War I he was accused of being a Japanese spy, but those charges were not confirmed.

"The newspaper accounts of those times, as now, are selective, likely reflecting the socio-economic conditions and attitudes of that era. Whereas Northerners then as now accept most individuals based on individual abilities, it has not always been so by federal standards. Alaska Natives were only accorded U.S. citizenship in 1915, and then only provisionally. Until 1922, non-whites weren't allowed citizenship through naturalization. These factors might have obscured the presence and exploits of individuals like Wada."

Alaskan Sled Dog Tales

The 2007 Yukon Quest honored Wada with an exhibit of photos and newspaper clippings of his achievements in the north. The official press release read in part: "'Mr. Wada traveled by dog team along what is now the Yukon Quest Trail over 100 years ago when it was a traditional travel route. He learned his survival skills and travel routes through the assistance of the aboriginal people in the north,' said Lillian Nakamura Maguire, educator for the Yukon Human Rights Commission. "'He was respected for his hardiness, dog care and good character, although, as a Japanese man he experienced racism due to the strong anti-Asian sentiments in the early 1900s,' Nakamura Maguire said.

"'The Yukon Quest is dedicated to honouring the traditions of travel by dog team in the North and the equal treatment of all dogs and people taking part in the race. Mr. Wada embodied the love and respect for his dogs that is one of the founding principles of the Yukon Quest,' said Stephen Reynolds, Yukon Quest (Canada) Executive Director. 'We are honoured to help bring Jujiro Wada's incredible story to the world.'"

In an article for the *Fairbanks News-Miner* in June, 2011, author and historian Dermot Cole wrote: "Jujiro Wada, who promoted many mining ventures, traveled great distances across Alaska by dog team. He also helped blaze the trail from Seward to Iditarod."

In 1912, the *News-Miner* took note of the rocky reception given to Wada in early 1903 and explained what transpired afterwards in an article which helped to secure his status as an explorer, adventurer, and intrepid musher: "True, when the Dawsonites moved over the winter trail and viewed Felix Pedro's strike the majority of them were in favor of hanging Wada, but the hardy little brown musher has since been vindicated. His estimate of the camp was the correct one and those of that first stampede who remained have mostly prospered."

The online encyclopedia Wikipedia details Wada's continuing travels in later life: "Wada returned to Seward in November 1912. He brought

Alaskan Sled Dog Tales

with him two sled loads of mining equipment, another sled load of miscellaneous supplies, and four Japanese companions who would serve as assistant dog drivers. The Japanese and their twenty dogs then drove to the Bear Creek strike. Wada remained at the Bear Creek site until February 1913.

"Wada went to Seattle for a short while, then he returned to Alaska in May 1913. That same year, he was described in John Underwood's *Alaska, an Empire in the Making* as one of Alaska's best long-distance dog sled drivers.

"In 1915, a man named Ernest Blue wrote in the *Cordova Daily Times* that Wada was a Japanese spy, asserting that Blue had seen cash and a

Alaskan Sled Dog Tales

map of Alaska in Wada's possession. This story reappeared in 1923 and during WWII. During May 1915, Wada was in San Pedro, California, working at Van Camp's tuna packing plant, but left town swiftly after receiving a phone call. As with many stories about Wada, the published accounts are contradictory. In the *Seattle Times* on May 15, 1916, Wada insisted the phone call was a job offer in Alaska, and he traveled to New York. However, on page 217 of *Tani*, 1995, Wada wrote a letter to his friend Sunada, written on Van Camp Sea Food Company stationery. that reads, "Sorry to say but I am compelled to leave here... otherwise they will kill me."

Alaskan Sled Dog Tales

"During 1917-1918, Wada resumed prospecting in the Yukon, mostly along High Cache Creek. In 1919, he went to the Northwest Territories.

"On September 6, 1920, he entered New York State via Niagara Falls. He listed his last residence as Herschel Island, Northwest Territories, and his employer as E.F. Lufkin. He listed his height as 5'2", his hair as black, and his complexion as dark.

"From 1920-1923, he was trapping foxes on the Upper Porcupine. He also searched for gold around Herschel Island and for oil around Fort Norman (modern Norman Wells). His business partners during this time included the veteran trader Poole Field.

"Wada left Canada in April 1923. On May 3, 1923, he arrived at Ketchikan aboard the *SS Princess Mary*. He listed himself as a citizen of Canada, but was not allowed entry into Alaska because he had no passport.

"His subsequent whereabouts are not currently documented, but in 1930, he was in Chicago, Illinois. In May 1934, he was in Seattle, having recently arrived from San Francisco. During January 1936, he was in Green River, Wyoming. During the winter of 1936-1937, he was in Redding, California.

"He died at the San Diego County hospital on March 5, 1937. The cause of death was listed as peritonitis caused by diverticulitis."

Jujiro Wada was buried in an unmarked grave. A large bronze monument to the far-wandering traveler was established in 2007 in a park in Matsuyama City, Japan, celebrating the high points of his adventurous life. ~•~

A load of gold in front of the Pioneer Roadhouse. Knik, Alaska. 1916

Pioneer Roadhouse, Knik, F.B. Cannon, Proprietor

Alaskan Sled Dog Tales

FINDING GOLD ALONG THE IDITAROD TRAIL
"3,400 ounces of gold"

"Travel was so heavy that in one week in November, 1911 more than 120 mushers passed through Knik and out from Iditarod. Inbound freight and gold seekers to the Innoko-Iditarod gold fields passed outbound shipments such as the 1916 'Iditarod Gold Team' with 3,400 ounces of gold hauled by 46 dogs."
~Louise Potter, 'Old Times on Upper Cook's Inlet,' 1967

In his 1919 book, *Adventures in Alaska*, Samuel Hall Young, a Presbyterian clergyman who had accompanied John Muir when he discovered Glacier Bay, wrote about a trip by dog team from Iditarod to Seward, and he briefly mentioned staying at a roadhouse in Knik: "Four hundred miles from our starting point we put up at the 'Pioneer Roadhouse' in the little town of Knik at the head of Cook's Inlet. This was one of half a dozen small towns around Knik Arm and Turn-Again Arm, two prongs of Cook's Inlet. These towns had been in existence for fifteen or twenty years, with gold miners and their families living there…"

The history of gold in the Iditarod District is well-represented by newspaper articles of the day. The following news items relate the rich - and often grim - history of gold discovered along the Iditarod Trail.

Alaskan Sled Dog Tales

The Daily Missoulian
Missoula, Montana. September 29, 1909
Iditarod Stampede to Rival Dawson Rush

Fairbanks, Alaska, Sept. 28. – The stampede to the Iditarod country promises to rival the rush to Dawson in the days of the Klondike boom. The steamer Reliance, which arrived today from Innoko, fully confirms the report of rich placers on Otter creek, a tributary of the Iditarod, to which 1,000 miners have gone from Fairbanks during the summer. Fifteen hundred men are camped on the creek.

Pay is outlines one mile in length and 600 feet wide, 3 cents to $1.25 to the pan at a depth of three to five feet. There is gold in every hole sunk and bedrock is reached at 14 to 17 feet. Prices of supplies and food in the new camp are very high owing to the approach of winter.

The Salt Lake Herald-Republican
Salt lake City, Utah. November 8, 1909
Reported Strikes in the Iditarod Cause Many to Start for the Field

Seattle, Wash., Nov. 7. – According to S. H. Ewing, a prominent business man of Nome, who arrived on the steamer Senator today, a general exodus of miners is expected from the Seward peninsula to the new gold field on the Iditarod as soon as cold weather sets in. Navigation on the rivers has already closed, and hundreds of men who are anxious to go to the new diggings are waiting for a heavy fall of snow, so that trails may be broken and the long journey can be made overland.

The reports received at Nome and other Seward peninsula towns concerning the Iditarod strike have caused great excitement among the miners, and the stampede promises to eclipse the famous rush to the Klondike. The fever has spread to Fairbanks and the Tanana district, where many prospectors are pulling up their stakes and heading toward the Iditarod county.

Alaskan Sled Dog Tales

Iditarod, Alaska, 1911. Lomen Bros. photo.

Turtle Mountain Star
Rolla, North Dakota, March 3, 1910

Predictions of Great Activity in the Iditarod Placers

Seattle, Wash., Mar. 1. – To the Iditarod placer diggings men are now toiling over the snow trails in a wild chase for a share of the undoubted riches first found there last season. The placer fields of the Iditarod and Innoko rivers which are said to be larger even in extent than the Klondike fields, are sure to yield many large fortunes. If the field proves as rich as the present showing would indicate the district will have a population of 10,000 within a twelvemonth. Already there are 2,000 men where a year ago there were hardly a dozen. The excitement resulting will be great, and the romantic story of the Klondike and Nome will be repeated. But it would be most exceptional if ten years from now should see any important placer mining going on in that now almost unprospected region. It will simply be worked out.

Alaskan Sled Dog Tales

The Seattle Star, Seattle, Wash., January 28, 1910
3,000 Winter in the Iditarod

Dawson, Nov. 28. – It is estimated 3,000 people are wintering in the Iditarod country. Harold Malstrom, who has just arrived from there, claims very few people left the diggings this fall. Pay has been found in the Kuskokwim district, across the divide, and a general rush from Iditarod is expected, according to Malstrom. He states that the biggest cleanup in the Iditarod country was made by Frank Manley, who has realized in the neighborhood of $3,000,000 in the Marietta claim.

The Salt Lake Tribune, Salt Lake City, Utah, March 10, 1911
Body of Prospector Found Frozen on Trail
Death Comes to John Olson While Sitting on Sled in Wilds of Alaska.

Seattle, Wash., March 9 – Members of the Alaska road commission party which surveyed the proposed road between Nome and Seward arrived in Seattle today and reported finding the body of John Olson, a prospector, on the trail near Distaket [Dishkaket], sixty miles from Iditarod, late in January. The body, frozen stiff, was in a sitting attitude on a sled.

The proposed Nome-Seward wagon road, for which congress has appropriated $50,000, is to pass through the Kuskokwim and Iditarod diggings. The surveyors, eight men with a caravan of forty-two dogs, left Nome November 15 and reached Seward February 25. They lived in the open, the temperature sometimes reaching 60 degrees below zero.

Alaskan Sled Dog Tales

The road will be 513 miles long and the route is perfectly feasible. Hundreds of men are prospecting along the tributaries of the Kuskokwim and some have made good strikes. In the Iditarod there is a scarcity of food, which the Esquimaux mitigated by driving in 150 reindeer to be slaughtered. The supply of whiskey, beer and cigars is ample.

The Ogden Standard, Ogden, Utah, February 28, 1918
Gold Shipment from Iditarod

San Francisco, Feb. 27. – Details of the shipment of $500,000 in gold bullion, weighing 2500 pounds, through tremendous snow barriers from Iditarod, Alaska, to Seattle, a distance of 1045 miles, have been made known by the Alaska Commercial Company offices here. The shipment was started December 5, 1917, from the Riley placer holdings in the Iditarod district. Dog teams took it to Tanana, and regular horse-drawn stages to Fairbanks and Chitna [Chitina]. It was then loaded on the Copper River railroad for the seacoast, 131 miles distant.

At Parson's and Yost's stations between Iditarod and Tanana, there was one snowfall of thirty-six inches in twenty-four hours. Because of this it took the dogs twenty - four hours to make twelve miles one day and fifteen hours to make sixteen miles the next. During the battle with this storm, R. D. Menzie, who had charge of the shipment, dislocated his shoulder while aiding in shifting the load. He was forced to ride three and a half hours before he could obtain relief.

While it was being taken on the horse drawn stages the bullion had to be cached in the snow and left alone several times while the drivers went to distant road houses for fresh horses. The shipment reached Seattle February 2, 1918.

The stage between Chitna [Chitina] and Fairbanks, a distance of 310 miles, is drawn by four horses. A single horse stage line operates between Fairbanks and Tanana, a distance of 161 miles.   ~•~

Alaskan Sled Dog Tales

"Slim" Williams, International Trail Blazer, and his leader "Rembrandt."

Alaskan Sled Dog Tales

SLIM WILLIAMS
Alaska Highway Trailblazer

". . . he had blue eyes that looked miles away . . ."
~First Lady Eleanor Roosevelt

Clyde "Slim" Williams arrived in Alaska in 1900 at the age of 18 and spent the next thirty years trapping, hunting, and blazing trails throughout the frontier. In the early 1930's Williams became a strong proponent of the plan for a highway linking Alaska to the lower 48 states, and he boasted that he could drive his dog team along the proposed route and continue all the way to Chicago, Illinois, where the 1933 Century of Progress Exposition was planned as part of the World's Fair, celebrating man's innovations in architecture, science, technology and transportation. The Alaska Road Commissioner, Donald MacDonald, persuaded Williams that such a trip could be used to promote the building of an Alaska highway, and so in 1933 Slim traveled down the proposed route by dogsled, using only crude maps in what was previously unmapped territory.

An article for the *Uniontown News Standard* reported on December 11, 1933, "He started from Copper Center, November 20, 1932, without stove, tent or compass and with only the stars, the trees and the sun to guide

Alaskan Sled Dog Tales

him. His route carried him through Dawson City, White Horse, Atlin and Telegraph Creek and after covering 1800 miles through the wildest sections of Alaska and British Columbia he reached civilization at Hazelton, B.C. On sections of this trip he traveled as far as 500 miles without seeing one human being. Cooking over an open fire and sleeping in his sled were part of the journey which was tinged with tragedy when the wolves along Forty Mile river killed one of his favorite dogs."

It took Williams five months to reach the end of the then-existing highway system near Hazelton, British Columbia. When spring thawing made sledding impossible, he mounted four Model T Ford wheels on his dogsled in Smithers, B.C. and continued toward the Chicago World's Fair. By the time he reached Seattle, Williams and his wolf-dog team had become celebrities. Articles about his overland trek appeared in *Time* magazine, *The Washington Post, The Christian Science Monitor* and many others.

In Chicago, Williams and his dogteam made a popular Alaskan exhibit at the Century of Progress Exposition. A *Time* magazine article (October 2, 1933) reported that when former President Herbert Hoover visited the fair he chatted with Williams, and First Lady Eleanor Roosevelt described her meeting with Slim Williams as the most enjoyable part of her visit. A lecture brochure noted: "upon returning to Washington she told newsmen that what she liked best was a tall young man with blue eyes that looked miles away, who had driven his dog team all the way from Alaska."

After the World's Fair closed for the season, Slim and his team of half-bred wolf/dogs proceeded to Washington, D.C., bringing the total distance of his journey by dogteam to over 5,600 miles. He camped in a city park and spent the winter discussing Alaskan concerns with legislators, and even met with President Franklin Roosevelt to further promote the highway. Williams enjoyed a dinner with the President and

Alaskan Sled Dog Tales

While his trip was sponsored by The International Highway Association of Alaska and the Yukon Territory, Williams still sold postcards like this along his route. [Slim Williams Papers, UAF-207-59-17 University of Alaska Fairbanks]

the First Lady, still advocating for the proposed road. The President finally did set up a commission with Canada to explore building a highway to Alaska, but while the project was considered feasible it was deemed too costly and unnecessary at that time.

Later in life, Slim traveled around the country with his wife doing presentations and slideshows, and he enjoyed success as a popular lecturer, as described in the text of a lecture brochure: "The Adventurers Club of Chicago, where all famous explorers speak, say his talk is one of the most fascinating and thrilling they've had in years."

In 1956 an authorized biography of Slim Williams' adventures was published by Richard Morenus: *Alaska Sourdough: The Story of Slim Williams*. The book detailed Slim's 1933 solo dogsled adventure, and also his 1939 trip from Fairbanks to Seattle by motorcycle with 25-year-old John Logan. Their goal was the New York World's Fair, and just as with

Alaskan Sled Dog Tales

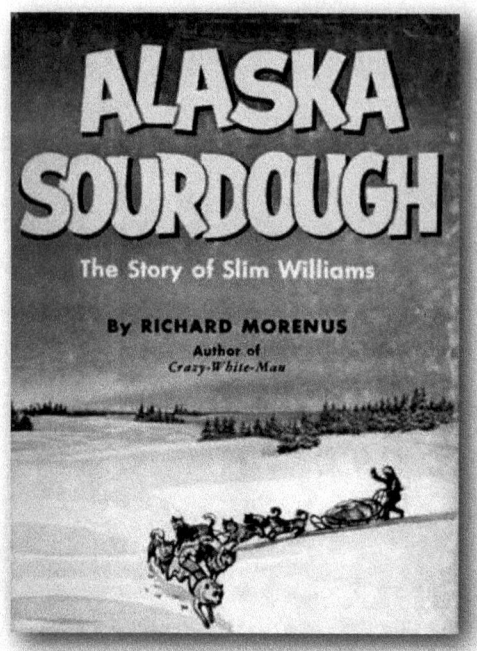

Above: 1956 book by Richard Morenus. Below: Coming into Tanana Crossing on 1933 trip to Chicago and Washington DC

Slim's 1933 trip, the purpose was to gain publicity for the need to build a road connecting Alaska to the rest of the United States. At that time, there still wasn't even a crude trail to follow for over 1,000 miles of the journey, so the adventurers crossed the wide rivers and daunting mountains in whatever manner they could, and their much-publicized journey once again spotlighted Alaska's need for a road to the 48 states.

In early 1942, when World War II made an overland route necessary, President Roosevelt signed the authorization, and on November 20, 1942, at Soldier's Summit near Kluane Lake, a ceremony marked completion of the first phase of construction. Today the road is a major artery to the north, and the Alaska Highway project is still heralded as one of the greatest engineering feats of the twentieth century. ~•~

Alaskan Sled Dog Tales

Above: Leaving a Roadhouse just out of Dawson City on the way to U.S.
Below: *Slim with his team at the Chicago Century of Progress Exposition, 1933*
[All photos: Slim Williams Papers UAF-2007-59 University of Alaska Fairbanks]

Alaskan Sled Dog Tales

DISTANCES EQUAL TO NOME-CANDLE CREEK RACE.

(Air Line.)
Cleveland to Evansville, Ind.
Cincinnati to Memphis, Tenn.
Denver to Ogden, Utah.
Dallas, Tex., to Jackson, Miss.
San Francisco to Los Angeles
Des Moines, Ia., to Chicago.
Tacoma to Boise, Idaho.

CHAPTER I.

Poke fun at John Johnson, crack "musher" of Alaska, and he will grin good naturedly; jibe at his dogs and his fighting blood is up.

Twice winner of the great $10,000 Nome-Candle Creek dog race, with an unbeaten record of 74 hours and 14 minutes over the 408-mile course, Johnson is known as "The Iron Man" for his amazing grit and endurance.

How he won the desperate race of 1910 with a "scrub" team, under the goad of derision, and became the hero of Alaska, Johnson here tells for the first time.

"The men who were betting their thousands looked us over—me and the dogs," began Johnson, "and they laughed! It was then I made up my mind to win or to run myself and the team to death."

Johnson is 40 years old, was born in Finland, sailed before the mast, prospected and faced death in Siberia, and went to Nome in the gold rush of 1900. In his face is the austerity of the north, in his speech the halt of men who have lived long in Arctic silences.

His love of dogs is like a religion.

"There were 14 dogs in the team I was driving for Colonel Fox Ramsey, an Englishman," Johnson resumed. "Most of them were his, but some belonged to me—shaggy little fellows who had gone over thousands of miles of perilous trail with me—especially Kolma, my blue-eyed leader.

"Ahead, to the northeast, stretched the bleak snows, over which we would race. Candle Creek was 264 miles away—the half-way point. It was Thursday, April 7th, and a clear day. A little too warm, though, meaning hard work breaking trail. This would be tough on me, for I was to start first, the others to follow at 10-minute intervals. I would have to pound snow for them.

"Around us 6,000 people were packed, watching. They jingled their gold. But little was bet on my 'scrubs.'

"Beside me stood 'Scotty' Allen, a great racer who had already won one sweepstake and come second in the other. He is a favorite in Nome—the 'King of the Arctic Trail.' As we waited for the start, 'Scotty' looked at me—squinting.

"'I'm going to run the heart out of you!' he said.

"And then my dogs leaped, at the signal, running low and whining with excitement."

(To Be Continued Tomorrow.)

The Tacoma Times, Tacoma, Washington, ran a series of articles about John "Iron Man" Johnson's All Alaska Sweepstakes races in the February, 1915 sports section.

Alaskan Sled Dog Tales

John "Iron Man" Johnson
1910 All Alaska Sweepstakes Champion
*"'Iron Man' of Arctic and Savage Huskies Leave Wilds to
See Land of Soft Delights" ~1915 newspaper headline*

San Francisco, Cal., Jan. 9, 1915–John Johnson, "The Iron Man of Alaska," and his pack of $30,000 Siberian wolf dogs, winners of the All Alaska Sweepstakes race, have come down here to loaf a little while in the land of soft delights. With Johnson is Bill Brady, another celebrity of the "land that God forgot," and his string of huskies, valued at $20,000.

John and Bill and their shaggy canine friends were a little shy and awkward when they tromped down the gangplank at the wharf here. Asphalt streets and skyscrapers were strange to feet and eyes accustomed to snows and the long, hard trails.

Lean and hard they were, both men and dogs, their bodies stripped to the fighting weight of bare muscle and sinew the Northland demands of its creatures. An extra pound of flesh may weigh like a ton in the strenuous sport. Johnson does not sleep. Only a few mouthfuls of food pass his lips, and scarcely any water. The dogs run the grueling race under the same conditions. In 1910 when he won his first Sweepstakes, John Johnson did not once stop to rest. This year he allowed himself a few minutes in breathing spells, finding that the short pauses benefitted him and his dogs. The man who can do that is quite naturally the idol of his fellows on the other side of '53.

Alaskan Sled Dog Tales

The dogs, too, come in for their share of worship–Those who live to drag themselves to the winning post. The drivers in the All-Alaska race, inaugurated by the Nome Kennel Club in 1908, may go as they please. The only condition is that they bring in every dog, dead or alive, with which they started. In one of his races Johnson finished in spectacular fashion with three exhausted dogs and one dead on his sled.

His record for the 408-mile course never beaten is 74 hours and 14 minutes, which is remarkable time when the rough country over which the trail leads is considered. On the way Johnson feeds his wolf hounds biscuits made of graham flour, eggs, cream and sugar, only small portions being doled out to sustain their fires of endurance.

"You can't get over the country on a full stomach," explained the greatest of northern dog mushers.

While in San Francisco, where Johnson and Brady expect to stage Alaskan dog-racing scenes at the 1915 exposition, the $50,000 beauties will be fed on a fish diet until they get accustomed to the rations of bread, milk, and biscuit it is intended to substitute after a time.

This is Johnson's first visit to San Francisco in 10 years. Formerly he often made this port as a sailor, having graduated from the foc'scle to champion dog driver a decade ago.

John "Iron Man" Johnson was a musher of great renown in early Alaska, having won the 1910 All Alaska Sweepstakes race and setting a record which would not be broken until the Centennial running in 2008, at a time when dogs were better bred, better fed, and better cared for on the trail.

When John "Iron Man" Johnson set the All Alaska Sweepstakes race record which would stand for more than 75 years, it was his peerless leader Kolyma who set the pace. In 1910, a Scottish nobleman named Fox Maule Ramsey went to Siberia to buy 70 Siberian huskies, and in that

Alaskan Sled Dog Tales

Above: Lead-in to The Tacoma Time's February, 1915 series of articles.
Below: In 1915 newspapers across the country excitedly touted "John Johnson 'The Iron Man of Alaska' and his pack of $30,000 Siberian wolf dogs."

Alaskan Sled Dog Tales

Above: With leaders Kolyma and Jodi.
Below: Johnson's famous leader Kolyma.

year's Sweepstakes race his dogs won 1st, 2nd and 4th place, with the first place team being Iron Man Johnson and his lead dog Kolyma.

At one point in the race, crossing the aptly-named "Death Valley," Johnson became snow-blind, strapped himself to his dogsled, and relied on Kolyma to keep the team on the trail. Upon winning the race Johnson was given a traditional victory wreath, but he took it off and placed the wreath on Kolyma, saying, "I did not win the race, this leader won it!"

Lake Tahoe's Winter Carnivals were much-anticipated and popular events in the early 1900's, and while dog sledding and racing began during winter carnivals in the late 1890's, the first and official sled dog race in the continental U.S. was reportedly held in Truckee, California, in 1915. Bert Cassidy, editor of the *Truckee Republican* (*Sierra Sun*), described the event: "Crowds of people had been arriving in Truckee on each train... all hotel accommodations had long since been taken... movie

Alaskan Sled Dog Tales

John "Iron Man" Johnson on his sled, with his friend, the famed novelist Jack London at center left, at a sled dog race held in Truckee, California in 1915.

cameramen were legion... all the bigger papers had sent sports editors."

After arriving in Seattle with his dog team during the latter part of 1914, John Johnson traveled to San Francisco to enter some races and display his dogs at various shows. He and his team entered the race in Truckee, and were billed as an All Alaska Sweepstakes champion team of "Siberian Wolf Dogs" competing against a team of "Huskies" driven by Ed Parker, and a team of Malamutes driven by Bill Brady.

Johnson was photographed with the famed novelist Jack London, a spectator at the event who would return to the area twenty years later for the filming of the movie version of his book, *The Call of the Wild*. While at Truckee, Johnson and his dogteam would be featured in a movie titled "*The Deathlock*," a silent film by the Mutual Film Corp. starring Fred J. Butler, Wilma Wilkie, and David W. Butler in a story of Alaskan prospecting, gambling, claim jumping, and of course, romance. ~•~

Alaskan Sled Dog Tales

Allan Alexander "Scotty" Allan with Baldy of Nome

Alaskan Sled Dog Tales

BALDY OF NOME
Scotty Allan's Legendary Lead Dog

"Scotty's famous leader"
~The Great Dog Races of Nome

In Esther Birdsall Darling's classic book, *Baldy of Nome*, a story is told of a driverless dog team in the 60-mile-long Solomon Derby, a race between Nome and Solomon along the coast of the Bering Sea. The young leader of the team, realizing his driver is missing, turns the team around and returns along the trail, searching...

"Far away in the whiteness, Baldy saw a black spot toward which he sped with mad impatience. It grew more and more distinct, till, beside it, he saw that it was his master, lying pale, motionless and blood-stained in the trail. From a deep gash on his head a crimson stream oozed and froze, matting his hair and the fur on his parka. Baldy stopped short, quivering with an unknown dread. There was something terrifying in the tense body, so still, so mute. He licked the pallid face, the cold hands, and placed a gentle paw upon the man's breast, scratching softly to see if he could not gain some response. There was no answer to his loving appeal; and throwing back his head, there broke from him the weird, wild wail of the Malamute, his inheritance from some wolf ancestor. The other dogs

Alaskan Sled Dog Tales

joined the mournful chorus, and then, as it died away, he tried again and again to rouse his silent master. Moment after moment passed, the time seemed endless; but finally the warm tongue and the insistent paw did their work; for there was a slight movement, a flicker of the eyelids, and then Scotty lifted himself upon his elbow and spoke to them."

The incident is based on an actual event, when Scotty, leaning over his sled to look at a broken runner, hit his head on an iron trail marker and was knocked unconscious. Scotty Allan's team, with Baldy in the lead, went on to win the race, and Baldy's rescue made him a hero. The story is even more remarkable because Scotty Allan's regular lead dog, named Kid, had passed away only the evening before the race, and Baldy, who had never led in a race before, had been selected to take his place.

Allan Alexander Allan had been known as Scotty since he was a lad in his native land, where he won the Scottish Grand National Sheep Dog Trials with a remarkable border collie named Dandy. Allan was also a horse trainer, which led him to be chosen to accompany a Clydesdale stallion to his new owners in the United States in 1887.

A few years later, attracted by news of the Klondike gold strike, Allan set out for the northern goldfields and found work moving supplies over the dangerous trails to the mining camps, earning a reputation in the Dawson area as a top notch dog driver. His first leader was a Mackenzie River Husky named Dubby, who came from the stock of the Hudson's Bay Company.

When gold was discovered on the beaches of Nome, Scotty, like many others, traveled down the frozen Yukon River some 1,200 miles to the newest goldfields. Scotty Allan didn't strike it rich in Nome, so he focused on his specialty, training dogs. He took in dogs others didn't want and trained them to race, saying, "Dogs are the most intuitive creatures alive. They take the disposition of their driver. That is why I never let my dogs know that I am tired. At the end of the day…, I sing to

Alaskan Sled Dog Tales

the little chaps and whistle so they always reach the end of the trail with their tails up and waving."

In 1907, the dog drivers in Nome banded together to form the Nome Kennel Club to improve the care and breeding of sled dogs. Around this same time Scotty reputedly purchased a sled dog named Baldy from a young boy who could no longer afford to care for him. As Scotty wrote in his autobiography, *Gold, Men and Dogs*, he was one of the founders of the All-Alaska Sweepstakes, the first organized sled dog race, which ran from Nome to Candle, a distance of 408 miles, from the shore of the Bering Sea to the shore of the Arctic Ocean

The first All Alaska Sweepstakes race took five days to finish and was won by John Hegness. The next year Scotty Allan and Baldy took first place, repeating the win again in 1911 and 1912, and they placed in the top three a total of eight times. In five other races, they finished either second or third, and they became famous beyond Alaska, all across the

Alaskan Sled Dog Tales

Scotty Allan's team won the fifth running of the All Alaska Sweepstakes, 1912. Baldy is one of the two dogs right behind the leaders, in the swing position.

United States. Their race entries were followed and reported in national newspapers such as *The New York Times*.

As Allan and Baldy gained fame, Allan partnered with his sponsor, Esther Birdsall Darling, to form the Allan and Darling Kennel, which became one of the best-known racing kennels in Alaska. Allan's dogs were so well known that when the United States entered World War I, the government commissioned dogs from the Allan and Darling Kennel to haul supplies for the French military. Twenty-eight of Baldy's sons and grandsons were chosen, bringing the total dogs from Nome to over 100. When they were ready to leave Nome, the whole group of dogs were put on a single 350 ft. gangline, and Scotty Allan's lead dog Spot led the 106-dog team through the streets of town to board the waiting ship.

Scotty Allan would go on to be elected to the Alaska Territorial Legislature in 1917 and 1919, and Admiral Richard Byrd sought out

Alaskan Sled Dog Tales

Scotty to train the dogs for Byrd's 1928 Antarctica Expedition. Scotty and his family moved to California prior to the 1925 Diphtheria Epidemic in Nome, which resulted in the famous Serum Run. They took the venerable old leader Baldy with them, and the famous sled dog lived out the remainder of his days in the warm California sunshine.

On April, 15th, 1922 *The New York Times* reported Baldy's death to their readers: "Berkeley, Cal., April 14.-- Baldy of Nome, famed for the races he won in Alaska, his heroic deeds that have been twenty-eight Malamute sons and grand-put in prose and verse, and for the sons he gave to France for the World War, was buried here today. He died in a dog hospital of old age and his final resting place is under the rose-bushes in the garden of 'Scotty' Allan, whose life he once saved. Baldy was 15 years old. He was two years old when Allan 'mushed' him through the first of his seven races for the All-Alaska Sweepstakes of 418 miles. With Baldy as the leader, Allan was brought in winner six times."

"Baldy of Nome"
"Scotty" Allen's famous Leader.
Winner of $25,000 in Sweepstake prizes.
© Winter & Pond Co.
Juneau, Alaska.

Alaskan Sled Dog Tales

Alaskan Sled Dog Tales

KING OF THE ARCTIC TRAIL
Allan Alexander "Scotty" Allan

"King of the Arctic Trail"
~The Great Dog Races of Nome

From the *Wenatchee World*, Wenatchee, Washington, June 29, 1909:

"SCOTTY" ALLAN, DOG TRAINER

Winner of All-Alaskan Sweepstakes an old-time resident of Chelan County and well known here

The *Seattle Post-Intelligencer* of Monday night contained an interesting story regarding "Scotty" Allan, who won the All-Alaskan Sweepstakes dog team race. The story in itself is an interesting one, but is especially so for the fact that "Scotty" lived in this country for several years, making his home in Leavenworth and is very well known in this city. Allan was practically raised by P.D. Sutor, of Burch Flat. The following is the P-I story:

Greatest of all dog drivers in the world, winner of the classic All-Alaskan Sweepstakes dog race at Nome last April, A.A. Allan, "Scotty" Allan, as he is known to friends and all Alaskans, came down from Nome on the St. Croix to spend a well-earned vacation at the exposition. A wiry little Scotchman, standing five feet four and one-half inches is this

Alaskan Sled Dog Tales

Scotty Allan was among the headlines in Wenatchee, Washington, June 29, 1909.

"Scotty." At 42 he is as spry as a high school boy, and every pound of the 150, which makes his weight, is filled with an energy which makes the whole a tireless machine.

It was a pleasant greeting that occurred between "Scotty" Allan and Jake Berger, the owner of the team which the former drove over a blizzard-driven trail of 408 miles, last April, to victory, when the St. Croix pulled into her dock. With $8,000 in gold, a cup valued at $2,500, and with the second prize of $2,500 to his credit, which he won with the Berger No. 2, Mr. Berger has been anxiously awaiting full details of the race, having been in Montreal when it was run. When "Scotty" came down the gang plank the dog race was begun and run all over again, and the two men went over every foot of the way until Mr. Berger knew the whole affair as if he had been there in person.

Little Profit for Victor

By the time the two men reached the Butler Annex, where they are registered, Jake Berger found that while his two teams had won and he

Alaskan Sled Dog Tales

was $10,000 to the good, much of the money had been expended in purchasing and training dogs during the long winter and that he was just about even with the game. It mattered not, however, for he has a comfortable fortune, a paystreak which has not had the ends tapped as yet, and above all he is a true sportsman.

Ever since his boyhood days in Scotland, Allan says, he has been fond of horses and dogs. He made companions when a lad, and when he came to North Dakota with blooded horses in 1887, he liked the wild free life of the men and animals. He says he loved the range horses just for their wildness. Then he came to Seattle in later years with the Great Northern railway, for all his life he has followed work with a pen, while his pastimes have been with animals. Then came the stampede in 1897 to the Klondike and "Scotty" Allan was the first to go. It was his first sight of dogs working in harness, and from the moment he first looked at them until the present day "Scotty" Allan has always had a string of dogs. Although he is president of the school board at Nome, secretary of the Darling & Dean Hardware company, and an official of several other companies and societies, he will always leave his business cares to enter a racing competition.

"Scotty" Trains the Dogs

When Mr. Berger came out last fall he entrusted his dogs, a score in number, to "Scotty," leaving a good sized bank account to see that they were properly trained. During the winter the latter tried all the dogs and with the purchase of a few selected animals entered Berger's two teams. He also did something which was the surprise of everyone in Nome. All winter he kept using a big heavy basket sled in training his team. He was laughed at, but told all that he wanted a sled that would stand any kind of usage. About a half hour before the race he brought out a sled that has never had an equal in the north. Although twelve feet long it weighed but

Alaskan Sled Dog Tales

31 pounds, and a feature of its construction was the use of every D violin string that could be purchased in Nome, which were used for lashing the joints. This spring there was a lack of music owing to this. His dog harness weighed nine ounces per dog, and his whole outfit of muklucks for himself and dogs, blankets for the animals and tugs and other equipment totaled, sleigh included, weighed only 42 pounds.

There were 14 entries in the race. The pick of human racing machinery was selected for the test of endurance, skill in the handling of dogs, and and judgement in the methods of travel. The best dogs of eastern Siberia and Alaska faced the starter's stand on the ice of the Bering Sea on April 1.

Allan, with Berger's team, made the 408 miles through a blizzard in 82 hours and 2 minutes, and Blatchford in 82 hours and 18 minutes. The Siberian team, third in the race, made the run in 89 hours.

Mr. Allan says that after years' experience with dogs he decided that a cross between a setter and the native Alaskan dog proves the best traveler. Each animal for racing purposes should weigh between 70 and 90 pounds.

Mr. Allan has made 17 trips from the interior of Alaska to the coast ports, covering every one that leads to a ship connection and over some of which, in the early days, he had to break trail.

So much does Allan love his dogs that they also have the kindest love for him and it is told that during the race not one of his dogs would lie down until it saw their master retire to his room. Dubby, a dog he has had for ten years and perhaps the best known animal on Seward peninsula, is the constant companion of Allan at all times and although too old to race followed Allan's team out several miles on the road and when distanced cried and howled for an hour before returning to Nome.

Allan says $4,000 has already been subscribed for next year's race.

Alaskan Sled Dog Tales

Alaskan Sled Dog Tales

Excerpts from an article by Florance Willoughby, titled 'Interesting Westerners: The King of the Arctic Trail,' which appeared in *Sunset Magazine*, volume 46, February, 1921:

In the golden days of Nome, a city icebound from November until June, there were no cross-country trails or roadhouses. Even among the most fearless adventurers it was difficult to find one brave enough to carry the mail across fifteen hundred miles of trackless empire to Valdez, where steamers from the States called. With nothing but a map–often inaccurate–and a compass to guide him, Scotty Allan was the first to set out with his huskies on the long, dangerous journey. Man and dogs battled for every mile of the way that slipped behind their shining runners. Three dollars and more for each letter carried was paid in those days, but money had no purchasing power on a trip where for hundreds of miles there was not a stick of wood to make a fire and not a habitation in which to seek shelter.

But the return to Nome! There must have been some compensation in the welcome. To those awaiting news of their loved ones in the States there was no sight in all that land of beauty and majesty that could thrill them as did the first glimpse of Scotty, frost-covered but undaunted and debonair, at the handle-bars of his sled, dashing down that last stretch of the silver trail, every decorative tail on his parka dancing, every sleigh-bell ringing, every pointed-nosed, pink-tongued huskie in his team laughing and waving a proud plume of a tail! To the cheering Northerners mail-day was an epoch and Scotty a hero.

Alaskan Sled Dog Tales

In the northern road-houses 'o winter nights, when the adventurers gather about the roaring air-tight stove while their shoe-pacs and parkas dry out for the next day's travel, the talk will sooner or later drift round to Scotty and Baldy, and many and wonderful are the tales they tell of this heroic pair. Baldy was too old to go to the war zone with his master but in the service flag presented to the old dog there are twenty-eight stars, one for every son he sent. Baldy did his part by appearing at lectures and raising money for the Red Cross. On state occasions he wears the cross presented to his sons by France.

~ ~ ~

A seat in the Alaska Legislature, a successful business and some inventions pertaining to sleds and arctic travel are minor incidents in Allan's picturesque career. He has a home now in Berkeley, California, where his daughters and a stalwart son are attending the University. With the whole-hearted hospitality of the trail he entertains hosts of friends from the North. So many little Indian, Eskimo and half-breed namesakes are scattered throughout Alaska that after the last census the number caused him some embarrassment.

"I suppose I ought to settle down—men do at my age," he said, in answer to a question. A wistful look came into his poet's face, clean-cut and young-looking under a heavy thatch of hair as white as the snow on his own loved mountains. "But there's nothing to fight down here. I long for a blizzard once in a while. If only a heavy sea would storm in here and tear up the beach a bit!"

He shrugged his powerful muscled shoulders, the only mark about him of the fighter, and his blue eyes, full of dreams, fell affectionately on Old Baldy lying at his feet, dim eyes raised ever and anon to his master's face, a deaf old ear lifted to catch, perhaps, the call to the Trail. One thought of caged eagles. ~•~

Alaskan Sled Dog Tales

Arthur Walden with his favorite dog, Chinook, around 1922.

Alaskan Sled Dog Tales

A DOG-PUNCHER ON THE YUKON
Arthur Treadwell Walden

"Let me tell you about this man Walden. He reached the country of the Yukon in the early part of '96, when Circle City was the center and the Birch Creek mines the magnet. Always an understanding companion of dogs, he was soon hauling freight across the white wilderness with dog-team.

"This was the Alaska before the days of the Klondike, the frontier of the miners' meetings and the sourdough, the land of justice and order without laws or statutes, the period of the gambling hall that was strict and square. Walden saw and took part in it all." -author and anthropologist Walter Collins O'Kane, from the Introduction to *A Dog-Puncher on the Yukon*

Arthur Treadwell Walden was a pioneering dog driver, a Klondike Gold Rush adventurer, developer of the Chinook sled dog breed, founder of the New England Sled Dog Club, and a major participant in the first Byrd Antarctic Expedition. He wrote a book about his adventures in Alaska and the Klondike, titled *A Dog-Puncher on the Yukon*, along with the instructive *Harness and Pack*, and *Leading a Dog's Life*.

Born in Indianapolis, Indiana, on May 10, 1871, he was the son of the Rev. Treadwell Walden, an Episcopal clergyman, and Elizabeth Leighton Walden. He was educated at Chattuck Military School in Faribault,

Alaskan Sled Dog Tales

Minnesota, and in 1890 he went to Boston, Massachusetts, where he visited the kin of his father's second wife, a well-to-do newspaper family named Sleeper. Through this connection Arthur Walden met Katherine Sleeper, and was hired as manager of her 1,300-acre Wonalancet Farm in New Hampshire.

In 1896, at the age of 24 and driven by a keen sense of adventure, Walden left Wonalancet and headed to the gold fields of Alaska. He worked at several jobs, including prospector, logger, stevedore, river pilot, and finally, hauling freight by dogsled, known in the Circle City area as 'dog-punching.' In his best-known book, *A Dog-Puncher on the Yukon*, Walden described the sleds and loads which were typical of the day: "The ordinary freight outfit consisted of three full-sized sleds, one behind the other, drawn up close and connected by cross-chains, making each sled follow in exactly the same track as the sled ahead of it. The sleds had to be so strongly made and heavily braced with iron that each weighed from sixty to eighty pounds, the front one being the heaviest. They were loaded for an average team with six hundred, four hundred, and two hundred pounds apiece, thus making a total of twelve hundred pounds, or about two hundred pounds per dog."

Arthur Walden saw the new century in carrying freight, supplies and mail on the Yukon River, and he was the first to bring news of the Klondike gold strike to Circle City, Alaska. He spent seven years freighting with dog teams, returning to Wonalancet and marrying Kate Sleeper in December of 1902. Having seen what sled dogs were capable of, Walden wanted to continue mushing, but in New England, horses and oxen were the draft animals of choice; quality sled dogs were not available. So Walden began a breeding program at Wonalancet, striving for dogs that possessed his ideal combination of strength, speed, endurance, and good nature.

While in the Yukon Walden had worked with a dog named Chinook, whose qualities he admired and wanted to develop in his line of sled

Alaskan Sled Dog Tales

A Chinook sled dog.

dogs. In January 1917 his efforts produced a trio of pups he named Rikki, Tikki and Tavi, after the brave mongoose in Rudyard Kipling's classic, *Jungle Book*. As he grew, Rikki exhibited the traits that Walden had been seeking, and he renamed the dog Chinook, honoring the dog that had so impressed him in the Yukon. A descendent of Admiral Peary's famous husky, Polaris, Chinook became the foundation stud of Chinook Kennels, and Walden's constant companion.

Walden was a born promoter, and soon his Chinook sled dogs were gaining renown far and wide. In 1922 he persuaded a local paper company to sponsor the first Eastern International Dog Derby of 123 miles, bringing the sport of dogsled racing to New England. Two years later he spearheaded the founding of the New England Sled Dog Club, serving as its first president. In 1927 at Poland Spring, Maine, Walden's

Arthur Walden (left) and Admiral Richard E. Byrd

team went up against Leonhard Seppala, hero of the Nome Serum Run, but he lost the race to Seppala's team despite a series of misadventures experienced on the trail by the All Alaska Sweepstakes champion and his dogs.

Around that same time, Walden heard of Rear Admiral Richard E. Byrd's plans for a major Antarctic expedition, and after meeting with Byrd, Walden was appointed the lead trainer and driver of dog teams for the expedition. During the winter of late 1927 and early 1928, the dogs and drivers gathered at Walden's Wonalancet Farm to begin training. Winter survival gear was tested in the harsh conditions of New Hampshire's White Mountains, and in September, 1928 the teams went to Antarctica.

The expedition landed on Christmas Day and for the next three months Walden and nine other drivers freighted 650 tons of gear from the ships to the base camp at Little America. Byrd wrote in his book, *Little*

Alaskan Sled Dog Tales

America: "Had it not been for the dogs, our attempts to conquer the Antarctic must have ended in failure. On January 17th, Walden's single team of thirteen dogs moved 3,500 pounds of supplies from ship to base, a distance of 16 miles each trip, in two journeys. Walden's team was the backbone of our transport. Seeing him rush his heavy loads along the trail, outstripping the younger men, it was difficult to believe that he was an old man. He was 58 years old, but he had the determination and strength of youth."

Unfortunately, midway through the expedition, on his 12th birthday, January 17, 1929, Chinook inexplicably disappeared. Walden had wanted to bury his great friend in his harness, but Chinook's body was never found. On January 24, 1929 the *Union-Leader* newspaper in Manchester, New Hampshire featured a story with the title, "Chinook, World Famed Dog, Reported Dead on Antarctic Ice Fields." The article went on, "Chinook, Walden's famous veteran of many sled dog races is now believed dead on the ice in the Antarctic. The Wonalancet dog, according to reports, wandered off across the ice fields and is believed to have succumbed to the rigorous climate. . . Throughout New Hampshire and Canada and even to several European countries where his fame as a sled dog leader spread, Chinook's death will come as a blow to dog lovers, especially in the North country where he was considered as a pet and more often treated as a human being than as a canine."

Upon returning to Wonalancet in 1930, Arthur Walden learned a highway was being developed on the old trail which Chinook had travelled with his team countless times over the years. Walden requested the road be named the Chinook Trail, the name it bears to this day.

Arthur Treadwell Walden spent the rest of his long life supporting and advocating sled dogs and the sport of mushing. He became a popular speaker at meetings and events, and Lorna Coppinger wrote of Walden in her classic tome for the International Sled Dog Racing Association (ISDRA), *The World of Sled Dogs*, "He lived to be 91 years old,

Alaskan Sled Dog Tales

straddling the animated decades from the 1870's into the 1960's. Without Arthur Walden, the lore and the lure of the sled dog would be much less than it is."

Clearly ahead of his time in anticipating the sport of mushing, Walden wrote in 1927: "People in general have an idea that dog driving is confined to racing, since sport of any kind is first to break into print, but this is not so. The greatest pleasure is the driving. The whole of northern New England lies open to the man who has a team of from two dogs up, at a time when some of its most attractive parts are practically closed for the winter months for all modes of travel except by dog team. The whole mountain section of northern Vermont, and the lake region of Maine are some of the most attractive sections for this health-giving sport of anywhere in America." ~•~

A team of Arthur Walden's big golden-coated Chinook sled dogs. Walden's breeding program combined his one-hundred pound leader, named Chinook and carrying the sought-after traits of intelligence, endurance, and personality, with a mixed Eskimo husky bitch, from which he selected the pups which most closely resembled their father. To maintain the purity of his new breed, Walden would not sell any dogs which could reproduce, letting them go only as pets or sled dogs.

Alaskan Sled Dog Tales

Arthur Walden with Chinook

Alaskan Sled Dog Tales

Archdeacon of the Yukon Hudson Stuck, circa 1914

Alaskan Sled Dog Tales

TEN THOUSAND MILES WITH A DOG SLED
Archdeacon of the Yukon
Hudson Stuck

"Dogs will usually stay with their sled; they seem to recognise their first allegiance to the load they haul, probably because they know their food forms part of it." ~Hudson Stuck, in Ten Thousand Miles with a Dog Sled

Hudson Stuck, an Episcopal clergyman and social reformer, was born in London, England in 1865. At the age of 20, eager for wide-open spaces, he tossed a coin: heads for Australia, tails for Texas. It landed tails, and over the course of the next twenty years Stuck earned a name for himself in the Lone Star State. In 1889 he enrolled to study theology, and became an Episcopal priest in 1892.

Once again seeking new adventures, he moved to Alaska in 1904, then nearly 40 years old. Appointed Archdeacon of the Yukon and the Arctic, he traveled incessantly throughout the interior of Alaska, by dogsled in winter and by boat in summer, ministering to those in need.

In 1913 he organized and co-led, with Harry Karstens, the first successful complete ascent of the highest peak in North America, the

Alaskan Sled Dog Tales

Striking across from the Tanana to the Kantishna, en route to Denali. Hudson Stuck, Harry Karstens, Walter Harper, Robert C. Tatum, Johnny, and Easias departed from Nenana on March 17, and reached the summit of McKinley on June 7, 1913.

South Peak of Mount McKinley (Denali), and it is that trek for which he is justifiably famous. But in the preface to his book on the historic climb, *The Ascent of Denali, The 1913 Expedition that First Conquered Mt. McKinley*, Stuck shared his perspective and his true concern: "The author would add, perhaps quite unnecessarily, yet lest any should mistake, a final personal note. He is no professed explorer or climber or 'scientist,' but a missionary, and of these matters an amateur only. The vivid recollection of a back bent down with burdens and lungs at the limit of their function makes him hesitate to describe this enterprise as recreation. It was the most laborious undertaking with which he was ever connected; yet it was done for the pleasure of doing it, and the pleasure far outweighed the pain. But he is concerned much more with men than mountains, and would say, since 'out of the fullness of the heart the mouth speaketh,' that

Alaskan Sled Dog Tales

his especial and growing concern, these ten years past, is with the native people of Alaska, a gentle and kindly race, now threatened with a wanton and senseless extermination, and sadly in need of generous champions if that threat is to be averted."

Hudson Stuck became a great champion for the native Alaskan Indians and Eskimos, traveling the great rivers, traversing the towering mountains, and guiding his dogteam across vast expanses of frozen tundra from village to village, seeking out the places where his services were most needed. His first trip, during the winter of 1905-06, went from Fairbanks to Circle, Fort Yukon, Bettles, Coldfoot, Kotzebue Sound, Nome and back to Fairbanks over the course of four and a half months. Three years later a shorter trip was made over the Koyukuk River to a new mission at Allakaket for Christmas. In the winter of 1909-10 a journey was made from Fort Yukon to Allakaket, Tanana, Rampart City, Nenana,

February, 1919. Substituting for Archdeacon Hudson Stuck. Enroute Allakaket. Ala Kellum and team of Archdeacon Stuck. F. B. Drane Collection UAF-1991-46-521

Alaskan Sled Dog Tales

Chena, Fairbanks, Salchaket, Eagle, Circle, and back to Fort Yukon during a very severe winter.

The winter of 1910-11, the Archdeacon traveled from Tanana to Iditarod and Fort Yukon. Archdeacon Stuck wrote about his travels: "So far as mere distance is concerned... there is nothing noteworthy in this record. There are many men in Alaska who have done much more. A mail-carrier on one of the longer dog routes will cover four thousand miles in a winter, while the writer's average is less than two thousand. But his sled has gone far off the beaten track, across the arctic wilderness, into many remote corners; wherever, indeed, white men or natives were to be found in all the great interior."

Hudson Stuck's accounts of travel methods, especially those pertaining to sled dogs, have become favorite passages among those who still race and travel with dogs. For example, his description of loading dogs is very instructive: "Five dogs are usually considered the minimum team, and seven dogs make a good team. A good, quick-traveling load for a dog team is fifty pounds to the dog, on ordinary trails. The dogs will pull as much as one hundred pounds apiece or more, but that becomes more like freighting than traveling. On a good level trail with strong big dogs, men sometimes haul two hundred pounds to the dog. These, however, are 'gee-pole propositions,' in the slang of the trail, and the man is doing hard work with a band around his chest and the pole in his hand. For quick traveling, fifty pounds to the dog is enough."

Hudson Stuck harbored an appreciation for the sled dogs who transported him across Alaska: "Indeed, any man of feeling who spends the winters with a dog team must grow to a deep sympathy with the animals, and to a keen, sometimes almost a poignant, sense of what he owes to them. There is a mystery about domestic animals of whatever kind. It is a mystery that man should be able to impose his will upon them, change their habits and characters, constrain them to his tasks, take up all their lives with unnatural toil. And that he should get affection and

Alaskan Sled Dog Tales

devotion in return makes the mystery yet more mysterious."

At the beginning of *Ten Thousand Miles with a Dog Sled* Stuck explains one of the most troublesome aspects of winter travel in the north country:

"The next day we were on the Chatanika River, to which Cleary Creek is tributary, and were immediately confronted with one of the main troubles and difficulties of winter travel in this and, as may be supposed, in any arctic or subarctic country—overflow water.

"In the lesser rivers, where deep pools alternate with swift shallows, the stream freezes solid to the bottom upon the shoals and riffles. Since the subterranean fountains that supply the river do not cease to discharge their waters in the winter, however cold it may be, there comes presently an increasing pressure under the ice above such a barrier. The pent-up water is strong enough to heave the ice into mounds and at last to break forth, spreading itself far along the frozen surface of the river. At times it may be seen gushing out like an artesian well,

Archdeacon Hudson Stuck and Walter Harper at Allakaket, March, 1917. [Frederick B. Drane Collection UAF-1991-46-531 Univiversity of Alaska Fairbanks]

223

rising three or four feet above the surface of the ice, until the pressure is relieved. Sometimes for many miles at a stretch the whole river will be covered with a succession of such overflows, from two or three inches deep to eight or ten, or even twelve; some just bursting forth, some partially frozen, some resolved into solid 'glare' ice. Thus the surface of the river is continually renewed the whole winter through, and a section of the ice crust in the spring would show a series of laminations; here ice upon ice, there ice upon half-incorporated snow, that mark the successive inundations.

"This explanation has been given at length because of the large part that the phenomenon plays in the difficulty and danger of winter travel, and because it seems hard to make those who are not familiar with it understand it. At first sight it would seem that after a week or ten days of fifty-below-zero weather, for instance, all water everywhere would be frozen into quiescence for the rest of the winter. Throw a bucket of water into the air, and it is frozen solid as soon as it reaches the ground. There would be no more trouble, one would think, with water. Yet some of the worst trouble the traveller has with overflow water is during very cold weather, and it is then, of course, that there is the greatest danger of frost-bite in getting one's feet wet. Water-proof footwear, therefore, becomes one of the 'musher's' great concerns and difficulties. The best water-proof footwear is the Esquimau mukluk, not easily obtainable in the interior of Alaska, but the mukluk is an inconvenient footwear to put snow-shoes on. Rubber boots or shoes of any kind are most uncomfortable things to travel in. Nothing equals the moccasin on the trail, nothing is so good to snow-shoe in. The well-equipped traveller has moccasins for dry trails and mukluks for wet trails—and even then may sometimes get his feet wet. Nor are his own feet his only consideration; his dogs' feet are, collectively, as important as his own. When the dog comes out of water into snow again the snow collects and freezes between the toes, and if not removed will soon cause a sore and lameness. Then a dog moccasin must

Alaskan Sled Dog Tales

"Rough ice on the Yukon." Hudson Stuck photo, circa 1910-11.

be put on and the foot continually nursed and doctored. When several dogs of a team are thus affected, it may be with several feet each, the labour and trouble of travel are greatly increased.

"So, whenever his dogs have been through water, the careful musher will stop and go all down the line, cleaning out the ice and snow from their feet with his fingers. Four interdigital spaces per foot make sixteen per dog, and with a team of six dogs that means ninety-six several operations with the bare hand (if it be done effectually) every time the team gets into an overflow. The dogs will do it for themselves if they are given time, tearing out the lumps of ice with their teeth; but, inasmuch as they usually feel conscientiously obliged to eat each lump as they pull it out, it takes much longer, and in a short daylight there is little time to spare if the day's march is to be made."

On October 10, 1920 Hudson Stuck died of pneumonia in Fort Yukon, and by his request, was buried in the native cemetery there. ~•~

Alaskan Sled Dog Tales

Lt. Billy Mitchell, U.S. Army, maintained over 200 sled dogs at Fort Egbert, near Eagle, on the Yukon River, around 1901. He used the teams for transporting materials and supplies when surveying and putting in the Washington to Alaska Military Cable and Telegraph System, better known as WAMCATS.

Alaskan Sled Dog Tales

MILITARY SLED DOGS
They received the Croix de Guerre

"28 dogs were hitched to 14 light sleds, and these were loaded with ammunition. Back over the forbidding trail they went, under artillery fire...."

When Joe Redington needed assistance relocating and marking the historic but long-forgotten Iditarod Trail in 1972, in preparation for the epic race he'd envisioned and was working to make a reality, he turned to the U.S. Army and forged a cooperative venture in which the Army helped put in the trail while gaining valuable wintertime maneuvers for their troops. Redington's history with the military had long been established: he'd spent many years doing contractual recovery work on military flights which had crashed in the remote reaches of the Alaskan back country.

In her book *Joe Redington, Champion of Alaskan Huskies*, Katie Mangelsdorf wrote of Joe's work for the military with his sled dog team: "Joe's job with Rescue and Reclamation took him around the territory for seven years, and later he contracted out for specific jobs. He was called whenever a plane went down. His job was to go out and rescue the survivors or bring back their remains and then recover the downed plane. Anything not of value had to be destroyed or buried. This was so

Alaskan Sled Dog Tales

that old wreckage sites would not be reported as new crash sites." And later she noted, "Joe also freighted materials and supplies for the Air Force to White Alice sites, U.S. Air Force telecommunications sites which dotted Alaska during the Cold War."

Joe Redington's use of sled dogs in service to the military was not the first time huskies had been pressed into action for the Army in Alaska. In the 1900's the U.S. Army Signal Corps laid an underwater telegraph cable from Seattle to the Alaskan port of Valdez. An overland line was necessary to relay telegraphed messages to the Army's outposts in the territory, but efforts at construction in the wild unexplored territory had made little progress. In the summer of 1901, Brigadier General A. W. Greely, head of the Army Signal Corps and a famous Arctic explorer, sent the son of a Wisconsin senator, 21-year-old first lieutenant William Mitchell, to Alaska to investigate the delays.

Mitchell observed that no one attempted to work in the winter for fear of the cold. But it soon became evident to Mitchell that "very little would

The mule barn at Ft. Egbert, showing the doghouses Lt. Billy Mitchell added to house the teams of huskies he used in his work for the U.S. Army, 1901.

Alaskan Sled Dog Tales

be accomplished if we attempted to transport material through this area in the summer, as a pack horse could carry only two hundred pounds fifteen or twenty miles a day; but in winter these same animals could pull from one to two thousand pounds over the frozen snow for even greater distances.... Although this was one of the coldest parts of the world, it seemed to me the thing to do was to work through the winter getting the material out: the wire, insulators, poles, food supplies, and forage; then to actually construct the lines in the summer, when we could dig holes in the ground and set telegraph poles."

As the winter set in, Lt. Mitchell journeyed to Fort Egbert, near the town of Eagle on the Yukon River, a lonely outpost which was to be his base for the next two years. He discovered there were no trails over the mountains where the telegraph lines were to go, and their course had not been definitely located, so his first task was to survey the route for the first line, which would be between Eagle and Valdez, a distance of almost four hundred miles through a trackless wilderness.

Mitchell would later write in his memoirs, "My orders specified that all transportation in the post should be turned over for my use, and I made preparations to get my outfits out on the trail as soon as possible. I began to buy dogs to use for light sledding and reconnaissance work, selecting each one myself. The first dog I obtained was a MacKenzie husky leader called 'Pointer,' owned by a squaw man named Jack Lawrence, a mail carrier. Pointer was the greatest dog I have ever seen. He weighed about 120 pounds and was perfectly sure on the trail. He could feel through the snow with his feet for an old trail and unerringly find it. We could depend on him to protect the sled and the team under all conditions. He was so fierce that we had to cut his fangs off to keep him from chewing up the other dogs. He became tremendously attached to me, and from that time on during every trip, Pointer was my constant companion and friend.

Alaskan Sled Dog Tales

"Gradually we got together wonderful teams. I selected the best ones, mated in size, gaits, and weight, and organized them into two teams. Taking a man named Emmet with me, I made a reconnaissance to see for myself where the lines should go and how we could stand the weather. When doing this advance reconnoitering, we always traveled light, often not carrying a tent but digging a hole out with a snowshoe and banking up a fire of logs opposite it, sleeping in the reflected heat of the embers. Sometimes we slept in a hole in the snow with the dogs lying on top of us."

Mitchell, who would later become known as the father of the U.S. Air Force, reportedly kept two hundred dogs, running loose in a huge pack, in a large corral at Fort Egbert. He learned the dog handling techniques of the indigenous peoples, used dog teams to scout the route of the telegraph line, and with the assistance of the sled dog teams Mitchell's workers finished the project three years ahead of the allotted five-year schedule.

All Alaska Sweepstakes legend A.A. Scotty Allan, winner of the 1909, 1911, and 1912 races, was so well-known and his dogs so respected that when the United States entered World War I the government commissioned dogs from the Allan and Darling Kennel. In *The World of Sled Dogs*, edited for the International Sled Dog Racing Association (ISDRA), Lorna Coppinger explained how Scotty Allan's dogs entered the First World War: "At the start of World War I two residents of Nome, Rene Haas and a man named Mufflet, left to join the French Army. Several months later Nome's most famous dog driver, Scotty Allan, received a message from Lieutenant Haas, asking him to secretly gather a hundred good sled dogs and all their equipment for use in the snow-choked mountains in France. Men, horses and mules were helplessly bogged down along the Vosges Mountains, and Captain Mufflet and

Alaskan Sled Dog Tales

Haas had convinced their superior officers that in Alaska the sled dogs kept the roads open in winter. They were sure they could serve the same purpose in France.

"Scotty Allan began casually buying up the best dogs he could find in the surrounding Eskimo villages, so that by the time Haas arrived Allan had assembled 106 dogs, plus sleds and harnesses and two tons of dried salmon for dog food. Twenty-eight of those dogs were sons or grandsons of Allan's famous racing lead dog, Baldy.

"To transfer the 106 dogs from Allan's kennel to the S.S. *Senator* Allan hitched up the longest towline ever used. Over three hundred feet of heavy rope, with iron rings for the dogs' harnesses every six feet along its length, was hitched to a big truck. French tri-color cockades decorated each dog's collar, and all the residents of Nome, including the school

A dog team ambulance in France during WWII.

Alaskan Sled Dog Tales

A newspaper clipping circa 1918

children, lined the streets to watch the longest dog team in the world. American's first unit in World War I had started on its journey."

The dogs Allan selected saw service hauling supplies over the Vosges Mountains between France and Germany during the severe winter of 1914-1915. Allan's teams reportedly delivered over 90 tons of ammunition to an artillery battery in only four days, a feat which had previously taken up to two weeks for horses and mule teams to accomplish. It was said that two seven-dog teams could do the work of five horses in the formidable terrain.

Alaskan Sled Dog Tales

In the March, 1919 issue of *The National Geographic Magazine*, in an article titled "Mankind's Best Friend," by Ernest Harold Baynes, the details of the sled dogs' heroic actions were explained: "In four days after a very heavy snowfall, one kennel of 150 dogs moved more than 50 tons of food and supplies from the valley below to the front line on the mountain above. In the Vosges Mountains more than a thousand Alaskan sled dogs helped to hold the Hun during the last year of the war."

The article continued, referring to Scotty Allan's kennel partner, Esther Birdsall Darling: "One woman brought back to America a Croix de Guerre awarded by France to her intrepid teams of sled dogs. The occasion that won them that honor was their salvation of a storm-bound, foe-pressed outpost in the French Alps. Dispatch bearers had been sent out repeatedly, but no succoring answer came, for the messengers were overwhelmed as they passed through the blinding blizzard.

"At last matters became desperate. The foe was pressing his advantage with dash and courage, and nothing but quick action could save the situation. So Lieutenant Rene Haas hitched his dogs to a light sled and started through a blizzard before which human flesh, in spite of the 'urge' of a consecrated patriotism, had failed. In 'Sweepstakes racing time' they covered the trip down the mountain over and over a perilous pass to the main army post.

"There the 28 dogs were hitched to 14 light sleds, and these were loaded with ammunition. Back over the forbidding trail they went, under an artillery fire, facing a bitter wind, and plowing through blinding clouds of snow. On the fifth day, at sunrise, the panting Malamutes reached the outpost, their burden of ammunition was rushed to the gunners, and the mountain was saved from the insolent foe."

Norman Vaughan, an American sled dog driver and explorer who participated in Admiral Byrd's first expedition to the South Pole in

Alaskan Sled Dog Tales

1928-30, was employed by the U.S. Army Air Forces Search and Rescue Division as a dog sled driver during World War II, engaging in many rescue missions in Greenland and attaining the rank of colonel.

Charles L. Dean recounts this history in his book, *Soldiers and Sled Dogs: A History of Military Dog Mushing*: "Hundreds of sled dogs were pressed into duty during WWII for search and rescue missions throughout Greenland, Canada and Alaska. But they also saw duty on the Western Front in one of the least-known stories of sled dog heroics that involved one of the most amazing adventurers Wintergreen has ever had the honor of being associated with.

"In December 1944 the German Army was making it's last stand, rolling across France and overwhelming American regiments in its path. Panzer troops drove on through bitter cold and heavy snow that rivaled the Arctic. When at last their drive was stopped by the bloody fight called the Battle of the Bulge, snows were hip deep. Motor ambulances found it impossible to rescue injured soldiers and many of the wounded lay dying in the drifts.

"Colonel Norman Vaughan sent out a rush call for dog teams. From throughout the Arctic, 209 dogs and their drivers were flown to France. Meanwhile, Vaughan experimented with the only option to get dogs to the battle front: parachutes. His superiors nixed the plan and it wasn't until Gen. Patton himself intervened that Vaughan was given the go ahead.

"By then clearing weather kept the plan from being fully deployed, but the operation had set a remarkable record and contributed to the lore of the war dogs. In fact, throughout the war, sled dogs were credited with retrieving 150 survivors, 300 casualties and millions of dollars worth of equipment."

In a review of Dean's book, Robert Kollar, an ex-scout-dog handler in the Vietnam War, succinctly describes the wartime involvement of dog

Alaskan Sled Dog Tales

teams: "During the Second World War America supplied equipment to Soviet and European allies via air routes over Alaska and the Bering Sea to Siberia and over Maine, Greenland and Labrador to Britain and later France. Search and rescue teams were vital when aircrews were forced down by extreme weather conditions in remote and harsh terrain. Survivors, casualties, and vital equipment had to be recovered and, in the days before helicopters, sled dogs were the only means available. It is estimated that 150 survivors, 300 casualties and millions of dollars of equipment were recovered. Sled dogs continued to be used by the Air Force after World War II for search and rescue until the mid-1950s when the helicopter finally closed the door.

"Sled dogs were also organized for combat. The 10th Mountain Division was created and trained for a proposed invasion of Norway. As

Army training dogs for the Air-Sea rescue operations.

Alaskan Sled Dog Tales

part of the planning, the 10th became the only army division to have a sled dog unit attached, the purpose of which was to bring in supplies and bring out casualties. The proposed invasion never occurred, and the sled dogs were no longer needed and were detached from the 10th.

"During the Battle of the Bulge in the spring of 1945, sled dog units came close to being sent in, but bureaucratic bungling kept the mission from going forward until snows melted and it was too late. Both of these tasks led to an expansion in the number and organization of military sled dogs. The Army had to develop doctrine; purchase dogs; design, construct, and test sleds; and train handlers."

The War Department even developed a field manual, titled *Dog Team Transportation*, for use by its drivers, which noted, "Sledge dogs have generally proved most reliable because of their ability to surmount the obstacles of uncertain weather, treacherous crevasses, and rough and hilly terrain."

According to Michael G. Lemish in his book, *War Dogs: A History of Loyalty and Heroism*, when the United States entered into WWII in December, 1941, the US Army had in effect only about 50 sled dog teams, based in Alaska and used for search and rescue, and transporting equipment, supplies, ammunition, and guns. By the end of WWII, there were over 200 active military sled dog teams available, and the three northern breeds, Siberian Huskies, Alaskan Malamutes, and Alaskan Huskies, had been identified as three of only seven breeds deemed suitable for combat due to their intelligence and agility.

In Alaska a special unit was organized by Colonel Marvin R. "Muktuk" Marston, who visited dozens of native villages and organized the Alaska Territorial Guard, more commonly known as the Eskimo Scouts. They served many vital strategic purposes to the entire Allied effort during World War II. In early 1943, when a promised plane failed to arrive after a week, Major Marston set out by dogsled on an epic 680-mile

Alaskan Sled Dog Tales

"A great dog. One of my lead dogs."
[from Men of the Tundra, Alaska Eskimos at War, by Muktuk Marston]

enrollment trip around the Seward Peninsula, surviving the coldest winter in 25 years by foregoing standard military survival training in favor of the native methods of his Eskimo Scout guide, Sammy Mogg. Thanks to Marston and Mogg's heroic effort, the Alaska Territorial Guard stood as a first line of defense for the terrain around the Lend-Lease route from America to Russia, against attack by Japan and the Axis Powers. This vital lifeline allowed the US to supply its Russian ally with essential military aircraft. ~•~

Alaskan Sled Dog Tales

Leffingwell with dogs at Flaxman Island, Canning District, Northern Alaska, ca. 1910

Alaskan Sled Dog Tales

ERNEST DE KOVEN LEFFINGWELL
Mapping Alaska's Arctic Coastline

"It always amazes me how much ground Leffingwell covered."
~Joe Henderson, author of *Malemute Man, Memoirs of an Arctic Traveler*

Ernest de Koven Leffingwell was a joint commander, with Ejnar Mikkelsen, of the 1906-1908 Anglo-American Polar Expedition, which established that, contrary to long-held myths and stories, there was no land north of Alaska.

Self-described as "the forgotten explorer," as his efforts went largely unrecognized in his own time, Leffingwell is credited for later mapping about 150 miles of the Arctic coastline, between Point Barrow on the northernmost point and Herschel Island, along with the adjacent Brooks Range, between 1906 and 1914.

Leffingwell, Mikkelsen, and the members of their expedition became stranded on the coast of the Arctic Ocean when their schooner, the *Duchess of Bedford*, became ice-locked near Flaxman Island, 250 miles east of Pt. Barrow, the northernmost point of Alaska. While Leffingwell, Mikkelsen, and the ship's physician, Dr. G.P. Howe, were exploring the coastline in March and April, 1907, the sailors in the expedition used

Alaskan Sled Dog Tales

*Above: Ernest de Koven Leffingwell.
Below: With cases of malted milk.*

wood from their badly-damaged ship to build a rough but serviceable cabin and other structures on Flaxman Island. For the next several years, Leffingwell stayed at the camp intermittently and conducted mapping projects with Inupiat guides, traveling by dog team in the winter and following the coastline in a small boat during the summer months

Leffingwell's cabin and several other buildings on Flaxman Island still stand, and a sign was placed on them in 1971 by geologist C. G. Mull for the Alaska Division of Parks which states: "From this base camp geologist Ernest D.K. Leffingwell almost singlehandedly mapped Alaska's Arctic coast during the years 1907-1914. He also identified the Sadlerochit - main reservoir of the Prudhoe Bay field." In 1978 Leffingwell's camp was listed as a National Historic Landmark.

Leffingwell's writings include many original journals and related papers from his expeditions. In 1909 he contributed to a book, *Conquering the Arctic Ice*, authored by his friend

Alaskan Sled Dog Tales

and expedition co-commander, Ejnar Mikkelsen (Philadelphia: G. W. Jacobs); in 1915 he wrote an article, "A Communication from Leffingwell," for the *University of Chicago Magazine*; and in 1919 he authored a 247-page Professional Paper on the Canning River Region for the U.S. Geological Survey.

In *Conquering the Arctic Ice* Mikkelsen described buying dogs for the two-month exploratory expedition which he, Leffingwell, and Dr. Howe undertook in the spring of 1907:

"Another serious question to be settled was that of the dogs, as several more of our pack had died, and some of those we had bought were useless. We had to get more and were willing to pay any price for them. We began at once to look about us for dogs in the possession of the Eskimos which we knew would stand us in good stead for the ones lost, but we had to pay exorbitant prices for them. For example, one which we bought from Kanara was paid for with two sacks of flour, 25 lbs. beans, 6 lbs. coffee, 20 lbs. dried potatoes, 12 lbs. cocoa, one shot-gun, 250 rounds of ammunition, and one broken-down tent; and another bought from Uxra with two sacks of flour, one sack of cornmeal, 5 lbs. coffee, 20 lbs. dried potatoes, 25 lbs. sugar, 4 lbs. prunes, 4 lbs. malted milk, 200 rounds of cartridges, and one hatchet file. The prices, as said above, were exorbitant, but the dogs were good, and what was more, we needed them."

Joe Henderson is a dog musher, author and arctic traveler who has explored the remote regions of Alaska over the past 30 years with his hardy team of twenty-two Alaskan Malamutes. During the winters of 2006-2008, Joe and his Malamutes made a series of unprecedented solo expeditions in the Brooks Range and the Arctic National Wildlife Refuge. Pulling three sleds in tandem with two tons of supplies, Joe and the team mushed entirely unsupported for up to five months at a time without seeing another human being.

Alaskan Sled Dog Tales

Henderson's expedition was a tribute to the "forgotten explorer," Ernest de Koven Leffingwell. Traveling with Leffingwell's journals as a guide, Joe covered much of the same country, camped in many of the same localities, and experienced some of the same weather and ground conditions that Leffingwell had a century before. On the third year of the expedition, Joe found Leffingwell's cabin during a whiteout blizzard.

Joe kept a detailed journal of his travels, and he wrote a three-part series of articles for *Mushing* magazine which appeared in three issues from 2006 to 2008. An excerpt: "It always amazes me how much ground Leffingwell covered. Leffingwell, along with some local Inupiat assistants, had spent six winters and nine summers surveying, mapping and studying Alaska's arctic environment. He traveled by dogteam or small boat over 4,500 miles, drew a sketch map of the entire coast between Point Barrow and the Canadian border, triangulated 150 miles of coast, and mapped the geographic features of 4,000 square miles of mainland. He also named several geologic formations, including the one that is the source of oil at the Prudhoe Bay oilfield. He journeyed 20,000 miles by ship, and he mentioned pitching camp 380 times! These are just a few of his extraordinary accomplishments." [Joe Henderson, 'Retracing Leffingwell,' *Mushing*, Nov/Dec, 2008. Henderson is also the author of *Malemute Man, Memoirs of an Arctic Traveler*.]

Ernest de Koven Leffingwell was awarded the Patron's Medal by the Royal Geographical Society and the Charles P. Daly Medal by the American Geographical Society, both in 1922. He was awarded an honorary Doctor of Science degree by Trinity College in 1923. Leffingwell Fork, a stream on Alaska's North Slope, Leffingwell Crags in Canada's Northwest Territories, and Leffingwell Nunatak in Greenland are named for him. When he died in 1971, he was believed to have been the oldest surviving polar explorer. ~•~

Alaskan Sled Dog Tales

Leffingwell's winter quarters, Flaxman Island, Canning District, 1910.

Ernest de Koven Leffingwell, Captain Eijnar Mikkelsen, and Dr. G.P. Howe, February, 1907, Anglo-American Polar Expedition, Canning District, Alaska.

ON A WORLD TOUR WITH A DOG TEAM

"Caribou Bill" of Nome, Alaska, Will Get $10,000 if He Makes the Trip in Four Years.

ADVENTURES ON THE WAY

His Life Saved by His Animal Friends —He's the Champion "Musher"— Due Here on Wednesday.

"Caribou Bill" Cooper, or William F. Cooper, to be really formal about him, is ing Nome, which put his courage and endurance to a severe test.

Mr. Seton says that after Bill and his dogs started from Nome they hadn't traveled far before they broke through the ice on one of Alaska's rivers, and had quite a tough time getting out. Also, according to Mr. Seton, Caribou Bill had the unpleasant experience of sleeping in "Dad" Weber's cabin one night in November of 1908 while the body of a man who had been frozen and partly devoured by wolves lay in the corner of the shack. "Dad" Weber's cabin is fifty-five miles from Mount McKinley.

There are many other experiences accredited to Caribou Bill by his friend Seton, one of which was a fall into a crevasse in Valdez glacier. Mr. Seton says that Bill's dogs pulled him out. Another time in the Winter of that same year, says Seton, Bill lost his way in a blizzard and his dogs found the way to an isolated cabin and saved their master's life. Mr. Seton is full of such stories of his friend Bill's exploits.

Caribou Bill reached Springfield, Mass., a few days ago and after a short stop headed for New York. Bill and his dogs will board a steamship here for Liverpool and will visit London, then go by boat to France, cross into Germany and Russia. There Bill and his dogs will follow the Russian-Siberian Railroad to Vladivostok and then trail along the coast line to East Cape, Siberia, cross Bering Strait on ice to Cape Prince of

"Caribou Bill" and "Missouri Kid" loading their photo supplies preparatory to starting on their overland trip from Valdez, Alaska, to Seattle, Wash. Dec. 9, 1908.

Alaskan Sled Dog Tales

CARIBOU BILL
World Tour with a Dog Team

*"'Caribou Bill' of Nome, Alaska, Will Get $10,000
if He Makes the Trip in Four Years."*

The New York Times, May 23, 1910: "'Caribou Bill' Cooper, or William F. Cooper, to be really formal about him, is expected here some time on Wednesday with his team of sixteen Eskimo dogs, with which he is 'mushing' around the world from Nome, Alaska, and back again. Caribou Bill says he is the champion dog 'musher' of the world, and out in Nome there are quite a few people willing to back his claim.

"Bill and his dogs started from Nome in October, 1908, on a four years' globe-trotting jaunt, and has since been trekking eastward, stopping now and then to rest himself and his animal friends and to have a little fun on the way.

"Incidentally, Bill's friends say he left Nome without a cent in his pocket, for one of the stipulations, if he is to win the purse of $10,000, said to have been offered by the Nome Sweepstakes Association, is that he must earn his own way around the world by Dec. 25, 1912. But Caribou Bill is quite a persistent person, and he is credited with a lot of courage as well as hardihood. In fact, according to the story told by one of his

Alaskan Sled Dog Tales

"Caribou Bill" in front of the Valdez Glacier, Valdez, Alaska.

friends, Fred R. Seton, who is now in this city awaiting Bill's arrival, the champion dog 'musher' has had some experiences since leaving Nome, which put his courage and endurance to a severe test.

"Mr. Seton says that after Bill and his dogs started from Nome they hadn't traveled far before they broke through the ice on one of Alaska's rivers and had quite a tough time getting out. Also, according to Mr. Seton, Caribou Bill had the unpleasant experience of sleeping in 'Dad' Weber's cabin one night in November of 1908 while the body of a man who had been frozen and partly devoured by wolves lay in a corner of the shack. 'Dad' Weber's cabin is fifty-five miles from Mount McKinley.

"There are many other experiences accredited to Caribou Bill by his friend Seton, one of which was a fall into a crevasse of the Valdez Glacier. Mr. Seton says that Bill's dogs pulled him out. Another time in the Winter of that same year, says Seton, Bill lost his way in a blizzard and his dogs found the way to an isolated cabin and saved their master's life. Mr. Seton is full of such stories of his friend Bill's exploits.

Alaskan Sled Dog Tales

"Caribou Bill reached Springfield, Mass. a few days ago and after a short stop is headed for New York. Bill and his dogs will board a steamship here for Liverpool and will visit London, then go by boat to France, cross into Germany and Russia. There, Bill and his dogs will follow the Russian-Siberian Railroad to Vladivostok and then trail along the coast line to East Cape, Siberia, cross the Bering Strait on ice to Cape Prince of Wales and down the Alaskan coast line to Nome.

"Bill, so his friend Seton says, has with him nearly a dozen and a half dogs, but drives only eight of them at a time. He has a sledge with a set of wheels which he uses when there is no ice or snow. About half of his journey across the continent has been made on snow and ice. The dogs which are not in harness trail along behind, and when the pullers become tired they swap places.

"Caribou Bill, so says Mr. Seton, was exiled from Russia many years ago by the Czar's order. He was also a member of a rescue party which dug for seventy-eight men entombed at White Horse Pass in Alaska in 1904, when an avalanche buried them. Bill, who speaks several

Caribou Bill's team traveled to the 1909 Alaska-Yukon-Pacific Exposition in Seattle.

languages, is said to be an expert with a moosehide whip thirty feet long, and Mr. Seton says the champion 'musher' can kill a cat or a rabbit at ten paces with the knotted thong at the whip end."

While in New York, Caribou Bill met some New Jersey film makers who were interested in his exploits. He subsequently abandoned his journey and went to Saranac Lake, New York to set up a movie camp. Five years later, in 1915, Bill secured $100,000 in capital and moved to Port Henry, New York, and created another film set, Arctic City, complete with a frontier town, mountain backdrops, and abundant snow for the dog team scenes. Numerous production companies leased the site for their filmmaking, and by the winter of 1920 three movie companies, the Charles Miller Production Company, the William Fox Film Company, and Goldwyn, were all making films at Caribou Bill's Arctic City. ~•~

Caribou Bill and his team at the 1909 Alaska-Yukon-Pacific Exposition in Seattle.

Alaskan Sled Dog Tales

After the Alaska-Yukon-Pacific Exposition in Seattle, Bill continued east across the U.S. This photo is captioned "Caribou Bill's Famous Dog Team in Butte, Montana"

Alaskan Sled Dog Tales

The Anchorage Daily Times splashed the film production across its front page.

250

Alaskan Sled Dog Tales

THE CHEECHAKOS
Alaska's First Motion Picture

"'Stupendous Epic of the Frozen North,' it was billed. There were fistfights, pistols, knives and whips. An explosion, a fire, a raging river, a calving glacier and a dogsled version of a car-chase scene. And in the end, there was Mother Nature serving the villain a heaping helping of exactly what he deserved."
~Debra McKinney, Anchorage Press, April 30, 2015

In 1923, dog teams dashing through the snowy countryside around Mount McKinley National Park were nothing unusual, because the land was full of people who depended on dog teams for getting around in winter. One of those often seen traveling with his dog team was Harry Karstens, the first superintendent of the park, who spent the winter of 1907-08 studying wildlife near the headwaters of the Toklat River with Charles Alexander Sheldon, an amateur naturalist who would become the father of Mount McKinley National Park. Karstens later gained fame as the climbing leader on the first successful summiting of Mount McKinley in 1913. When he became the superintendent of the park he established a kennel to provide sled dogs for patrolling the park's vast backcountry, so when a group of filmmakers went seeking a stunt man

Alaskan Sled Dog Tales

who could handle a dog team in a high-speed chase scene, Harry Karstens' well-known reputation made him an easy choice.

In the early 1920's there were many popular silent movies about Alaska and the north country, such as Rex Beach's 1918 *'Laughing Bill Hyde,'* with Will Rogers; the 1920 film *'Nomads of the North;'* the 1922 film *'Nanook of the North;'* and in 1923 *'The Grub-Stake,' 'The Frozen North'* with Buster Keaton, and Jack London's classic *'The Call of the Wild.'* But these films inevitably relied on locations far from Alaska's majestic landscapes, utilizing scenic sites in other places which their producers hoped would compare favorably with Alaska's grandeur.

In 1922 a group of Anchorage residents decided to go into the film-making business and bring the real Alaska to the big screen with a silent film about the gold rush days in the Klondike. Financed by Alaskan businessman and millionaire Captain Austin E. "Cap" Lathrop, a one-time prospector who owned a chain of movie theaters in several Alaskan towns, they formed a production company, the Alaska Moving Picture Corporation. With no prior experience in the field of film-making, the group sold stock at $10.00 per share and raised $75,000. They lured four Hollywood silent movie stars, along with a crew of about 30 professionals with six movie cameras, from California, Oregon, and New York. The film, originally titled *'The Great White Silence,'* would be written and directed by Portland, Oregon-based writer and director Lewis H. Moomaw.

The plot was standard fare for the day, and included heroes and villains, a damsel in distress, a cherubic child, and plenty of exciting action. After a disastrous fire aboard a north-bound steamship separates a mother and her young daughter, the child is taken in by two good-hearted prospectors bound for the Klondike, while the mother falls prey to the film's version of Snidely Whiplash, complete with cowering henchmen in his employ. Through a series of mishaps and deliberate

Alaskan Sled Dog Tales

Private railcars took the Alaska Moving Picture Corporation to Mt. McKinley Park.

misleadings by the villain, the mother and child travel parallel trails to what passes for the Klondike gold diggings, but which is in reality Maurice Morino's Mount McKinley Park Hotel, which was located near the present-day park entrance. The action includes the ship's sinking, boating down raging rivers, a fire in the gold camp, traipsing across dangerously calving glaciers, and the aforementioned high-speed sled dog chase.

After building a 7,000-square-foot studio in downtown Anchorage (on Third Avenue, later occupied by the Snow Goose Restaurant), the cast and production crew of the Alaska Moving Picture Corporation traveled by private cars on the newly constructed Alaska Railroad to the recently established Mount McKinley National Park, where they met Park Superintendent and musher Harry Karstens. He agreed that an all-Alaskan film would be good exposure for Alaska and the new national park, but he voiced concern that the production would not just be a "cheap melodrama."

Alaskan Sled Dog Tales

The leading stars in front of Maurice Morino's Mt. McKinley Park Hotel.

With reassurance that a quality movie was indeed the goal, Karstens and the film crews set about filming several dramatic winter scenes with dog teams. Among the most historically valuable is an arrival at the picturesque Mount McKinley Park Hotel, an unusually-constructed log building, originally a roadhouse, which opened on Thanksgiving Day, 1921. In July, 1923, only a few weeks after filming ended there, the hotel would see a visit by President Warren Harding and a 65-person Congressional delegation. Sadly, the historic building would be lost to fire in May, 1950.

A thrilling highlight of the film is the racing dog teams, where "two actors from the all-star cast will battle with one another, in one of the most startling episodes of the master production, featuring a grueling dogteam race, extending over many miles."

In his book *'McKinley Station'* (Pictorial Histories Publishing Co., 2009), Tom Walker describes Karstens' role in the film: "For this segment of the film, two legendary mushers, Frank Tondro, the famed 'Malemute

Alaskan Sled Dog Tales

Kid,' and Harry Karstens, the equally famous "Seventymile Kid,' doubled for the actors mushing their teams across the frozen terrain. Tondro, famous for his fur attire, mushed his dogs both at McKinley Station and through Broad Pass for pay. Karstens loaned eleven dogs, two sleds, and four days of his time, as public relations for the park."

A mock-up of a gold rush town was built in the vicinity of Seventh Avenue and L Street in Anchorage, and then, with a city fire truck on standby, was set ablaze for a climactic scene. To show the drama of the 1898 Klondike gold rush, the production company traveled to Girdwood, where they recreated the historic jumping-off town of Skagway. The April 4, 1923 *Anchorage Daily Times* reported: "The struggles of former years will once again be fought by real veterans of the early days, many of them still retaining and wearing the identical garments and packs, such as jackets, parkas, fur hats and pack boards used by their owners during the stampede days over the great Chilkoot Pass. Tandem dog teams will once again hit the trail with the Yukon sled in prominence. The vast illumination will portray sled loads of supplies of flour, bacon, salt, beans, sugar, coffee, tobacco and other bare necessities used by the prospectors."

Two weeks later, on April 17, 1923, the *Anchorage Daily Times* grandly announced, "All Aboard for Mile 52, the scene of the million-dollar picture which is destined to make Alaska famous… Advices from Mile 52 report some splendid pictures have been taken, but the big thing comes when the 250 Anchorage people arrive on the scene to take part in the mad gold rush of '98. Captain A.E. Lathrop, in charge of local affairs, invites the public to take part in the scene that so aptly shows Alaska during the olden, golden days. This is a free-for-all, and everybody is welcome. Hot coffee will be served on the trail, but guests are asked to take their own lunches."

And so a traincar full of extras was commissioned in Anchorage and taken to mile 52 on the Alaska Railroad, where the Bartlett Glacier stood

Alaskan Sled Dog Tales

in for the infamous Chilkoot Pass. The crowd donned their packs and walked in front of two airplane propellers to portray the men who had struggled over the pass en route to the Klondike only 25 years before. Footage was also shot on the Childs Glacier, north of Cordova on the Copper River.

After five months of filming the reels were sent for editing into an 86-minute movie. The beautiful inter-title cards for the film were done by Alaska's most prominent artist, then 58-year-old Sydney Laurence, whose painting of Denali from the hills above the rapids of the Tokositna River had already become his trademark.

The filmmakers held closed screenings in Los Angeles and Portland (Director Moomaw's home town), and finally 'The Cheechakos' triumphantly returned to Alaska and opened to the public at Anchorage's Empress Theater, owned by Cap Lathrop, on Dec. 12, 1923. The film then traveled to Fairbanks and played to packed houses all over the territory, heralded as "the best Alaska picture ever filmed."

Similar rave reviews greeted the film's gala debut for several hundred national critics at New York's Ritz-Carlton Hotel on May 1, 1924. When the film showed in Washington, D.C. the audience included President Calvin Coolidge and Secretary of Commerce Herbert Hoover. The film crossed the oceans, playing to crowds in many far-off lands who were undoubtedly impressed with the magnificence of the Last Frontier, but ultimately the film was not a commercial success; with the new talkies seizing the interest of moviegoers, silent films inevitably lost popularity and fell by the wayside.

Few people, even in Alaska, were aware of the old classic until 2000, when the film was restored at the University of Alaska Fairbanks and released on DVD. In 2003 the Library of Congress deemed the film "culturally, historically, or aesthetically significant," and it was selected for preservation in the National Film Registry, becoming one of the 50 films

Alaskan Sled Dog Tales

in the 4-disk boxed DVD set called "Treasures from American Film Archives (2000)", compiled by the National Film Preservation Foundation. The film is available on YouTube.

The Cheechakos (1924)

Production Company: Alaska Moving Picture Corp. Producer: Capt. Austin E. Lathrop. Director/Writer: Lewis S. Moomaw. Title text: Harvey Gates. Title art: Sydney Laurence. Photographers: Herbert H. Brownell and Raymond Johnson. Cast: William Dills ("Horseshoe" Riley), Albert Van Antwerp (Bob Dexter), Eva Gordon (Mrs. [Margaret] Stanlaw), Alexis B. Luce (Richard Steele), Gladys Johnson (Ruth Stanlaw), Baby Margie (Ruth as a child), Guerney Hays (Pierre). Running Time: 8 reels, 86 minutes. ~•~

Filming at a remote location, possibly along Turnagain Arm near Portage.

Alaskan Sled Dog Tales

Yost's Roadhouse on the Valdez-to-Fairbanks Trail

Alaskan Sled Dog Tales

MARGARET MURIE'S WILD RIDE
Over the Valdez-Fairbanks Trail

"In winter Yost's two-story log building was sometimes buried by a huge snowdrift, leaving only the stovepipe visible. Travelers had to look hard to find the stovepipe. Then they had to scout around to find the tunnel leading down to the roadhouse door." ~Jim Rearden in Alaska's Wolf Man: The 1915-55 Wilderness Adventures of Frank Glaser

In her classic memoir *Two in the Far North* (Knopf, 1962), about finding love and adventure in Alaska with the great naturalist Olaus Murie, Margaret Murie tells of traveling via dog team and horse-drawn wagon in 1918, over the trail which would become the Richardson Highway. The future author, ecologist, and environmentalist, who would be called 'the Grandmother of the Conservation Movement' by both the Sierra Club and the Wilderness Society, was only fifteen years old, but she was making the trip from her home in Fairbanks to Cordova, where she would meet her father and her brother.

At one point she is riding in the sled of a dog driver named French John, and after dinner and a few hours of sleep at the Black Rapids

Alaskan Sled Dog Tales

Young Margaret Murie, who would become an ecologist, environmentalist, author, and recipient of the Presidential Medal of Freedom, the highest civilian honor awarded in the US.

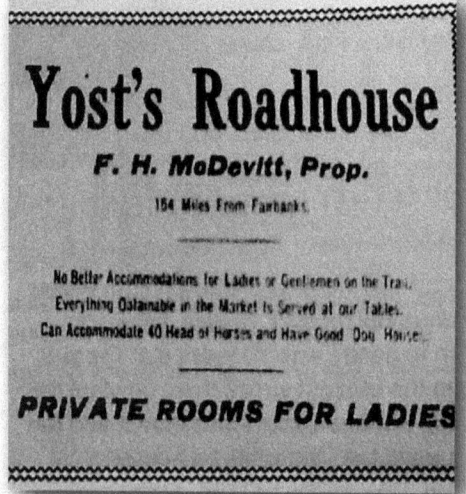

roadhouse, he awakens her to continue the journey south.

"I was tucked into a big wolfskin robe in John's basket sled sometime around midnight. For now the snow even high in the mountains was thawing and we must still travel at night. But not silently, for John poured forth one story after another of the North, of his dogs, even while he struggled to keep the sled on the thawing, sliding trail which led up and around and ever up, with the high peaks glistening above us.

Sometimes John talked to his seven beautiful Huskies in French, and I almost drowsed, snug in the furs, in spite of the bouncing and sliding of the sled on the soft trail. Once I roused suddenly with John's face close to mine; he was crouching under the side of the sled, his shoulder under the rim of the basket, his voice exhorting the dogs. He was fairly holding the sled by main strength from turning over and rolling down the mountainside, for here the way led across a steep mountain face and the trail had thawed away. 'Jus' sit still, don' be

Alaskan Sled Dog Tales

The tall pole on the left holds the bell which would guide lost travelers to the roadhouse, as described in Margaret Murie's book, 'Two in the Far North.'

scare. We soon get to Yosts now; dis place here de worse one. Ah! Dere's de bell!'

"Bell? I sat up. We had come onto a level pass, and out in the middle hung a large bell in a framework of heavy timbers. A few yards away there was a black hole in the snow, and above the hole, smoke.

"'Funny places in dis world, eh?' said John. 'You know, snow still very deep up here, roadhouse mostly covered. Dis is top of Alaska Range–summit. And dat bell, she is save much people since early days. Wind, she blow like son of gun here in winter–roadhouse always cover in snow. Bell, she only ting to tell us where Yost's is, see? Wind so strong she ring bell.'"

This first-person exchange is echoed in an article written in 2002 for the *Los Angeles Times*, titled *Finding Gold Rush Tales and Roadhouse Comfort on the Richardson Highway*. Writer Michael Parrish opens his article with some chilling history: "At least a dozen people died in the winter of 1913 along the old Valdez-Fairbanks Trail, lost in churning

Alaskan Sled Dog Tales

Above: An unidentified dog team on the Valdez-Fairbanks Trail.
Below: Yost's Roadhouse, 1916. A 1908 advertisement for this roadhouse notes: "Can Accommodate 40 Head of Horses and Have Good Dog House."

Alaskan Sled Dog Tales

blizzards as they struggled to find Yost's Roadhouse. The two-story log lodge in the central Alaska Range was often so buried in snow that only its stovepipe poked above the drifts. Yost's was 200 yards back from the trail, making it even harder to find in a storm."

He shares the story of the bell which would help lost travelers find safety and comfort: "The summer after that deadly season, a Lt. Dougherty of the U.S. Army Signal Corps installed a wire fence across the winter trail to steer blizzard-blind trekkers toward the front door, and a 150-pound bell mounted near the roadhouse would clang whenever the wind blew. Those innovations are said to have saved many lives."

Ken Marsh's history of the Richardson Highway, *The Trail* (Sluice Box Productions, 2008) shares more. Apparently built in 1905 at the confluence of McCallum Creek and Phelan Creek, on the north side of Isabel Pass, it was a small one-story log building operated by a Mrs. McCallum during the summer and winter of 1905-06. Known at that time as McCallum's Roadhouse, it was "at a pivotal spot... as well as a treacherous area during the winter." Marsh continues: "Charlie Yost took over McCallum's in the winter of 1906-07 and enlarged it with a two-story log building next to the old structure. The name was changed to Yost's Roadhouse, and Charlie was said to have dispensed a basic menu of hot cakes and beans to travelers at two dollars a meal."

Ken Marsh shared an excerpt from Hallock C. Bundy's 1910 guide to the Valdez-Fairbanks trail: "The roadhouse at Yost's is built right on the bank of the Delta River, at one of the most exposed portions of the winter trail, but at the place where it is most needed. At night the big light that is hung outside the door can be seen for a long distance by the travelers coming from Fairbanks and is a welcome beacon in stormy weather."

A flood of the Delta River in March, 1916 overran the roadhouse. The Alaska Road Commission reportedly used the site as a camp while working on improvements to the Richardson Highway during the 1920's and '30's, but nothing remains at the site today. ~•~

Alaskan Sled Dog Tales

The front and back sides of a 1906 postcard from the author's collection, showing the first superintendent of Denali National Park, Harry Karstens, who was also co-leader of the 1913 expedition which first summited what was then Mt. McKinley.

Alaskan Sled Dog Tales

DOG TEAM POSTCARDS
Sled Dogs in the Mail

"Here's a pretty picture for Leslie showing how we traveled to Salcha."
-from the back of a dog team postcard, 1929

The often romanticized vision of a sled dog team making its way across the trackless wilderness has always been a popular image for postcards from the north country. Whether colorized, hand-tinted or left in black-and-white, the postcard scenes of how dogs helped settle the vast northern frontier remain a sought-after collectible.

Dog team postcards such as the one on the opposite page were most often made from actual photographs, so they are an excellent record of the types of dogs to be found in harness, the always-interesting sleds and gear which were used, and the outfits of the dog drivers who took their teams across the trails. And of course they showed the land crossed by the mushers and their teams, a land which has not changed much over the years between then and now.

Old postcards are a fun collectible, and the handwritten messages on the backsides, with their often obscure and mysterious meanings, lend their own unique and one-of-a-kind charm. ~•~

Alaskan Sled Dog Tales

A popular colorized postcard ~ "Alaska Dog Team"

1907 postcard, postmarked Washington, D.C.: "I don't want you to melt in that Wash. heat so send you something cooling. Los Angeles hot too, but not sticky."

Alaskan Sled Dog Tales

"A Dog Team, Yukon River, Klondike, Alaska." Postcard circa 1910.

Postcard: "Yukon Dog Team Freighting Through Alaskan Canyon."

Alaskan Sled Dog Tales

Postcard: "Railroad track team, mile 1 out of Seward, Alaska."

Postcard: "Keystone Canyon, near Valdez, Alaska."

Alaskan Sled Dog Tales

Postcard: "Prize Dog Team in the Arctic."

Postcard: "Returning from a Polar Bear Hunt in Alaska."

Alaskan Sled Dog Tales

Postcard: "Dog teams hauling freight from steamer Corwin. Two miles out at sea, Nome, Alaska."

Postcard: "Alaska Dog Team"

Alaskan Sled Dog Tales

Postcard: "A Crack Dog Team, Alaska."

Postcard: "Tea on the trapline"

Alaskan Sled Dog Tales

A popular early Alaskan postcard showing Ben Downing's mail teams leaving Circle City for Fort Gibbon, about 150 miles down the Yukon River, circa 1899.

Postcard: "U.S. Mail Team"

Alaskan Sled Dog Tales

Postcard: "The Yukon mail at Eagle, Alaska."

Postcard: "U.S. Mail Dog Team on the Yukon River in Winter."

*Historic Biederman Camp on the Yukon River, ca. 1930s.
[UAF Archives, George Beck Collection]*

ED BIEDERMAN
Delivering Mail on the Yukon: Eagle to Circle

"The things Biederman has been through would fill a book. I suppose no man knows more about sled dogs, or winter weather, or making his way alone in wild country." — Ernie Pyle, 1937 Washington Daily News

Born in Bohemia in 1870, Max Adolphus "Ed" Biederman came to the United States at the age of thirteen and he was in San Francisco when the 1900 Nome gold strike happened. He arrived too late to stake a paying claim, so he took a job with the Northern Commercial Company as a dog team mail carrier on the Yukon River between Tanana and Rampart. In 1912 he received a route farther upriver, between the towns of Circle and Eagle, and by 1916 he'd built a log cabin and a camp roughly halfway between the two towns, across from the mouth of the Kandik River.

Alaskan Sled Dog Tales

Also around 1916 Ed Biederman met and married an Athabascan woman, Bella Roderick, from Medicine Lake near Circle Hot Springs. She was the granddaughter of the famous Yukon Flats chief Shahnyaati, who was said to have several wives and dozens of grandchildren. The Canadian explorer Alexander Murray said of him in 1847, "This Indian never saw Whites before we arrived. He has given us more fur and more meat than any other, was our Fort Hunter this spring, has great influence with his band, and is the person for whom the Red Coat is intended."

Ed and Bella had five children, and two of their sons, Charlie and Horace, learned the mail route and helped with the family business. In the summer mail was delivered along the river by steamboat, and the Biederman family boarded as many as sixty sled dogs for miners and trappers who did not want to care for their dogs in the off-season. Feeding their own team and those of the boarders required a great deal of salmon, and the Biedermans maintained twin fish wheels for their salmon drying operation, where they processed nearly three tons of fish each year.

Many mushers dog boarded their dogs for the summer at Biederman's Camp on the Yukon River, this photo is ca. 1935. [UAF Archives, George Beck Collection]

Alaskan Sled Dog Tales

In the winter the Yukon River camp became an overnight stop on the mail trail between Eagle and Circle; Biederman would reach it on the third night and switch dog teams, giving one team a rest while the other team continued the journey. The 160-mile route took six days one way and, after a rest day, six days back, and Biederman did this thirteen times each winter, covering 4000 miles of rough trail over the course of a season. He would start out from Eagle with a load of mail often exceeding 500 pounds. Traveling northwest, sometimes on the river and sometimes following overland trails, he followed a string of roadhouses located at intervals along the way. In her book *Yukon: The Last Frontier* (UBC Press, 1993) Melody Webb explained: "The first night out of Eagle he stayed at Miller's Camp, then Nation, home on the third night, Woodchopper on the fourth, either Twenty-Six Mile Waystation or Twenty-Two Mile

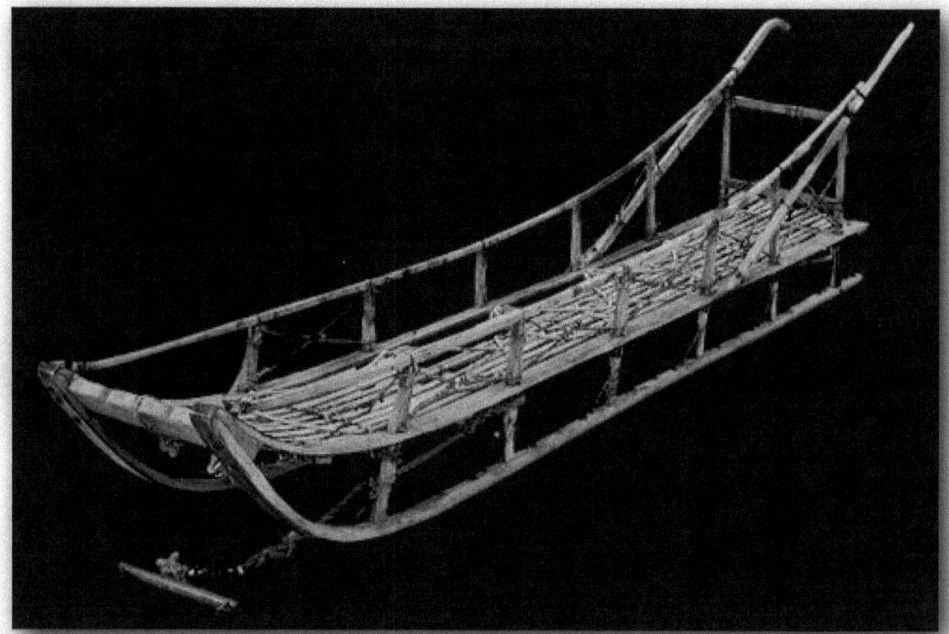

From the National Postal Museum: This sled, built in 1922, is an extraordinary reminder of this remarkable chapter in Alaskan postal history. Sam Olson hand-crafted this 13-foot-long dog sled out of hickory in 1922. Contract mail carrier Alfred "Ed" Biederman (1861-1945) used this hand-made hickory dog sled for his 160-mile route between Circle and Eagle, Alaska. It has moose hide lashings and iron runners, brake, and springs, with cotton cords for securing mail loads.

Alaskan Sled Dog Tales

Roadhouse on the fifth night, and finally into Circle. Resting only one day, he started back."

In 1925 Biederman's dog team was on a barge, being pushed upriver to Eagle to begin another season, when the barge hit a rock, capsized, and the entire team drowned in the Yukon River. Without his well-experienced trail dogs, Biederman was forced to borrow dogs from a musher in Eagle. Another tragedy struck when he drove the team through overflow and thoroughly soaked his moccasins. He was only four miles from the Twenty-Two Mile Roadhouse, and thought he could make it, but his feet froze before he reached the roadhouse, and parts of both feet had to be amputated. Biederman was back at work hauling the mail the following winter, wearing triple layer socks with rabbit fur stuffed in the empty toes of his footwear. When Ernie Pyle, a reporter for the *Washington Daily News,* stopped by the camp in 1937, he described Biederman as "a footless dog-team postman who's tough as nails."

Pyle noted, "The things Biederman has been through would fill a book. I suppose no man knows more about sled dogs, or winter weather, or making his way alone in wild country."

Ed Biederman's son Charlie took over the mail contract until 1938, when he was finally outbid by an air carrier. ~•~

Above: Ed and Bella Biederman, circa 1935. Below: "Cap" Adolphus, an Athabascan who worked tending sled dogs. [Both UAF/George Beck Collection]

Alaskan Sled Dog Tales

ESTHER BIRDSALL DARLING
Alaskan Author

An article from an unknown publication, circa maybe late 1920's?

Esther Birdsall Darling, an early day Nome resident, was a staunch supporter of sled dog racing. She was the daughter of the late Frederick Birdsall who arrived in Sacramento in the spring of 1850. He built and operated the first quartz mill in Dayton, Nevada. After his marriage in Ohio in 1869, he established his home in Sacramento and commuted to Nevada. It was there Esther was born.

Around the time that San Francisco was having its famous earthquake, Esther Birdsall met Charles Edward Darling. She married him on his return from Europe in June of 1907 and went to Nome, Alaska as a bride. Her husband was a member of the Darling and Dean mercantile firm that sold everything from fly paper to mining machinery.

For the next ten years, Esther Birdsall Darling called Nome home.

In 1908, the Nome Kennel Club was organized to help improve the breed of sled dogs and to promote a characteristic Arctic sport in the 'All Alaska Sweepstakes Race.'

Alaskan Sled Dog Tales

Esther Birdsall Darling

Alaskan Sled Dog Tales

THE GREAT DOG RACE OF NOME—1912

ESTHER DARLING

There are three yearly events from which time is generally reckoned in Nome. The opening of navigation, in June, when after eight long months the floes of Arctic ice which have separated this part of Alaska from the rest of the world, drift to the northward and permit the arrival of vessels. The close of navigation, usually toward the end of spite of its long nights and its days of weird twilight, passes quickly; holidays, fittingly observed, come and go. And then, in April, is the third real event of the year—the great dog race of the north. This race from Nome to Candle, on the Arctic, and return, has taken its place at the very head of sports requiring courage, skill and endurance. The Mar-

With the late Scotty Allan, one of the best dog men in the north, Esther entered teams in the famous annual race. The Darling-Allan teams met with many success stories in the 408-mile races across the frozen wastes.

The wonderful lead dog of that team, 'Baldy of Nome,' became the hero of Esther's book, *'Baldy of Nome.'* The book, published in 1916, was very successful. It brought in royalties for many years.

Esther Darling also wrote *'Boris, Grandson of Baldy,' 'The Break Up,' 'Navarre of the North,'* and *'Luck of the Trail.'* Another of her books, *'No Boundary Line,'* told the story of a spoiled girl whose father decided she must spend the winter in a sparsely settled town in northern Alaska. Critics spoke highly of the book.

Mr. and Mrs. Darling left Alaska in 1918 and moved to Berkeley, California, as did Scotty Allan.

Twenty-eight of Baldy's sons and grandsons served with the 'Alpine Chasseurs' in World War I. With others of the sled dog division, they were given the French Croix de Guerre for valiant service. Thus 'Baldy's' fame found its way not only to Berkeley, where he participated in various civic events, but also to the battlefields of Europe.

'Baldy' died in Berkeley in 1922. Esther Darling and Scotty Allan obtained a special permit from the City of Berkeley to bury the famous dog in the back yard of the Allan home on Gerber Street. A little rose bush was set out as 'Baldy's monument.'

Alaskan Sled Dog Tales

Esther's husband died in 1922. Then Esther lived alone in an apartment at 2412 Durand Street. There she had pictures of Alaska all over the walls. She also displayed several big solid silver cups won by her lead dog, 'Baldy of Nome.'

There was one rare photograph that Esther cherished. It showed Will Rogers, the famed humorist; Wiley Post, noted airman; Leonhard Seppala, famed sled dog musher and 'All Alaska Sweepstakes' winner and Joe Crosson, famous bush pilot from Alaska. The quartet was standing in front of Wiley Post's plane which half an hour later crashed near Barrow, killing Rogers and Post.

Esther Birdsall Darling, by her writing, helped keep the stories of early day sled dog racing in print so others could enjoy the history of sled dog racing. ~•~

Alaskan Sled Dog Tales

Esther Birdsall Darling with Tom, Dick, and Harry—aka the Tolman Brothers. Tom is in the middle. Handwritten on the back: "For Constance and Leonhard with best wishes from their affectionate friend Esther Darling. Nome—1916."

Alaskan Sled Dog Tales

THE GREAT DOG RACES OF NOME
Esther Birdsall Darling

"A sport unequalled in history for excitement, speed, and endurance..."
~Esther Birdsall Darling

The All Alaska Sweepstakes was the first organized sled dog race, held in Nome, Alaska in 1909 and running to the mining camp of Candle, 204 miles to the north, and returning to Nome. The course followed the coastline of Norton Sound east to Safety and Dickson, then turned north and inland toward Council and traversed the forbidding Seward Peninsula, a land so remote and treacherous that few travelers dared cross the wide and wind-blown expanse. The First World War interrupted the race, and it was not run between 1917 and 1983. The last running, after a 25-year break, was the Centennial Race in 2008.

In 1916 Esther Birdsall Darling wrote this 16-page commemorative booklet celebrating the race which her kennel partner, the three-time champion A.A. 'Scotty' Allan, had helped to create in 1908.

THE START OF THE FIRST TEAM IN THE FIRST ALL ALASKA SWEEPSTAKES, 1908

Alaskan Sled Dog Tales

The Great Dog Races of Nome

Held Under the Auspices of the Nome Kennel Club, Nome, Alaska

OFFICIAL SOUVENIR HISTORY

By
ESTHER BIRDSALL DARLING
(President, 1916)

Photographs by Lomen Brothers, Nome

THE DOG RACES OF NOME

THE ALL ALASKA SWEEPSTAKES

Since out of the far North have always come tales of adventure and achievement, hardship and heroism, it is not strange that out of the far North have come also the records of a Sport unequalled in history for excitement, speed and endurance—the records of the famous Dog Races of Nome.

The winter season here extends from the departure of the last boat of the open season late in October, to the arrival of the first boat early in June, and during this time the people of Northwestern Alaska are cut off from the rest of the world by a barrier of over a thousand miles of ice and snow; the only direct communication with the "Outside" being by the weekly Government Dog Team Mails, and the Wireless Telegraph System.

The men and women of this shut-in community, unusually active mentally and physically as is always the case in any frontier civilization, need an outlet for their superabundant energy in some diversion that is characteristic of their surroundings—for many pleasures are geographically impossible. This diversion they have found in these thrilling contests over the snow-swept wastes of Seward Peninsula.

In this country where dogs have always been an indispensible factor in the work of discovery and settlement, it is hardly surprising that they should be, as well, an indispensable factor in the most popular and representative sport; and it was because of a desire to make this sport a recognized part of the life of the community that the Nome Kennel Club was organized in 1908 with Albert Fink as its first President.

From the very beginning there was much enthusiasm, and generous purses have been offered that have ranged from ten to three thousand dollars, according to the financial conditions prevailing, not only in Alaska, but generally—for many contributions come from liberal friends "Outside."

It was early seen that not only would the races furnish much of the winter entertainment, but that there would also be a consistent effort on the part of the dog owners and dog drivers to improve the breed of sled dogs, which up to this time had been but little considered; an effort to instill into all dog users an intelligent understanding of the accepted fact that care and kindness to their dogs bring the quickest and surest returns from all standpoints. This has resulted in the development of such a high standard for dogs that not alone is their worth acknowledged throughout Alaska, but their supremacy is conceded the world over.

When Amundsen contemplated making a dash to the North Pole, it was to Nome that he wrote for dogs; and while he subsequently gave up the voyage, the dogs selected for him were afterwards used by Leonard Seppala in a team which twice won the All Alaska Sweepstakes, and the Ruby Derby.

Vilhjalmur Stefansson, too, turned to Nome for dogs when he went at the head of a Canadian Expedition to search for unknown lands and chart unknown waters in the ice floes of the Arctic; and the dogs which "Scotty" Allan bought for that intriped explorer have been of untold assistance in his great achievments.

Alaskan Sled Dog Tales

WINNERS OF THE FIRST ALL ALASKA SWEEPSTAKES, 1908. ALBERT FINK, OWNER; JOHN HEGNESS, DRIVER

THE DOG RACES OF NOME

Perhaps the most signal tribute of all to the remarkable reputation of the Nome Dogs was the fact that in 1915 the French Government sent Lieutenant Rene Haas nearly ten thousand miles to secure Nome dogs for service in the Vosges Mountains; and these "little auxiliaries of a great war" as they were called by the celebrated French writer, Leon de Tinseau, were so carefully and wisely chosen by "Scotty" Allan for Lieutenant Haas that they are now recognized as an indispensable addition to the Alpine Corps in the matter of transportation where the use of horses and mules is impossible.

The first great race took place with all the pomp and ceremony that marks the carnival time in sunnier lands. There was a holiday spirit in the very air; schools and the courts adjourned, and business houses were practically closed for there was no demand for anything but "inside information" or "straight tips" during these famous Dog Days of Nome.

The surging crowds that pushed their way through the narrow streets, laughing and care-free, proudly wore the colors of their favorite teams. Pennants and streamers of the Kennel Club, gold and green, fluttered everywhere in the keen, crisp air. Heralds with their silver-toned bugles announced the coming of a chosen Queen and her many Maids of Honor, fur-clad from head to foot, and brought in state to the decorated stands of the Kennel Club officials in sleds drawn by powerful huskies.

Then followed the excitement of the starts when the teams, mad with the desire to be gone, plunged and barked and howled, straining at the harness, and held only with the greatest difficulty by men who strove in vain to calm their impatience.

The drivers, motionless, yet alert and watchful, waited the final signal through the tense moments of silence before the flag in the hands of the Queen should drop, and the dogs, released, should dash forward in their head-long flight—spurred on by wild and echoing cheers. Cheers that died away only as each team disappeared down the white trail that leads from Nome on Bering Sea, to Candle on the Arctic Ocean, a course of 408 miles over one of the bleakest and most desolate regions of the North.

These celebrations have now become a Tradition in Nome, and the interest has grown as the capabilities of the dogs have developed, and the skill of the drivers increased, till the races are the greatest events of the year to the sport-loving enthusiasts whose support makes them possible. Not alone that, but they are now considered of national and international importance—the progress and results of the various events being telegraphed in detail, and published in all of the great newspapers of the world.

The course lies along a telephone line so that the messages from road-houses, camps, and villages are constant, and bulletins telling of the condition of the men and dogs are posted up in public places, clubs, and the theaters; and when the thrill of the start is over, and the wild excitement has simmered down to a keen attention, the town waits day and night for reports on the where-abouts and welfare of the racers.

As early as November the prospective entries, men and dogs, begin to train for the event which takes place always in April, the exact date being determined by the climatic conditions of the season. As a matter of fact, the men who go into it are usually those who are never quite out of training; men whose days are often spent in work that hardens the muscles, followed by evenings devoted to indoor base ball, or other forms of exercise that will give them strength and suppleness. Smoking and drinking have no place in their routine, and frequently a rigid diet is observed.

Alaskan Sled Dog Tales

WINNERS OF THE SECOND ALL ALASKA SWEEPSTAKES, 1909. J. BERGER, OWNER; "SCOTTY" ALLAN, DRIVER

THE DOG RACES OF NOME

The dogs, which have been carefully selected for strength and fleetness, are driven daily increasing distances until a little spin of a hundred miles or more at a time is a mere trifle.

The number of dogs driven in a team is entirely optional with the driver, and varies according to his personal idea of how many can be used to advantage—it being desirable to select enough to keep up to the required standard in all things, yet not too many for efficient team work. Of late years the teams have averaged from ten to twenty dogs each.

That there shall be no cruelty to dogs that might, by chance, become lame or exhausted or in any way a drag upon the others, an invariable rule of the Kennel Club makes it obligatory to return with every dog, alive or dead, with which the team started. In this way it is to every driver's obvious advantage to so treat his dogs that he may not be forced to carry on his sled the extra weight of a dead or disabled dog.

The drivers can also use their own discretion about the number and length of the stops to be made—only one being stipulated at Candle, 204 miles from Nome, and the end of the first half of the race. Here the teams are examined and checked up by judges appointed by the Club.

Not the least scientific feature of the race is the ability to realize how much rest a driver can afford to take himself and give his dogs, without the loss of a single valuable moment.

These stops are made at relay stations, and here all of the food for all of the contestants is distributed by commissary teams controlled by the Kennel Club; and is so divided into separate allowances that no time is lost in preparing and allotting it.

Throughout the year the dogs are fed on a general diet in which rolled oats, dried salmon, household scraps, and the flesh of the white whale make up the list. The latter is oily and full of nutriment, and is fast becoming one of the most popular of dog foods. But during the race they are fed the most nourishing and sustaining combinations such as chopped mutton and beef, mixed with eggs. This, having been carefully prepared, is then frozen to be kept as long as may be necessary.

The only equipment carried on the light racing sleds, which are made of hickory and lashed with reindeer sinew or walrus hide, is an assortment of furs and water boots for the men, and certain necessities for the dogs in the way of canton flannel moccasins for their feet should they encounter icy trails; dark veils for their eyes if the sun is too strong, and blankets in case of a cutting wind.

In every resting place the dogs are considered first, and no man thinks of himself till his dogs are rubbed with alcohol, fed and bedded. In case of any stiffness, liniments are applied and a thorough massage given. Many of the drivers sleep on the floor of the road-house with their dogs to better note their condition, while others share their bunks with the leader of the team.

It should be thoroughly understood that as dogs are not driven with reins, but by spoken orders, the leader of a team must understand all that is said to him and guide the others accordingly. An intelligent leader is, therefore, an absolute necessity and in most teams there will be found several dogs capable of filling that important post.

A driver rarely sits in his sled for any great length of time during the race, but runs behind pushing as hard as possible, jumping on and off the runners at the rear—generally riding down, and shoving up, the grades.

Alaskan Sled Dog Tales

WINNERS OF THE THIRD ALL ALASKA SWEEPSTAKES, 1910. COLONEL RAMSAY, OWNER; JOHN JOHNSON, DRIVER

THE DOG RACES OF NOME

The best of feeling exists between the drivers in the contest, and they are invariably willing to help one another, if necessary, in any way possible.

In the second Sweepstakes, that of 1909, a team of Siberian dogs, owned by Goosak, and driven by Thrustrup, attracted much attention for various unusual attributes.

Fox-Maule Ramsay, a young Scotchman, interested in mining in Nome, and a keen sportsman, saw their possibilities, and during the following summer went over to the coast of Siberia, a distance of less than 150 miles; and going some way up the Kolima River procured a large number of the best type of these Siberian dogs, bringing with them to Nome, two men who understood them thoroughly.

In the race of 1910, in which Ramsay entered one team in the name of Colonel Charles Ramsay of London, one in the name of Stuart Weatherly, also of London, driving a third himself, they showed their capabilities beyond the most sanguine anticipation of their backers, and attained an enormous popularity which has never waned.

These Siberian dogs, generally and erroneously called "Siberian wolf hounds," in the "Outside" papers, are suggestive neither of hounds nor wolves. On the contrary they have much more the appearance of the fox, with pointed noses, prick ears, and bushy tails curled up over their backs. They are wonderfully even and steady in their work, gentle and tireless, requiring comparatively little food, and but little time in which to digest it. Any number of them can be turned loose together in a corral or stable, with hardly any fear of their fighting. Their allegiance is given to the one who feeds them.

The Alaskans, a comprehensive name used for convenience, to distinguish them from the distinct type of Siberians, may be malamutes or huskies (native Alaskan dogs) or they may be setters, pointers, collies, hounds, airedales or what-not, with or without a strain of the malamute or huskie. These dogs are far more individual, less like machines, in their characteristics, than are their rivals the Siberians; less easy to manage, too, but exceedingly intelligent and responsive, showing much pride in their work, and a deep and abiding affection for their masters, as well as great fleetness.

Each type has distinct and obvious advantages, and each, as may be readily understood, has its enthusiastic supporters and staunch admirers —and for good cause.

Sometimes, however, despite the known skill of a driver and the acknowledged merit of his team, despite months of training and years of experience, luck may be against a man; and a slight accident to his sled, or to a dog, a sudden blizzard which strikes him alone because of his position on the trail, or some other untoward incident, quite out of any human reckoning, may turn an anticipated victory into an overwhelming defeat.

The race of 1908 was in many ways more or less experimental, and much was learned that resulted in numerous changes in methods and rules; one of the most important things altered being in regard to the starts. At first these had been made two hours apart, each man's time being counted from the moment of departure to the moment of return; but with so many teams it was found that some of them ran into unfavorable weather that others wholly escaped. The next year the time between the starts was reduced to fifteen minutes, then to ten, later to five, and after 1912 they were made one immediately after the other and considered even.

The time of any particular race depends not so much upon the speed of the dogs as upon the weather and trail conditions that prevail during their run.

Alaskan Sled Dog Tales

WINNERS OF THE FOURTH ALL ALASKA SWEEPSTAKES, 1911   ALLAN AND DARLING OWNERS; "SCOTTY" ALLAN, DRIVER

THE DOG RACES OF NOME

The route varies constantly—from hour to hour—from a narrow passage between the towering ice hummocks of Bering Sea, to wide plains of unbroken snow; from the steep slopes of Topkok Hill, to the desolate, storm-swept wastes of Death Valley; from the pleasant winding road through the wooded Council district, to the trackless and treacherous ice on rivers and lakes.

With so much hinging on climatic changes and the temporary state of the trail, it may be conceded that the winning of this great race lies one-third in the driver, one-third in the dogs, and one-third in Chance. It is the uncertainty of the result, the possibility of unexpected developments, that keep up the interest in the race; and arouse an enthusiasm that prompts the entire town, no matter what the hour of night or day, to be ready to greet the returning Victor, and his faithful dogs, with the cordial welcome that is always freely given to those who have triumphed in the greatest sporting event that the world has ever known. So—

When the boom of the gun at Fort Davis
Tells the news that the Winner is near,
With whistles and bells all ringing,
There's the sound of a rousing cheer.

A cheer for the man who has conquered,
For the dogs that have set the pace
Of the strength and speed, at their master's need,
In Alaska's Sweepstakes Race.

And there's honor for all awaiting—
For whether they win or fail,
They're Heroes still, in the eyes of the North,
For their pluck on the Arctic Trail.

THE SOLOMON DERBY

The Solomon Derby is, next to the All Alaska Sweepstakes, the most important event of the racing season in the North, and is generally held sometime during February.

The comparatively short distance of this race does not tax the staying qualities of the men and dogs, nor the generalship of the drivers, as do the longer ones, but is more a question of great speed.

Many of the racing teams enter practically all of the winter events, and often the Solomon Derby develops material that proves valuable in the Sweepstakes later. As in the latter, the time depends largely upon weather and trails, and in 1912, over a perfect trail, and in perfect weather, Charles Johnson, with a string of trim Siberians, made the 65 miles from Nome to Solomon and return, in the record time of 5 hours, 47 minutes, and 24 seconds.

Later, three times in succession, Fred Ayer was the Derby winner, with his magnificent team of Alaskans (of foxhound and malamute strain) but in not one of these three races were the conditions as favorable as they had been with Johnson.

It was agreed that should such a thing as an ideal day occur, an attempt would be made to lower Johnson' time; and on March 24, 1916, under a cloudless sky, with weather cold but calm, and a trail of unusual smoothness, four entries: Webb, Vincent, Delzene and Ayer, each man driving his own team, were ready for the contest. There was an enormous amount of interest manifested, as many firmly believed that Johnson's record was unbreakable. It was, however, broken not only once, but twice: Fred Ayer making the 65 miles in the almost incredible time of 5 hours, 32 minutes and 3 3-5 seconds, beating Johnson's time over 15 minutes; William Webb completing the course in 5

Alaskan Sled Dog Tales

WINNERS OF THE FIFTH ALL ALASKA SWEEPSTAKES, 1912. ALLAN AND DARLING, OWNERS; "SCOTTY" ALLAN, DRIVER.

THE DOG RACES OF NOME

hours, 44 minutes, and 40 seconds, nearly three minutes faster than Johnson. Webb's team had never before been driven further than 45 miles at a stretch, and this great accomplishment was a revelation to all of the speed and strength of his team of sinewy youngsters.

While each season brings to light dogs of much promise, it is predicted that it will be many a year before Fred Ayer's time will be equalled or exceeded; and his achievement, as well as that of William Webb, in the race of 1916, will have set a high standard indeed for the Solomon Derby.

THE FORT DAVIS RACES

Short races from Nome to the Fort Davis Bridge and return, a distance of 6 1-3 miles, are of frequent occurrence, and offer much diversion because of the number and varied qualifications of those who take part in them.

This course enables the drivers to show their skill in "navigating" through the more or less crowded main street of Nome as well as to give evidence of great speed on the unobstructed trail which stretches almost in a straight line to the turning point at the Bridge.

Over this course, and under the rules and auspices of the Nome Kennel Club, the Annual High School Race, for both girls and boys, and the Ladies' Race are held, as well as many impromptu contests that have no regular place in the winter schedule.

On December 31, 1915, the Fifth Amateur Boschen Cup Race created much interest because the almost impossible conditions attached to the winning of the Cup which had been put up by Lieutenant Boschen, U. S. A., made it seem practically unattainable. It was, however, "landed" permanently by Ernest driving Harry Riley's speedy Alaskans (of Scotch stag-hound and malamute strain), and in view of the fact that the day was very stormy and the trail exceedingly heavy, their time of 24 minutes 11 3-5 seconds was considered excellent.

The record for this run was made on January 22 by Fred Ayer in the phenominal time of 21 minutes, 39 seconds.

After the great races for the season are over, and just before the spring break-up when the rivers and creeks burst their icy bonds making travelling dangerous as well as uncomfortable, there is always a "joy race" to Council, via Solomon, a distance of 75 miles, the Kamoogan Handicap Burden Race. In this race a prospective driver, if not a dog owner, uses any team in Nome that he can annex legally; and carries as his Burden the fair lady of his choice. As may be readily imagined, the time of this event is of but little importance, while the excitement and amusement count for much. Perhaps its most delightful feature is the boundless hospitality accorded by the residents of both Solomon and Council to the contestants; just as, in the All Alaska Sweepstakes, the people in Candle and all along the line, prove their good will in every conceivable manner, and show themselves possessed of a spirit of courtesy to the men and kindness to the dogs that appeals to all true Alaskans.

NOME'S WINNING ENTRY IN THE RUBY DERBY OF 1916

While Nome was the first city in Alaska to organize a Kennel Club, and establish dog racing as a permanent feature of life in the far North, the enterprising town of Ruby on the Yukon has also, in the past few years developed a Kennel Club whose material, both men and dogs, compels attention and admiration.

Alaskan Sled Dog Tales

WINNERS OF THE SIXTH ALL ALASKA SWEEPSTAKES, 1913. BOWEN AND DELZENE, OWNERS; FAY DELZENE, DRIVER

THE DOG RACES OF NOME

So, when a most cordial invitation came from the Ruby Kennel Club to the Nome Kennel Club to enter a team in the great Annual Ruby Derby of 1916, Nome was proud indeed when the invitation was accepted by Leonard Seppala, the winner of the Sweepstakes of 1915; and all felt that no more worthy nor popular representative could have gone to give battle for the Ruby laurels.

To accept this invitation, it must be remembered, he had to drive his dogs about 450 miles over frozen sea and mountain passes, for enormous stretches on the glare ice of the Yukon, through mighty forests, and over trackless wastes of snow. But Leonard Seppala, a "hardy Norseman" of the finest type, modest and unassuming, but absolutely fearless, was a thorough trailsman; and to him this long and desolate journey of 450 miles seemed merely a desirable preparation for a contest in which he would be pitted against rivals of splendid attainments.

The course of the Ruby Derby, from Ruby to Long City, was over a trail that was both steep and rough, and the 1913 record of Joe Jean was thought to be unbreakable, but Seppala lowered it 8 minutes and 31 seconds, covering the 58 miles in 5 hours, 26 minutes and 18 seconds; and that, too, with four of the ablest mushers with four of the best teams on the Yukon contesting his victory.

Ruby, cordial in her invitation, had been the perfection of hospitality in the treatment of her honored guest; and now proved her claim to superlative sportsmanship when she tendered to him a veritable ovation after the race.

This good fellowship has established an "entente cordiale" between the Kennel Clubs of Ruby and Nome; and Nome is not more gratified with Seppala's victory than with Ruby's gracious attitude toward the Nome winner of the Ruby Derby.

ALL ALASKA SWEEPSTAKES RECORDS

First Annual All Alaska Sweepstakes, 1908

1. Paul Kjegstad, owner and driver.
2. Harry Lawton, owner and driver.
3. Charles Herron, owner; Tiepelman, driver.
4. Coutu, owner and driver.
5. Cavey, owner; Major Renny, driver.
6. Bob Adams, owner; Bob Griffis, driver.
7. Ben Derrick, owner and driver.
8. Morte Atkinson, owner; Percy Blatchford, driver.
9. J. Berger, owner; A. A. ("Scotty") Allan, driver.
10. Albert Fink, owner; John Hegness, driver.

Winners

First—Fink (Hegness driving). Time: 119 hours, 15 minutes, 12 seconds.

Second—Berger ("Scotty" Allan driving). Time: 120 hours, 7 minutes, 52 seconds.

Third—Atkinson (Blatchford driving). Time: 123 hours, 17 minutes, 57 seconds.

Alaskan Sled Dog Tales

WINNERS OF THE SEVENTH ALL ALASKA SWEEPSTAKES, 1914. JOHN JOHNSON, OWNER AND DRIVER

THE DOG RACES OF NOME

Second All Alaska Sweepstakes, 1909

1. J. Berger, owner; Blatchford, driver.
2. J. Berger, owner; "Scotty" Allan, driver.
3. Frank Waskey, owner; Coutu, driver.
4. Albert Fink, owner; Hegness, driver.
5. Brown and McCarty, owners; Bob Brown, driver.
6. Brown of Candle, owner; Brown, driver.
7. Cary and Derrick, owners; Cary, driver.
8. Lang, owner and driver.
9. Joe Crabtree, owner; Aleck Holmsen, driver.
10. W. A. Gilmore, owner; Peter Berg, driver.
11. Fox Ramsay, owner and driver.
12. The Syndicate, owner; "Sport" Smith, driver.
13. Goosak, owner; Thrustrup, driver.

Winners

First—J. Berger ("Scotty" Allan driving). Time: 82 hours, 2 minutes, 41 seconds.
Second—J. Berger (Blatchford driving). Time: 82 hours, 18 minutes, 42 seconds.
Third—Goosak (Thrustrup driving). Time: 89 hours, 46 minutes, 15 seconds.

Third All Alaska Sweepstakes, 1910

1. Colonel Charles Ramsay, owner; John Johnson, driver.
2. Colonel Weatherly Stuart, owner; Charles Johnson, driver.
3. Allan and Darling, owners; "Scotty" Allan, driver.
4. Solomon Syndicate, owners; Blatchford, driver.
5. M. J. McCarthy, owner; Bilby, driver.
6. Fox Ramsay, owner and driver.
7. Joe Crabtree, owner; Hegness, driver.

Winners

First—Colonel Ramsay (John Johnson driving). Time: 74 hours, 14 minutes, 37 seconds.
Second—Fox Ramsay (self driving). Time: 76 hours, 19 minutes, 22 seconds.
Third—Allan and Darling ("Scotty" Allan driving). Time: 76 hours, 33 minutes, 27 seconds.

Alaskan Sled Dog Tales

WINNERS OF THE EIGHTH ALL ALASKA SWEEPSTAKES, 1915. LEONARD SEPPALA, OWNER AND DRIVER

THE DOG RACES OF NOME

Fourth All Alaska Sweepstakes, 1911

1. Allan and Darling, owners; "Scotty" Allan, driver.
2. Johnson and Madsen, owners; John Johnson, driver.
3. Bowen and Delzene, owners; Delzene, driver.
4. Coke Hill, owner and driver.
5. Charles Johnson, owner and driver.
6. Captain Martin Crimmins, U. S. A., owner; E. O. Eastaugh, driver.

Winners

First—Allan and Darling ("Scotty" Allan driving). Time: 80 hours, 49 minutes, 41½ seconds.

Second—Coke Hill (self driving). Time: 82 hours, 10 minutes, 2½ seconds.

Third—Charles Johnson (self driving). Time: 82 hours, 54 minutes, 46 seconds.

Fifth All Alaska Sweepstakes, 1912

1. Charles Johnson, owner and driver.
2. Allan and Darling, owners; "Scotty" Allan, driver.
3. Alec Holmsen, owner and driver.
4. A. G. Oliver, owner; Blatchford, driver.

Winners

First—Allan and Darling ("Scotty" Allan driving). Time: 87 hours, 27 minutes, 46 2-5 seconds.

Second—Holmsen (self driving). Time: 87 hours, 58 minutes, 17 3-5 seconds.

Third—Charles Johnson (self driving). Time: 88 hours, 55 minutes, 38 2-5 seconds.

Alaskan Sled Dog Tales

WINNERS OF THE NINTH ALL ALASKA SWEEPSTAKES, 1916. LEONARD SEPPALA, OWNER AND DRIVER

THE DOG RACES OF NOME

Sixth All Alaska Sweepstakes, 1913

1. John Johnson, owner and driver.
2. Neuman and Johnson, owners; Illayok, driver.
3. Bowen and Delzene, owners; Delzene, driver.
4. Allan and Darling, owners; "Scotty" Allan, driver.

Winners

First—Bowen and Delzene (Delzenne driving). Time: 75 hours, 42 minutes, 27 seconds.

Second—John Johnson (self driving). Time: 77 hours, 18 minutes, 10 3-5 seconds.

Third—Allan and Darling ("Scotty" Allan driving). Time: 78 hours, 47 minutes, 34 seconds.

Seventh All Alaska Sweepstakes, 1914

1. John Johnson, owner and driver.
2. Fred M. Ayer, owner and driver.
3. Leonard Seppala, owner and driver.
4. Allan and Darling, owners; "Scotty" Allan, driver.

Winners

First—John Johnson (self driving). Time: 81 hours, 3 minutes, 45 seconds.

Second—Allan and Darling ("Scotty" Allan driving). Time: 90 hours, 26 minutes, 40 seconds.

Third—Fred Ayer (self driving). Time: 101 hours, 39 minutes, 20 seconds.

Alaskan Sled Dog Tales

THE FINISH OF THE WINNING TEAM IN THE ALL ALASKA SWEEPSTAKES OF 1916

THE DOG RACES OF NOME

Eighth All Alaska Sweepstakes, 1915

1. Dr. Kittilsen, owner; Holmsen, driver.
2. Council Kennel Club, owners; Murphy, driver.
3. Paul Kjegstad, owner and driver.
4. Allan and Darling, owners; "Scotty" Allan driver.
5. Leonard Seppala, owner and driver.

Winners

First—Seppala (self driving). Time: 78 hours, 44 minutes, 57 seconds.

Second—Allan and Darling ("Scotty" Allan driving). Time: 80 hours, 25 minutes, 55 seconds.

Third—Council Kennel Club (Murphy driving). Time: 85 hours, 43 minutes, 49 seconds.

Ninth All Alaska Sweepstakes, 1916

1. F. M. Ayer, owner and driver.
2. Leonard Seppala, owner and driver.
3. Bobby Brown, owner and driver.
4. Bowen and Delzene, owners; Delzene, driver.
5. Paul Kjegstad, owner and driver.

Winners

First—Seppala (self driving). Time: 80 hours, 38 minutes, 3 seconds.

Second—Bowen and Delzene (Delzene driving). Time: 82 hours, 14 minutes, 55 seconds.

Third—Ayer (self driving). Time: 84 hours, 21 minutes, 4 seconds.

Alaskan Sled Dog Tales

BOARD OF TRADE BULLETIN FOR THE ALL ALASKA SWEEPSTAKES OF 1913

These Bulletins are carefully kept during each race, and record all of the changes of position of the various teams from hour to hour during the entire run of 408 miles, the returns being telephoned from the camps along the route.

THE DOG RACES OF NOME

RULES GOVERNING ENTRIES

(From Article 3, Rules and Regulations of the Nome Kennel Club)

Rule 1. The race will be started at.........o'clock, April............, on Front Street opposite Barracks Square, Nome Alaska; but the Judges may, by unanimous consent, on account of stormy weather, postpone the race until a later date.

Rule 2. The route will be from Nome to Safety; thence to Dixon; thence to Topkuk Hill; thence over or around Topkuk Hill; thence to Timber Road House; thence to Council; thence over the head of Melsing Creek to Boston Creek, across the Fish River Valley to Telephone Creek, over the divide to Death Valley; thence across Death Valley to Camp Haven; thence to First Chance; thence over the divide into Gold Run; thence to Candle, and from Candle to Nome over the same route.

Rule 3. Teams will start one minute apart, the first team leaving at............o'clock, and the time of each team starting be reckoned as at............o'clock.

Rule 4. Each team must take all of the dogs with which it started to Candle and return with the same dogs, and none others, to the starting point in Nome.

Rule 5. The team accomplishing this in the least time will be declared the winner of the race, and the team accomplishing this in the second best time will be declared second, and the team accomplishing this in the third best time will be declared third.

Rule 6. When any team in the race meets another, the right of way shall belong to the homeward bound team, and it shall be the duty of the person driving the out-going team to get out of the way of the homeward-bound team and assist it in passing.

Rule 7. When one team shall overtake another team going in the same direction, the team behind shall have the right of way, and it shall be the duty of the driver in front to pull out of the trail and assist the driver of the team behind in passing; and in the event that one team shall pass another, and the team behind shall hang on to the team in front for half an hour, then the team behind shall have the right of way, and upon demand of the driver behind, the team ahead shall pull out of the trail and assist the team behind in passing; except that this rule shall not apply on the homeward stretch from Fort Davis to Nome.

Rule 8. Each team shall have the choice of its own sled, subject only to the condition that some kind of a sled must be drawn; and at the option of the drivers, sleds may be changed during the race.

Rule 9. At all Road-houses and public stopping places along the route, the first team arriving shall have the choice of public stable room, and any interference by any parties afterward arriving, is strictly prohibited.

Rule 10. During the race each team and its driver shall have all of the assistance he desires, subject, however, to the following limitations:

First—During the race no team shall be allowed at any time in any manner to use any other dogs than those started with.

Second—Pacing in any and all of its forms is strictly prohibited; nor shall any team connected in any way with any team in the race, follow any racing team until all of the racing teams shall have passed the next telephone station; nor shall any such team precede any racing

Alaskan Sled Dog Tales

FRED AYER AND HIS DERBY RECORD BREAKERS, 1916

THE DOG RACES OF NOME

team on the trail by a less distance than one telephone station; and said team or teams shall at all times be subject to the directions of the judges of the race.

Third—No team shall be allowed to secure any other team to haul any of its dogs or its driver.

Fourth—No team shall have any person other than the driver take hold of the sled while the team is in motion, which interference is in the driver's power to prevent.

Fifth—No teams shall have any person or persons to instruct the driver while his team is actually traveling.

Rule 11. The cruel and inhuman treatment of dogs by any driver is strictly prohibited under penalty of losing the race and forfeiture of the owner's team.

Rule 12. Every person entering or driving a team in the race will be required to conduct himself in a perfectly fair and honorable manner, under penalty of forfeiture of the prize and his dog team, and expulsion from the Club.

Rule 13. In awarding the cup and prize money, these rules shall be interpreted by the judges according to their spirit; it being understood that the race is to be awarded on merit, and not on technicality.

Rule 14. The driver of any team quitting the race shall report the same to the judges in Nome before he makes any movement toward returning to the starting point; and thereafter his movements shall be subject to the direction of the judges.

Rule 15. The race shall not be decided by the judges until all of the teams starting in said race have returned to Nome, or the owners thereof waive the right of protest in writing; and in no event shall such decision be rendered until twenty-four hours after three teams shall have finished the course.

Rule 16. In the event of a driver of a team in the race being behind and away from his sled and team at the finish of the race, the finishing time of such team shall be the time the driver crosses the tape.

Rule 18. In consideration of the premises and the mutual promises herein contained, each party agrees with the Nome Kennel Club to abide by the rules of the race as herein set forth, otherwise to forfeit his team to the Nome Kennel Club; and for such purpose agrees to make, or cause to be made, a bill of sale covering his team if so demanded by the Judges of the race, and as evidence of such agreement hereto sets his hand and seal.

Dated at Nome, Alaska, this.......... day of April, 19......

Alaskan Sled Dog Tales

A TROPHY CUP OF THE ALL ALASKA SWEEPSTAKES

"SCOTTY" ALLAN, THE VETERAN OF ALASKA DOG RACING, who has been in eight of the All Alaska Sweepstakes, and never "out of the money," having finished three times first, three times second, and twice third. Allan was selected by the Great Explorer Stefansson to buy the dogs for his Canadian-Arctic Expedition, and by the French Government to select dogs for use in winter warfare in the Vosges Mountains. "Scotty's" famous leader "Baldy of Nome."

JOHN JOHNSON, THE "IRON MAN," whose incredible endurance made the record for the All Alaska Sweepstakes in the race of 1910, in which he covered the 408 miles to Candle and return, in 74 hours, 14 minutes, 37 seconds. He was also the winner of the great race of 1914. To the left is his noted "Blue-eyed leader," Kolma, whose tireless pace was a marvel to the dog-loving North.

LEONARD SEPPALA, THE "HARDY NORSEMAN," whose splendid achievement, as winner of the All Alaska Sweepstakes of 1915 and 1916, was augmented by his victory in the Ruby Derby of 1916. His three most celebrated leaders.

Alaskan Sled Dog Tales

THE DOG RACES OF NOME

THE PRIDE OF NOME

Do you know our North, with its wintry wastes,
Its mountain heights and its frozen sea—
A lifeless land in a shroud of snow,
Where the Arctic winds blow wild and free?

Do you know the men of this Northern land—
The men, who whether in toil or play,
Will reach their goal, though the task be hard;
Who will face the danger and find the way?

Do you know our dogs—the dog of the North—
A beast of burden, a faithful friend;
Wolf-like in wisdom, human in love,
Patient in service, fierce to defend?

Have you traveled the trail, in this lone bleak land
The trail that is endless, silent, white;
That dazzles at noontide, or faintly shows
A ghostly path in the Northern Light?

Well, that is Alaska's Sweepstakes course—
Four hundred and eight long miles the run;
Do you wonder the fame of this Race has spread
To the Southern Cross from the Midnight Sun?

Do you wonder our April Racing days
Are the gala days of Nome's whole year;
With school, and business and work forgot,
And crowds that gather from far and near?

Is it strange—our pride—in these Trailsmen true,
When the Racers are safe once more at home?
Our pride is just; for the whole world's Best,
In Dogs and Drivers, you'll find in Nome.

Alaskan Sled Dog Tales

Alaska Nellie, by Nellie Neal Lawing.
Published in 1940 by Seattle Printing & Publishing Company. Seattle, WA.

Alaskan Sled Dog Tales

~ Bibliography and References ~

It's difficult to include every book, news article, interview, or other source of information and inspiration about Alaskan sled dogs, but I have tried to include as many of the resources I found helpful as possible, for those who may want to know more, or continue the research. My apologies to any who were quoted in this book but inadvertently missed in this listing. I've also included publications which may be long out of print, but with the title and author the reader may be successful in tracking down copies or additional information through the internet or a library system.

~ Books and Publications ~

Allan, Allan Alexander. *Gold, Men and Dogs.* New York: G.P. Putnam Sons, 1931.

Anderson, Eva Greenslit. *Dog-Team Doctor, The Story of Dr. Romig.* Caldwell, Idaho: Caxton Printers, 1940

Bleakley, Geoffrey. *Selected Residents and Visitors to the Wrangell-St. Elias Mountain Region, 1796-1950.* Last updated 2006.

Bundy, Hallock C. *The Valdez-Fairbanks Trail: The Story of a Great Highway.* (1st Annual). Seattle: Alaska Publishing Co., 1910.

Caldwell, Frank. *Wolf the Storm Leader, A Story of Alaskan Mail Trails.* Dodd Mead & Co., New York, 1910.

Clark, M. *Roadhouse Tales, or Nome in 1900.* Girard, Kansas: Appeal Publishing Company. 1902.

Coppinger, Lorna. *The World of Sled Dogs: From Siberia to Sport Racing.* New York: Howell Book House, 1977.

Darling, Esther Birdsall. *Baldy of Nome, An Immortal of the Trail.* A.M. Robertson Publishing, 1913.

Alaskan Sled Dog Tales

Darling, Esther Birdsall. *The Great Dog Races of Nome*. Nome Kennel Club, 1916.

Dean, Charles L. *Soldiers and Sled Dogs: A History of Military Dog Mushing*. Lincoln, NE: University of Nebraska Press, 2005.

Gallaher, Aileen and Samme. *Sisters, Coming of Age and Living Dangerously in the Wild Copper River Valley*. Seattle: Epicenter Press, 2004.

Goodwin, Colonel Walter L. *Official Iditarod Trail Survey and Recording Report to the Alaska Road Commission*, April 16, 1908.

Greiner, Mary. *Mary Joyce, Taku to Fairbanks: 1,000 Miles by Dogteam*. Bloomington, IN: AuthorHouse, 2007.

Hegener, Helen. *Alaskan Roadhouses*. Wasilla, Alaska: Northern Light Media, 2015.

Hegener, Helen. *Along Alaskan Trails: Adventures in Sled Dog History*. Northern Light Media, 2010.

Hegener, Helen. *The All Alaska Sweepstakes*. Wasilla, Alaska: Northern Light Media, 2012.

Hegener, Helen. *The First Iditarod: Mushers' Tales from the 1973 Race*. Northern Light Media, 2015.

Hegener, Helen. *The Yukon Quest Trail*. Northern Light Media, 2014.

Hubbard, Bernard R., S.J. *Mush, You Malemutes!* New York: The American Press, 1932.

Lawing, Nellie Neal. *Alaska Nellie*. Seattle Printing and Publishing Co. 1940.

Lemish, Michael G. *War Dogs: A History of Loyalty and Heroism*. Silver Spring, Maryland: Potomac Books, 1999.

Lynch, Alice J. *A Preliminary Inventory of Cultural Resources of Iditarod Trail between Rainy Pass and Unalakleet*. Anchorage, Ak: Bureau of Land Management, 1979.

Alaskan Sled Dog Tales

Marsh, Kenneth L. *The Trail: The Story of the Historic Valdez-Fairbanks Trail that Opened Alaska's Vast Interior*. Trapper Creek, AK: Sluice Box Productions, 2008.

Marston, Marvin R. "Muktuk." *Men of the Tundra, Alaska Eskimos at War*. New York: October House Inc., 1972.

Mitchell, Brigadier General William. *Billy Mitchell in Alaska*. An article in *American Heritage* magazine, February, 1961.

Morenus, Richard. *Alaska Sourdough, the Story of Slim Williams*. Rand McNalley Co. 1956.

Murie, Margaret. *Two in the Far North*. New York: Knopf, 1962.

Orth, Donald J. *Dictionary of Alaska Place Names*. Washington D.C.: U.S. Government Printing Office, 1967.

Patty, Ernest. *North Country Challenge*. New York: David McKay Co., Inc., 1969.

Pearson, Grant. *My Life of High Adventure*. New Jersey: Prentice-Hall, 1962.

Ricker, Elizabeth M. *Seppala, Alaskan Dog Driver*. Boston: Little, Brown Co. 1930.

Salisbury, Gay; Laney Salisbury. *The Cruelest Miles: The Heroic Story of Dogs and Men in a Race against an Epidemic*. New York: W.W. Norton & Company, 2003.

Schneider, William S. *On Time Delivery, The Dog Team Mail Carriers*. Fairbanks: University of Alaska Press. 2012.

Walden, Arthur Treadwell. *A Dog-Puncher on the Yukon*. Boston, MA: Houghton Mifflin Co., 1928.

Stuck, Hudson. *Ten Thousand Miles with a Dog Sled*. New York: Charles Scribner's Sons. 1914.

Stuck, Hudson. *The Ascent of Denali, The 1913 Expedition that First Conquered Mt. McKinley*. New York: Charles Scribner's Sons. 1918.

Alaskan Sled Dog Tales

United States War Department. *Dog Team Transportation Basic Field Manual.* Washington: United States Government Printing Office, 1941.

University of Alaska Fairbanks. *Anthropological Papers of the University of Alaska.* Vol. 13, No. 1, Winter, 1965.

Walker, Tom. *Kantishna: Mushers, Miners, Mountaineers - The Pioneer Story Behind Mount McKinley National Park.* MT: Pictorial Histories Publishing Co. 2006.

Walker, Tom. *McKinley Station: People of the Pioneer Park that Became Denali.* Missoula, Montana: Pictorial Histories Books, 2009.

Walker, Tom. *The Seventymile Kid: The Lost Legacy of Harry Karstens and the First Ascent of Mount McKinley.* Seattle, WA: Mountaineers Books, 2013.

Waid, Jack. 354th Fighter Wing Historian at Eilson Air Force Base, Alaska. Two articles, March, 2014: *Alaskan War Dogs: Not Forgotten* and *Heroism Defined.*

Webb, Melody. *Yukon: The Last Frontier.* Vancouver, British Columbia, Canada. UBC Press, 1993.

Wickersham, Hon James, *Old Yukon: Tales-Trails-Trials.* St. Paul, Minnesota: West Publishing Co., 1938.

Willoughby, Barrett. *The Trail Eater: A romance of Alaska and a famous dog race.* New York, NY: G.P. Putnam Sons. 1929.

Willoughby, Florance. Article in *Sunset Magazine*, February, 1921: *Scotty Allan, The King of the Arctic Trail.*

Wirt, Loyal. *Alaskan Adventures: A Tale of Our Last Frontier, and of 'Whiskers', Gallant Leader of the First Dog Team to Cross Alaska.* New York: Revell. 1937.

Young, Egerton Ryerson. *My Dogs In The Northland.* NY: F.H. Revell Co., 1902.

Young, S. Hall. *Adventures in Alaska.* New York: Fleming H. Revell Company. 1919.

Alaskan Sled Dog Tales

~ PHOTOGRAPH SOURCES AND COLLECTIONS ~

Alaska's Digital Archives
http://vilda.alaska.edu/
Alaska's Digital Archives presents a wealth of historical photographs, albums, oral histories, moving images, maps, documents, physical objects, and other materials from libraries, museums and archives throughout our state.

Alaska State Library
http://library.alaska.gov/
Search for books, music, movies and more! Over 1 million items in libraries throughout southcentral and southeast Alaska.

Atlantic Richfield Co. Photograph Collection 1904-1910
http://library.alaska.gov/hist/hist_docs/finding_aids/PCA199.doc
Includes 49 views selected and copied from two albums owned by the Atlantic Richfield Co. Photographers include Albert J. Johnson, George G. Cantwell, P. S. Hunt, and Clarence Leroy Andrews.

Carpenter, Frank G., Photograph Collection
Library of Congress, Washington, D.C.
http://www.loc.gov/pictures/item/2003653070/
About the photographer: Frank George Carpenter (Mansfield, Ohio, May 8, 1855, – Nanking, June 18, 1924) was an author, photographer, lecturer, collector of photographs. With his daughter Frances, Carpenter photographed Alaska between 1910 and 1924. Frank Carpenter died in 1924 in Nanking, China, during his third trip around the world. A collection of over 5,000 images were donated to the Library of Congress by Frances at her death in 1972. The collection at the Library of Congress totals approximately 16,800 photographs and about 7,000 negatives.

Carrie McLain Museum, Nome
http://www.nomealaska.org/department/index.php?structureid=12
The Carrie M. McLain Memorial Museum is dedicated to collecting, preserving & showcasing the Nome Gold Rush, Bering Strait Eskimo, aviation as well as contemporary history & culture associated with Nome, Alaska & the Bering Strait region of Western Alaska.

Alaskan Sled Dog Tales

Circle Mining District and Historical Museum, Central
http://steesehighway.org/steesehistory.html
 Online photograph album for the historically important gold mining areas of Central and Circle. Several mushing and dog team mail photos.

Cook Inlet Historical Society
http://www.cookinlethistory.org
 Established in 1955, the Cook Inlet Historical Society is a private non-profit historical society focused on the Anchorage area.

Hope and Sunrise Historical Society
http://www.hopeandsunrisehistoricalsociety.org
 The Hope and Sunrise Historical Society is dedicated to preserving photographs, documents, and artifacts related to the gold rush communities of Hope and Sunrise, Alaska. The first claim was staked on Resurrection Creek in 1893.

Kenai Mountains-Turnagain Arm (KMTA) National Heritage Area
http://www.kmtacorridor.org
 The designation of Alaska's Kenai Mountains-Turnagain Arm as a National Heritage Area recognizes the compelling history and culture of an area that cradles some of the most influential crossroads of Alaska's history.

Library of Congress, Washington, D.C.
https://www.loc.gov/
 The Library of Congress is the nation's first established cultural institution and the largest library in the world. A notable resource used in this book is the Frank and Frances Carpenter Collection of Photographs: http://www.loc.gov/pictures/collection/ffcarp/

National Archives, Washington, D.C.
http://www.archives.gov/
 The National Archives is the U.S. Government's collection of documents that records important events in American history.

National Park Service - Alaska
https://www.nps.gov/state/ak/index.htm
 A state page on the National Park System website with links to the National Parks, Preserves, Historic Landmarks, Heritage Sites, Natural Landmarks, and public lands in Alaska. Many include local histories and notable people.

Alaskan Sled Dog Tales

Seward Community Library and Museum
http://www.cityofseward.us/index.aspx?nid=379
The Seward Community Library & Museum is a combined public library, museum, archives and community center.

Smithsonian Institution/National Postal Museum 1898 Gold Rush Exhibit
http://postalmuseum.si.edu/gold/index.html
The National Postal Museum celebrated the 1998 Klondike/Alaskan gold rush centennial with an exhibit that explored the last great gold rush of the 19th century and the unforgettable role of the mail carriers who provided contact between those so far from home and the families they left behind. Although the exhibit is no longer on view in the museum, it continues in an online format.

University of Alaska-Fairbanks Elmer E. Rasmuson Library
Alaska and Polar Regions, PO Box 756808, Fairbanks, AK 99775-6811
http://library.uaf.edu/apr
The Alaska and Polar Regions Collections & Archives (APRCA) holds exceptional resources for the study of Alaska's history, politics, and culture, as well as significant international Polar research materials.

University of Washington Special Collections Division
Alaska, Western Canada and United States Collection.
http://digitalcollections.lib.washington.edu/cdm/specialcollections

Wasilla Knik Historical Society
http://www.wkhsociety.org/
The Wasilla Knik Historical Society is a non-profit association that maintains the historic building housing the Knik Museum, and collects, preserves and interprets the history of the Knik settlement from the late 1900s - 1918 and Alaska Natives in the area, including recognition of the Alaska Native settlement as an integral part of the Knik settlement.

Alaskan Sled Dog Tales

INDEX

~ A ~

A Dog-Puncher on the Yukon 211
Adolphus, "Cap" 277
Adventure 131
Adventures in Alaska 62, 86, 179
Alaska Central Railway 55
Alaska Commercial Company 34, 183
Alaska Days with John Muir 58
Alaska Dispatch 14
Alaska Engineering Commission 148
Alaska Highway 15, 77, 184-189
Alaska Legislature 20
Alaska Magazine 14
Alaska Moving Picture Corporation 250-257
Alaska Nellie 146-157, 300
Alaska Nellie 146-157
Alaska Peninsula 83
Alaska Railroad 107, 146-157, 250-257, 268
Alaska Road Commission 6-11, 55, 185, 263
Alaska Sourdough: The Story of Slim Williams 187, 188
Alaska Sportsman, The 130, 132, 133
Alaska Steamship Co. 79, 85
Alaska Territorial Guard 236, 237
Alaska Territorial Legislature 200
Alaska Trail Dogs 14, 19
Alaska's Silver Millions 82
Alaska's Wolf Man 259
Alaska, maps of 6-11
Alaska-Yukon-Pacific Exposition 244-249
Alcan Highway 78
Aleutian Islands 124, 127
All Alaska Sweepstakes 14, 40, 45, 89, 96-105, 115, 117, 126, 127, 137, 143, 159, 190-195, 230, 278-299
Allakaket 221
Allan and Darling Kennels 99, 100, 200, 230, 289, 290
Allan, A. A. "Scotty" 15, 18, 20, 97-105, 117, 119, 127, 159, 196-209, 230, 231, 233, 280, 283, 285, 287, 289, 290, 298
Along Alaskan Trails 14
American Boy 132
American Kennel Club 162
Anchorage 18, 255
Anchorage Daily Times 13
Andersen, Karsten 140
Anderson, Eva Greenslit 94-95
Aniakchak 81, 83, 84
Antisarlook, Mary 125
Anvik Mission 107, 120, 124
Appetite and Attitude (DVD) 14
Archdeacon of the Yukon 218-225
Arctic City film set 248
Arctic coast 238-243
Arctic National Wilfelife Refuge 241
Arctic Ocean 199, 239
Athabaskan U.S. mail carriers 41
Attla, George 13
Atwater, Ben 71, 110, 112
author's preface 12
Ayer, Fred 127, 297

~ B ~

Baird, John 170, 172
Baldy of Nome 15, 16, 18, 20, 87, 99, 100, 127, 196-209, 231, 232, 280, 281
Baldy of Nome 197, 280
Baleena 164, 169

Alaskan Sled Dog Tales

Balto 139, 158-163
Balto statue 127
Barnette, E.T. 165, 173
Barrow 22, 165, 281
Bartlett Glacier 255
Beach, Rex 252
Beaton, John 55
Beautiful Joe 16
Berger, Jake 204
Bering Sea 44, 45, 110, 111, 197
Bering Sea ice 41
Bering Sea villages 123
Bering Strait 247
Berry Roadhouse 68
Bettles 221
Biederman's Camp 275
Biederman, Ed 274-277
Big Creek 67
Big Red 16
Bishop Mountain 41
Bishop Rowe 33
Black Rapids Roadhouse 259
Bluff 41
Bluff Roadhouse 41
Bonanza Roadhouse 66
Bone, Governor 40-45
Boris, Granson of Baldy 280
Boys' Life 130
Brady, Bill 191, 195
Breeze, William 61-75
Broad Pass 255
Brooks Range 239, 240
Brower, Charlie 165
Brown, Gus 48
Buckner, General Simon Bolivar 157
Butcher, Susan 111
Byrd Antarctic Expedition 211-215
Byrd, Admiral Richard E. 90, 200

~ C ~

Caldwell, Elsie Noble 14, 19
Caldwell, Fenton 46-52
Caldwell, Frank and Brownie 46-52
Calhoun, Alice 157
Call of the Wild, The 16, 17, 51, 85, 195, 252
Canadian Arctic Expedition 140-145
Candle 96-105, 190-195, 283
Canning River 238, 241
Canyon City 107
Caribou Bill 244-249
Caribou Bill's Arctic City 248
Carsh 34
Cavanaugh, U.S. Marshal 154
Central Park statue 163
Chandalar River 168
Charley River Indian Roadhouse 31
Charley, Chief 31
Chatanika River 223
Cheechakos, The 250-259
Cheenik Post Office 136
Cheenik Village 45
Chena 222
Chicago World's Fair 1933 186, 189
Childs Glacier 256
Chilkoot Pass 61, 255, 256
Chinook 210-217
Chitina 183
Circle City 33, 37, 46, 108, 211, 212, 221, 272, 274-277
Circle Hot Springs 275
Cleary Creek 223
Clum, John P. 107
Coal Creek Roadhouse 31
Col. Walter L. Goodwin 54-57
Coldfoot 221
Cole, Comer 106

309

Alaskan Sled Dog Tales

Cole, Dermot 174
Collman, Henry 146-157
Conquering the Arctic Ice 240, 241
Cook's Inlet 72
Coolidge, President Calvin 256
Cooper, William F. 244-249
Copper Basin 300 14
Copper Center 185
Copper River 256
Copper River Railroad 183
Coppinger, Lorna 14, 115, 215, 230
Cordova 61, 64, 256, 259
Corwin, S.S. 25
Council 135, 283
Country Gentleman 130
Crane, Al 100
Croix de Guerre 227, 233, 280
Crosson, Joe 281
Crouch, Ed 26, 30
Crow Creek Pass 55, 73
Cruelest Miles, The 19, 38-45, 119, 135, 137
Crumrine, Josephine 79, 85
Curry 157
Curry, Gladys 102
cyclometer 54, 55

~ D ~

Dalzell Gorge 56
Dalzene, Fay 102, 103
Darling, Esther Birdsall 87, 98, 99, 100, 127, 197, 200, 233, 278-299
Dawson City 12, 34, 37, 46-48, 61, 108, 112, 165-168, 170-171, 186, 189
Dead Horse Roadhouse 157
Dean, Charles L. 234
DeArmond, Robert 62
Deathlock, The 195

Delta River 263
Delzene, Fay 291
Denali 69, 219, 246, 251, 256, 264
Denali National Park 264
DeWolfe, Percy 112
Dexter's Roadhouse 41, 134-139
Dexter, John 134-139
Dickson 283
Dikeman, William A. 55
diphtheria epidemic 38-45, 114, 115, 119, 127, 158-163
Dishakaket 56, 182
dog breeds 108
dog stable 32
Dog Team Doctor 94-95
dog team mail delivery 106-113, 115
Dog Team Transportation field manual 236
dogs in the military 200
Downing, Ben 12, 31, 108, 113, 272
Dr. Curtis Welch 38-45
Dubby 198, 206
Dyea Trail 21

~ E ~

Eagle 27, 30, 37, 61, 107, 108, 112, 113, 222, 226, 229, 230, 273, 274, 274-277
Eagle River 12, 13, 55
Eaton Reindeer Station 124
Egypt Mountain 69
Emiu 140-145
epidemic 38-45, 114, 115, 119, 127, 158-163
Esias 220
Eskimo Roadhouse 41
Eskimo Scouts 236, 237

Alaskan Sled Dog Tales

~ F ~

Fairbanks 15, 22, 24, 54, 75, 76, 126, 183, 221, 259
Fairbanks gold strike 165-168
filmmakers, 248, 250-257
Fink, Albert 285, 286
First Iditarod, The 54
Fish Lake 41
Flat City 66
Flaxman Island 238-243
Fort Egbert 226, 228, 229, 230
Fort Gibbon 18, 272
Fort Hamin 34, 36
Fort Richardson 12
Fort Yukon 34, 107, 221, 225
Fourth of July Creek 37
freighting with dogs 212, 222, 270
French Joe 69
French John 258-263
Fritz 158-163
Fur-Fish-Game 133

~ G ~

Galena 41
Gambell 110, 111
Gane Creek 56
gee-pole 30, 34, 65, 222
Girdwood 255
Glacier 74
Glacier Creek 55
Glacier Priest 80-85
Glennallen 15
gold bullion 154
gold nugget necklace 154
gold rushes 114-117
gold shipment from Iditarod 183
gold strike at Iditarod 54-57, 114, 169, 178-183
gold strike in Fairbanks 165-168, 170-171
gold strike in Tanana 165-168, 170-171
Gold, Men and Dogs 97, 119, 199
Golovin 41, 134-139
Golovnin Bay 135, 139
Golovnin, Mikhailovich 135
Goodwin, Col. Walter L. 54-57
Governor Bone 40-45
Grandview Roadhouse 148-157
Great Dog Races of Nome, The 98, 197, 203, 278-299
Great Race of Mercy 38-45, 159
Green, Dr. and Mrs. 68
Greiner, Mary Anne 78
Grenfell, Dr. Wilfred 121
Griffiths, Bob 154
Guggenheim Trust 28

~ H ~

Haas, Lt. Rene 230-233, 286
Haley, Jack 154
Half-way Roadhouse 33
Hall Young of Alaska 62
Happy River 56, 70
Happy River roadhouse 71
Harding, President Warren 254
Harper, Walter 220, 223
Healy, Captain Michael A. 123, 124
Hegness, John 101, 199, 286
Heim, Patricia A. 154
Hell's Acres 146-157
Henderson, Joe 239-243
Herschel Island 141, 239
Holy Cross 83
Hoover, President Herbert 186

311

Alaskan Sled Dog Tales

Hubbard, Father Bernard R. 80-85
Hudson's Bay Company 198
Hunter Trader Trapper 130, 131, 133
Hunting and Fishing 131

~ I ~

ice, Bering Sea 41
Iditarod 14, 56, 66, 117, 222
Iditarod gold discovery 54-57, 114, 169
Iditarod gold shipment 183
Iditarod Historic Trail Alliance 144
Iditarod River 55, 56, 181
Iditarod Trail 15, 18, 38-45, 51, 54-57, 58-75, 108, 112, 117, 124, 135-139, 144, 145, 146-157, 172, 174, 178-183
Iditarod Trail distances table 57
Iditarod Trail Sled Dog Race 100, 113
Iditarod Trail, blazing 172, 174
Iditarod Trail, scouting 1908 54-57
Iditarod, town of 56
Innoko River 181
Inouye, Ronald 173
Irwin, U.S. Marshal 154
Isaac's Point 41, 43, 138

~ J ~

J.P. Morgan 28
Jackson, Frank 55
Jackson, Sheldon 118-127
Japanese musher 15, 117, 145, 164-177
Jesson, Ed 30
Joe Redington, Champion/Alaska Huskies 227
Johnny 220
Johnson's Roadhouse 33
Johnson, Erick 152
Johnson, G.H. 98

Johnson, John "Iron Man" 101, 102, 103, 145, 190-195, 288, 292, 298
Jonrowe, Dee Dee 112
Joyce, Mary 15, 76-79
Juneau 20, 46, 76

~ K ~

Kaasen, Gunnar 127, 139, 160, 162
Kaiyuk Slough 56
Kallands 41
Kaltag 41, 56, 120, 124
Kaltag Portage 38-45
Kandik River 274
Karluk 142
Karstens, Harry 219, 220, 250-259, 264
Katma 82
Katmai 83, 85
Keaton, Buster 252
Kenai Lake 157
Kenai peninsula 74
Ketchikan 46
Keystone Canyon 15, 268
King, Jeff 103, 104
Kinney, R.J. 55
Kjellmann, William 124
Klondike Clan, The 62
Klondike Gold Rush 55, 61, 126, 180, 181, 211, 250-257, 198
Knik 56, 72, 178-183
Knik Arm 56, 72, 73
Kokrines 41
Kolyma 15, 190-195, 298
Koonce, Egbert 65
Kotzebue 124
Kotzebue Sound 221
Koyukuk, post office 107
Koyukuk River 221
Kuskokwim 170, 172

Alaskan Sled Dog Tales

Kuskokwim gold strike 182, 183
Kuskokwim River 56, 69
Kuskokwim Valley 62, 64, 68
Kuskokwim, South Fork 69

~ L ~

Lassie Come Home 16
Last Frontier Magazine 14
Lathrop, Austin E. "Cap" 250-257
Laurence, Sydney 256, 257
Lawing, Bill 157
Lawing, Nellie Neal 146-157
Lawrence, Jack 229
Leffingwell, Ernest de Koven 238-243
Lemish, Michael G. 236
Little McKinley 135, 139
Lombard, Doc 13
Lomen, Carl J. 125
London, Jack 16, 17, 51, 85, 195, 252
Longstreet, Hattie 87
Luck of the Trail 280

~ M ~

MacDonald, Donald 185
MacKenzie River Husky 64, 198, 229
Mackey, Dick 14
Mackey, Lance 14, 103, 104
magazine covers 128-133
Mageik 80-85
mail carrier rescue 146-157
mail carriers 12, 13, 16, 18, 24, 34, 36, 46-52, 106-113, 115, 208, 212, 229, 272, 273, 274-277
mail delivery, dog team 106-113
mail teams, description of dogs 108
mail, weight 109
malamute dog team 22
Malamute Man, Memiors of an Arctic Traveler 239, 242
Malamute Saloon 47
Malemute Kid 145, 254, 255
Malstrom, Harold 182
Mangelsdorf, Katie 227
Manley Hot Springs 41
Manley Roadhouse 41
Manley, Frank 182
maps 6-11
Marsh, Ken 263
Marston, Marvin R. "Muktuk" 236, 237
Mary Joyce, Taku to Fairbanks 77
McCallum Creek 263
McCallum's Roadhouse 263
McGrath 56, 113
McGrath Mail Trail Race 113
McGrath's 56, 113
McGuire, Lillian Nakamura 174
McIlhenny, Edward Avery 170
McKinley Mountains 68
McKinley Station 254, 255
McKinley, President 27, 61
McKinney, Debra 251
Medicine Lake 275
Men of the Tundra, Alaska Eskimos at War 237
Menzie, R.D. 183
Mikkelsen, Einar 239, 240, 243
military sled dogs 200, 226-237
Miller's Camp 276
Minto roadhouse 41
mirages 33
Missouri Kid 244-249
Mitchell, Lt. Billy 226, 228, 229, 230
Mogg, Sammy 237

Alaskan Sled Dog Tales

Montauk Roadhouse 31, 37
Moomaw, Lewis H. 250-257
Moon Craters of Alaska, The 84
Moore Creek Roadhouse 67
Morenus, Richard 187, 188
Morino, Maurice 253, 254
Mount Egypt 69
Mount Foraker 69
Mount McKinley 69, 219, 246, 251, 256, 264
Mount McKinley National Park 251, 264
Muir, John 58-61, 179
Murie, Margaret 258-263
Murray, Alexander 275
Mush, You Malamutes! 80-85
Mushing Magazine 14
Mushing Parson, The 58-75, 86

~ N ~

Nation River 37
Nation River Roadhouse 31, 276
National Geographic 84
National Historic Landmark 240
National Postal Museum 276
Natkusiak 140
Navarre 100
Navarre of the North 280, 281
Nenana 38-45, 83, 221
New England Sled Dog Club 89
news reporting 114-117
Nine Mile Cabin 41
No Boundary Line 280
Noice, Harold 142
Nome 15, 25, 37, 38-45, 46-52, 54-56, 61, 96-105, 107, 108, 115, 119, 124, 126, 136, 139, 143, 159, 182, 190-209, 221, 244, 247, 270, 278-299
Nome gold rush 198

Nome Kennel Club 96-105, 126, 192, 199, 278-299
Nome Nugget 114
Nome Sweepstakes Association 245
Nome-Seward Wagon Road 182
Noongwook, Chester 110, 111
Noongwook, Nathan 110, 111
North Slope 238-243
Northern Commercial Company 24, 274
Northern Light Media 14
Northern Lights 300 14
Norton Bay 43
Norton Sound 38-45, 135, 137
Norton, Captain Ulysses Grant 145
Norwood, Captain H.H. 164
Nulato 40-45, 41, 83, 113
Nunivak 37

~ O ~

Ode to Mushing 86
Old Knik 55, 56, 73
Old Times on Upper Cook's Inlet 179
Old Woman Shelter 41
Old Yeller 16
Old Yukon, Tails, Trails, Trials 3, 26-37
Oldfield, Jim 36
Olson Roadhouse 41
Olson, Charlie 139
Olson, John 182
Olson, Sam 276
Olympics, Winter 1932 88-93
Ophir Creek 56
Orphans of the North 78
Outdoor Life 131
overflow 30, 223, 224
Overland Mail Trail 56

Alaskan Sled Dog Tales

~ P ~

Parson's Roahouse 183
Pass Creek 56
patch, Nome Kennel Club 102
Pedro, Felix 167-168, 170-171
Percy DeWolfe Memorial Mail Race 112
Peters, Emmitt 13
Phelan Creek 263
Pioneer Roadhouse 178
Point Barrow 239
Pointer 229
polar bear hunt 269
Pollard, Doc 106
Ponto's Road House 22
Port Safety Roadhouse 41
Portage 257
Post, Wiley 22, 281
postcards 12, 15, 264-273
Potter, Louise 179
preface 12
Prudhoe Bay oilfields 238-242
Pulham, Geo. E. 55
Pyle, Ernie 277
Pyramid Mountain 69, 107

~ R ~

Rainy Pass 112
Rainy Pass roadhouse 70
Rampart 28, 36, 37, 61, 65, 107, 221, 274
Ramsay, Col. Fox Maule 102, 192, 288
Raven Creek roadhouse 73
Rearden, Jim 259
Redington, Joe 13, 227, 228
Reindeer Act 125
Reindeer King 125
reindeer mail teams 118-127
Reindeer Queen 125
Reindeer Research Program 127
Rembrandt 184-189
Reynolds, Stephen 174
Richardson Highway 258-263
Richardson Trail 18
Ricker, Elizabeth M. 20, 159, 161, 162
roadhouses 6-11, 56-57, 108, 157
roadhouses, Iditarod Trail 56, 57
Roderick, Bella 275
Rogers, Will 23, 157, 252, 281
Rohn River 56
Romig, Dr. Joseph 94-95
Roosevelt Roadhouse 157
Roosevelt, Eleanor 185, 186
Roosevelt, President Franklin 88, 186, 188
Roosevelt, President Theodore 47, 49-52
Roosevelt, Quentin 47, 49, 52
Rowe, Bishop 33
Ruby 41, 54
Russian-Siberian Railroad 247

~ S ~

S.S. Corwin 25, 270
Safety 283
Salcha 265
Salchaket 222
Salisbury, Gay and Laney 19, 38-45, 119, 135, 137
Salt Creek 36
Samuelson, Hans 127
Saturday Evening Post 17, 84, 128, 133
Savoonga 110, 111
Schidel 34
Schultz, Jeff 112
sea ice 44, 45
Seavey, Mitch 103, 104

Alaskan Sled Dog Tales

Seeley, Eva 90
Seppala, Alaskan Dog Driver 38-45, 162
Seppala, Leonhard 15, 20, 38-45, 88-93, 100, 102, 103, 127, 134-139, 158-163, 214, 281, 293, 294, 298
Serum Run 15, 38-45, 114-119, 158-163, 201
Serum Run transfer points 41
service flag, Baldy of Nome 232
Seton, Fred R. 246-248
Seventeen Mile Cabin 33
Seventy-Mile River 37
Seventymile Kid 254, 255
Seward 15, 18, 38, 55, 65, 73, 74, 108, 113, 147, 169, 172, 174, 182, 268
Seward and Susitna Mail Team 151
Seward Peninsula 38-45, 96-105, 237, 283
Seward to Nome Mail Trail 55
Shahnyaati 275
Shaktoolik 41, 43
Sheldon, Charles Alexander 251
Shepherd, Ed 110, 111
Siberia 123, 124
Siberian huskies 102, 158-163
silent films 248, 250-259
Sinrock Mary 125
Skagway 255
Skwentna River 56
sled dogs in war 226-237
Sleeper, Kate 212
Smith, Eli A. 46-52
Smith, Elmer and Mrs. 68
snowshoeing 31
Soldiers and Sled Dogs 234
Solomon 45, 197
Solomon Roadhouse 41
Sourdough Mary 48
South Fork of Kuskokwim 69
Spanish influenza 145

Split-the-Wind 140-145
Sports Afield 132
Spot 200
St. Godard, Emile 88-93
St. Lawrence Island 110, 111
St. Michael 34, 124
stable, for dogs 32
Star Roadhouse 30, 107
Stefansson, Viljhalmur 140-145, 285
Stickeen, The Story of a Dog 60-61
Stuck, Hudson 15, 19, 107, 118-127, 218-225
Sunrise City 74
Sunset Magazine 208
Susitna River 56, 157
Susitna Station 56
Susitna Valley 62, 64
Suter Trophy 96
Swenson, Rick 103, 104

~ T ~

Tacotna 68, 71
Tacotna River 56
Taku Lodge 76-78
Taku River 78
Tanana 18, 41, 47, 107, 183, 221, 222, 274
Tanana gold strike 165-168, 170-171
Tanana River 38-45, 108
Tatum, Robert C. 220
Taulnian, Fred 73
Teller 61
Ten Thousand Miles with a Dog Sled 15, 19, 119, 218-225
The Break Up 280
The First Iditarod 54
This Week 132
Togo 15, 20, 38-45, 134-139, 158-163
Togo, retirement 45

Alaskan Sled Dog Tales

Tokositna River rapids 256
Tolman Brothers 282
Tolovana Roadhouse 41
Tombstone, Arizona 107
Tondreau, Frank 145, 254, 255
Tonzona River 56
Trail Eater, The 127
Trail, The 263
Tulasak River 170, 172
Turnagain Arm 55, 74, 257
Twenty-Six Mile Waystation 276
Twenty-Two Mile Roadhouse 276, 277
Two in the Far North 258-263

~ U ~

U.S. Army 226, 227, 228
U.S. Mail 16, 18, 24, 41-45, 106-115, 117-127, 146-157, 272, 273, 274-277
U.S. Mail Reindeer Service 117-127
U.S. Revenue Cutter *Bear* 123, 124
Unalakleet 38-45, 56, 83, 124
Up in Alaska 281

~ V ~

Valdez 15, 22, 24, 47, 48, 65, 107, 208, 228, 229, 244, 246, 268
Valdez Glacier 246
Valdez to Fairbanks Trail 24, 258-263
Valley of Ten Thousand Smokes 82, 83, 85
Vaughan, Col. Norman D. 90, 233

~ W ~

Wada, Jujiro 15, 117, 145, 164-177
Walden, Arthur 210-217
Walker, Tom 254, 255
WAMCATS 226, 229
War Department Field Manual 236
War Dogs: History/Loyalty and Heroism 236
Washington, D.C. 15, 46-52
Webb, Melody 276
Webber's Roadhouse 32
Weber, "Dad" 246
Welch, Dr. Curtis 38-45
Wetzler, Edward 41
Whiskey Creek 41
White Fang 16
White Horse Pass 247
White Mountain 135
White Pass Route 46
White, Tim 92
Whitehorse 46
Wickersham, James 3, 26-37
Williams, Slim 15, 184-189
Willoughby, Barrett 83, 127
Willoughby, Florance 208
Willow Creek 34
Wolf 15, 79
Wolf, The Storm Leader 46-53
wolves 186, 246
Woodchopper Roadhouse 32, 276
World of Sled Dogs, The 14, 115, 215, 230

~ Y ~

Yentna River 56
Yost's Roadhouse 183, 258-263
Yost, Charlie 263
Young, Rev. S. Hall 58-75, 86, 179
Yukon Fox 13
Yukon Quest 14, 174
Yukon River 12, 18, 26, 38-46, 56, 61, 81, 83, 108, 112, 165, 198, 212, 226, 229, 267, 272, 273, 274-277
Yukon: The Last Frontier 276

Alaskan Sled Dog Tales

ABOUT THE AUTHOR

Helen Hegener has written books about all three major Alaskan sled dog races: The Iditarod, the Yukon Quest, and the All Alaska Sweepstakes, which saw its centennial (and final) running in 2008. She has lived in Alaska off and on since 1964, when her parents moved to Alaska from Arizona, and she has been a full-time resident since 1984. Five generations of her family have now made their homes in Alaska, including four great-grandchildren.

Helen has written books about the history of Alaska and the Matanuska Valley, including *Alaskan Roadhouses*, *The 1935 Matanuska Colony Project*, and *The Stained Glass Dog Team*. She has coordinated two international conferences on the history of mushing, has been a speaker at the Alaska State Fair and numerous historical society meetings and gatherings, has been interviewed on radio and television, and has written articles for many different publications over the years, including *Alaska Dispatch*, *Alaska Magazine*, *Last Frontier Magazine*, *Mushing Magazine* and others.

When not writing her interests include travel, camping, gardening, and watercolor painting, and her constant companion is a large gray and white Alaskan husky much like the one described in the preface. ~•~

The author's Alaskan husky, Chena.

Alaskan Sled Dog Tales

Additional copies of this book are available for $24.95 plus $5.00 shipping and handling:

    Northern Light Media
    PO Box 870515
    Wasilla, Alaska 99687

    http://northernlightmedia.wordpress.com
    email: northernlightmedia@gmail.com

Other titles available from Northern Light Media
- *Alaskan Roadhouses*
- *The First Iditarod*
- *The Stained Glass Dog Team*
- *The Matanuska Colony Barns*
- *The 1935 Matanuska Colony Project*
- *The All Alaska Sweepstakes*
- *The Yukon Quest Trail*
- *Long Hard Trails and Sled Dog Tales*
- *The Beautiful Matanuska Valley*
- *The Matanuska Colony Album*
- *Appetite & Attitude: A Conversation with Lance Mackey (DVD)*

    Contact us via email for information about wholesale orders.

www.ingramcontent.com/pod-product-compliance
Lightning Source LLC
Chambersburg PA
CBHW071654160426
43195CB00012B/1469